Ecomedia

Ecomedia: Key Issues is a comprehensive textbook introducing the burgeoning field of ecomedia studies to provide an overview of the interface between environmental issues and the media globally. Linking the world of media production, distribution, and consumption to environmental understandings, the book addresses ecological meanings encoded in media texts, the environmental impacts of media production, and the relationships between media and cultural perceptions of the environment.

Each chapter introduces a distinct type of media, addressing it in a theoretical overview before engaging with specific case studies. In this way, the book provides an accessible introduction to each form of media as well as a sophisticated analysis of relevant cases. The book includes contributions from a combination of new voices and well-established media scholars from across the globe who examine the basic concepts and key issues of ecomedia studies. The concepts of "frames," "flow," and "convergence" structure a dynamic collection divided into three parts. The first part addresses traditional visual texts, such as comics, photography, and film. The second part of the book addresses traditional broadcast media, such as radio and television, and the third part looks at new media, such as advertising, video games, the Internet, and digital renderings of scientific data.

In its breadth and scope, *Ecomedia: Key Issues* presents a unique survey of rich scholarship at the confluence of Media Studies and Environmental Studies. The book is written in an engaging and accessible style, with each chapter including case studies, discussion questions, and suggestions for further reading.

Stephen Rust is Adjunct Professor at the Department of English at University of Oregon and the School of Writing, Literature, and film at Oregon State University, US.

Salma Monani is Associate Professor at the Department of Environmental Studies at Gettysburg College, US.

Sean Cubitt is Professor of Film and Television at Goldsmiths, University of London, UK; Professorial Fellow of the University of Melbourne, Australia; and Honorary Professor of the University of Dundee, Scotland.

"This is a timely, well-conceived, and impactful addition to the growing field of ecologically based cultural studies. *Ecomedia: Key Issues* powerfully demonstrates how media and the environment are intrinsically linked. Media texts reflect back to us and shape our perceptions of and engagement with the environment. But equally, if not more importantly, this volume illustrates how media systems are materially imbedded in ecological systems: dependent on natural resources for their existence and complicit in the contemporary ecological crisis we face. Collectively, the essays in this collection aptly untangle these complex ecological webs of connectivity, revealing the impact of a diverse set of media texts and practices on planetary health. Adopting a global and interdisciplinary approach, the editors leave no media unturned. Each chapter focuses on a single media, ranging from film, television, radio, advertising and photography, to comic strips, video games, the Internet and data vitalization. Divided in three sections offering engaging analyses of particular media, each chapter is well supported by case studies, up-to-date scholarship, and discussion questions. *Ecomedia* is a must for anyone seeking to deepen their understanding of and reflection about contemporary media culture and practices, and an essential contribution to unpacking the environmental consequences of the digital revolution."

Paula Willoquet-Maricondi, *Champlain College, USA*

"So much media and communications scholarship is needed to address the importance of facing up the 'global challenge' of our age – namely Climate Change and environmental issues generally. This exciting new volume certainly fills a gap, in focusing across aspects of music, games, comics, radio, television as well as film and much else besides.

The overall scope is impressive, covering so many interrelated media formats and is effectively structured using the prism of frames, as well as the concept of flow, which is effectively used to analyse broadcast media, while the notion of convergence captures the interconnecting nature of media formats. It is very useful also to have tightly framed environmental questions accompanying each chapter.

I highly recommend this book for its broad range of contributions and insights across this multi-disciplinary research agenda, focused on a broad range of environmental concerns that will interest scholars and students at all levels."

Pat Brereton, *Dublin City University, Ireland*

Key Issues in Environment and Sustainability

This series provides comprehensive, original and accessible texts on the core topics in environment and sustainability. The texts take an interdisciplinary and international approach to the key issues in this field.

Low Carbon Development
Key Issues
Edited by Frauke Urban and Johan Nordensvärd

Sustainable Business
Key Issues
Helen Kopnina and John Blewitt

Sustainability
Key Issues
Helen Kopnina and Eleanor Shoreman-Ouimet

Ecomedia
Key Issues
Edited by Stephen Rust, Salma Monani and Sean Cubitt

Ecomedia

Key issues

Edited by Stephen Rust,
Salma Monani and Sean Cubitt

Routledge
Taylor & Francis Group
LONDON AND NEW YORK

from Routledge

First published 2016
by Routledge
2 Park Square, Milton Park, Abingdon, Oxon OX14 4RN

and by Routledge
711 Third Avenue, New York, NY 10017

*Routledge is an imprint of the Taylor & Francis Group,
an informa business*

British Library Cataloguing-in-Publication Data
A catalogue record for this book is available from the British Library

Library of Congress Cataloging-in-Publication Data
Ecomedia : key issues / edited by Stephen Rust, Salma Monani and
    Sean Cubitt.
        pages cm
    Includes bibliographical references and index.
    1. Mass media and the environment. 2. Environmentalism
in mass media. I. Rust, Stephen, editor. II. Monani, Salma,
editor. III. Cubitt, Sean, 1953– editor.
    P96.E57E35 2016
    302.23—dc23
    2015009676

ISBN: 978-1-138-78153-5 (hbk)
ISBN: 978-1-138-78155-9 (pbk)
ISBN: 978-1-315-76982-0 (ebk)

Typeset in Sabon
by Apex CoVantage, LLC

Printed and bound in Great Britain by
TJ International Ltd, Padstow, Cornwall

Stephen: To my loving and supportive parents

Salma: To family near and far (both human and more-than-human)

Sean: To my brother Terry

Contents

Figures

Boxes

Acknowledgements

This collection would not be possible without the inspiration and work of many. We extend our thanks to our wonderful contributors who agreed to the textbook format, our colleagues and students who inspired this collective vision, our institutions that supported our research and teaching, and to our editors at Routledge/Earthscan – Louisa Earls who encouraged us to submit our proposal, Helen Bell who answered many questions, Annabelle Harris, and all the others in the editorial and production offices whose work ensured our ideas can be shared with readers. We give thanks to the many, human and nonhuman, whose lives and labor (willingly or unwillingly) share a part of this endeavor. And last but by no means least, we extend a special thanks to you, our reader, whose dialogue with the collection we hope will further Ecomedia Studies' goal of developing ecologically resilient futures.

Foreword
An idea whose time has come

Ecomedia studies is an idea whose time has come, as Victor Hugo didn't exactly say.* We need ecomedia studies, and here's why.

There are two powerful and increasingly important discourses about the media and the environment. The first asks how the *bourgeois* media cover environmental issues. The second questions how to communicate such matters effectively and efficiently to citizens and consumers through public-service announcements and the like.

All well and good. These are significant things to worry about; worth-while concepts that are important for democracy and happiness.

But such perspectives focus ineluctably on representation and consciousness. As a consequence, they have their limits. Problems arise when we think about the media exclusively in those terms and give them a free pass as industries.

What about the media as purposive actors – as agents of climate change, for example, through their extraordinary carbon footprint?

That insight informs the book you are about to read.

But it has not been achieved at the cost of asking and answering the similarly significant questions I touched on earlier.

For this volume cogently, nimbly, even guilefully, blends all these approaches. It knows that representation, communication, and materiality matter equally, that they are coeval elements of how we must understand the media in environmental terms.

Apart from the fact that I learnt many new things empirically from *Ecomedia: Key Issues*, the chapters are innovative in their design and execution, with the prose alternately chilling and enlivening.

The three broad topics and approaches covered in the book – frames, flow, and convergence – touch on core concerns of the contemporary moment: how our past, present, and future ecological disaster is understood; the place of meaning on a continuum of specialization and generality, from text to genre, from story to medium; and why we imagine, or actualize, mergers of old, middle-aged, and new cultural technologies.

The other neat aspect of this volume is that it disobeys the banal dictates that tell us there is a comprehensive and necessary distinction between top-down and bottom-up (hullo, boys!) elements, as claimed by cybertarian takes on culture. These authors know we need to study up, down, and sideways if scholars, activists, citizens, and other participants in this struggle are to understand what needs to be done and be equipped to do it. They know the life of the commodity sign is complex and that it must be engaged by semioticians, audience researchers, environmentalists, and political economists alike, preferably in collaboration.

Ecomedia people seek to draw on all those components in their work. And *Ecomedia* the book illustrates their alertness to the necessity for such a blend of approaches. It offers a mixture of established and emergent scholars and discourses; pays attention to the theories of activists and the actions of theorists; and disobeys the infantile yet venerable borders that separate the humanities, the sciences, and the social sciences. Bravo.

Toby Miller

Notes

* Hugo wrote 'On resiste à l'invasion des armées; on ne résiste pas à l'invasion des idées' in *Histoire d'un crime: Déposition d'un témoin* (Paris: Nelson, 1907), 554. This is often rendered in English as the *cliché* I have just used. The next sentence is, 'La gloire des barbares est d'être conquis par l'humanité; la gloire des sauvages est d'être conquis par la civilization.' It translates as 'The glory of barbarians is to be conquered by humanity; the glory of savages is to be conquered by civilization.' Thanks for sharing, Vic.

Toby Miller is Emeritus Distinguished Professor at the University of California, Riverside; the Sir Walter Murdoch Professor of Cultural Policy Studies at Murdoch University (40%); Profesor Invitado at the Universidad del Norte (25%); Professor of Journalism, Media and Cultural Studies at Cardiff University/ Prifysgol Caerdydd (20%); and Director of the Institute of Media and Creative Industries at Loughborough University in London (20%). He can be contacted at tobym69@icloud.com and his adventures scrutinized at www.tobymiller.org.

Introduction

Ecologies of media

Stephen Rust, Salma Monani, and Sean Cubitt

The last 40 years of media's history is one of leaps and bounds. The *digital revolution* that fuels and drives a network of media production, distribution, and consumption has become so extensively global that many in the US, Europe, Brazil, India, China, and across the world now have access to media experiences that were in the realm of science fiction not so long ago. Yet even as the Internet and other products of this global revolution fuel social change and increase communications, we know that media technologies rely on an enormous amount of energy consumption – from the extraction of raw materials used in manufacturing and the energy grids that power our devices to the landfills and electronic waste facilities where our discarded technologies inevitably end up. In short, our love of media and media technology has become part and parcel of our *global environmental crisis*. We are, after all, living in a time in which human industrial activities are taking an unprecedented toll on our earth's systems. Deforestation, ocean acidification, species extinction, toxic pollution, and global climate change are all facets of this human-propelled crisis.

For most people in the developed world, and for an increasing number of people in the developing world, media technology is at our fingertips. As our students in the United States and Great Britain have told us again and again, "We can't live without our cell phones." In our current media-saturated lives, such everyday dependence is what environmental historian James Farrell would call our *common sense* – "everyday knowledge, what we think when we're not really thinking about things, the stuff that everybody knows" (2010, 5). We "know" we need cell phones, laptops, and other media devices to thrive in our twenty-first century. This everyday knowledge feeds into our day-to-day habits, which appear beguilingly "natural" because they are just what we do, what everyone does. Yet as Farrell and many other *ecocritics* point out, such common sense is fueled by social, cultural, and political systems that often don't support "nature" itself or the ecological thinking necessary to uncover and change humanity's troubling relationship with the planet.

Ecomedia studies, which the chapters of this book will familiarize you with, is a practice of media analysis that helps us move beyond the notion of common sense to what Farrell describes as **commons sense**. The idea of the commons is central to ecocritical work. It is based in the profound belief that we share the world in common with one another and with other non-human organisms and processes. By drawing our attention to the seemingly inaudible and invisible background static of our everyday media routines, the contributors to this collection invite us to shift our perceptions of the global commons. Taken together, the chapters of this book – from analysis of photography to exploration of satellite data imaging – emphasize two central themes. First, media, society, and the environment are inextricably entangled together, both in how media texts represent the environment (even absence suggests a representational practice of erasure) and in the inevitable ways that media texts and systems are materially embedded in natural resource use and abuse. Second, in untangling these ecological webs of connectivity that go far beyond media's common-sense notion of having easy access to one's friends, entertainment, sports, news, or weather, theoretical and critical engagements can enrich both our intellectual lives and our ability to act in the face of contemporary ecological crises.

Theme one: media as ecologically entangled

It is crucial to keep in mind that media are inextricably bound up in society. If we take the keyword **media** at its broadest level as a means of mass communication, there can be no society without media. Just as our students cannot imagine a world without cell phones, we cannot imagine a society without language – without printed laws, printed and electronic money, codes for dressing and acting in social settings, etc. Media and society are synonymous: societies are made of the media that bind us together and media exist only where there are societies for them to bind. This is why media analyses are constantly immersed in questions of economics, politics, power, gender, race, identity, and culture.

However, through the colonial dominance of European philosophical traditions, much of mainstream global culture has learned to speak about society as an exclusively human phenomenon. We place society on one side and nature over on the other, whether we think of nature as the external environment or the instinctive and biological aspects of being human. Over the last forty years, **environmental humanities**, however, has questioned this division, and the central mission of **ecocritics** is to critically interrogate such dualism and expose its fallacies. Society cannot exist without the environment, which it inhabits and from which it derives. Humans are animals, and thus need access to natural resources (for example, sun, air, water, and food) much like our biological kin. A similar logic reveals that even though media are artifacts of human civilization, they are not entirely divorced from nature and the environment. Just as speaking requires a human body capable of articulating sounds, writing, drawing, and musical instruments require paper from plants or animal skins. We use plastic in pens and other media tools that we derive from the oil we get from ancient deposits of dead plants and animals or metals extracted from the earth and refined by human hands. Similarly, broadcasting and cellular networks require the extraction and manufacturing of raw materials from the earth by human bodies and machines, and our radio spectrum for transmission is also occupied by cosmic radiation and the electrical fallout from lightning.

The planet's human population has doubled in the past forty years, and the number and hours of use of media have increased even more. Thus the impact of media practices on the environment and environmental understandings are more important to consider today than at any point in history. To take just two examples: first, the most financially successful motion picture of all time, *Avatar* (2009), considers humanity's mistreatment of the environment as its central theme. Hyped through the Internet, the film generated some of the most chatter of any recent Hollywood blockbuster. Yet at the time of that film's release, the server farms that allow the Internet to operate and that provide cloud-based digital computing had surpassed the airline industry in terms of the amount of carbon dioxide released into the earth's atmosphere (Boccaletti, Löffler, and Oppenheim 2008). Such statistics speak all too clearly about media's contributions to global climate change. Second, today we can understand the behaviors of plants, animals, and even the weather in ways that were unimaginable to previous generations of humans. From thermometers and weather satellites to earthquake monitors and medical technologies, we use science to mediate between the human and nonhuman worlds. If we understand media as the physical devices of mediation, then we can see that media pervade both human and nonhuman worlds. In essence, the idea of an absolute division between human society and our environment is no longer tenable when we begin to analyze media from an ecocritical perspective.

Theme two: media and ecocritical studies

To explore the second central theme of this book, it is important to note that ecocritical inquiry as a scholarly discipline is a relatively recent phenomenon. The pioneering studies of Leo Marx (1964) and Raymond Williams (1973) were oddly alone until the foundation of organizations such as the American Society of Environmental History (ASEH) in 1977, the Association for the Study of Literature and Environment (ASLE) in 1992, and the International Association for Environmental Philosophy (IAEP) in 1998. Subsequently, pioneering works of ecocriticism appeared in history (for example, Cronon 1982), literature (for example, Buell 1995), the fine arts and high culture (for example, Schama 1995), and philosophy (for example, Callicott and Nelson 1998). In addition, considerable scholarly attention in communication studies was paid to the relationship between news media and public understandings of environmental and ecological issues (for example, Anderson 1997 and Neuzil 2008). The development of ecocritical and environmental humanities organizations across the globe (e.g., the International Environmental Communication Association [IECA] and the various affiliates of ASLE) as well as recent growth of international consortiums (e.g., the Environmental Humanities network) attest to the vibrancy of recent ecocritical inquiry.

Despite this multi- and cross-disciplinary attention to ecocritical inquiry across the humanities and social sciences, it is only in recent years that ecocritics have really expanded their focus to consider popular media texts. Cinema, popular music, and television have all become important subjects of analysis (for example, Cubitt 2005, Ingram 2010, and Molloy 2011). Most contemporary ecocritics recognize that popular cultural artifacts are at least as significant mediators of the human–environmental relationship and its attendant anxieties and joys as are literature and the fine arts (for example, Meister and Japp 2002; Dobrin and Morey 2009). Indeed, popular media have several important sociocultural qualities (such as their broad consumption and appeal to multiple segments of society) that make them potentially finer antennae than the fine arts for sensing the changing moods and tendencies in cultural perceptions of environmental relationships and concerns.

While our previous collection *Ecocinema Theory and Practice* (Rust, Monani, and Cubitt 2013) confirmed the expansive purview and viability of ecocritical film studies, this collection responds to a clear need in the scholarship for a volume bringing together a far more diverse set of media texts and contexts. A marked increase in course offerings, journal articles, doctoral dissertations, and conference presentations all attest to the need for a definitive collection introducing readers to Ecomedia Studies. The collection brings scholars from around the globe with interests and expertise in everything from comic strips and photography to radio and social media into one space to better integrate ecocritical work into media studies.

Our book benefits from significant new work undertaken in interdisciplinary **environmental studies.** One of the most telling accusations against environmentalism and Green Party politics has been that it is a single-issue campaign based on the interests of the upper-middle class and wealthy, or at least those who are comfortable enough to worry about more than survival. However, as the "environmentalism of the poor" movements in the Global South has demonstrated, it is the poor who suffer most from toxic waste, air pollution, and climate change (for example, Martinez-Allier 2002). Demands for environmental justice have become central to contemporary ecocriticism, such as articulated in Joni Adamson, Mei Mei Evans, and Rachel Stein's foundational *Environmental Justice Reader* (2002) and Rob Nixon's more recent work (2011) on environmental degradation as *slow violence*. Indigenous speakers have cast off the New Age demand that they should teach us how to live, instead campaigning for an end to the exploitation of their lands and the restitution of the commons (for example, Tuhiwai Smith 2012; Pulitano 2012). At the same time, ecofeminism has been a growing force, increasingly influential since the publication of

Carolyn Merchant's *Radical Ecology* (1992), and eco-queer studies has followed suit (for example, Seymour 2013). Combining with both electoral and direct-action environmental politics, these ways of reconsidering how humans make themselves and the more-than-human world suffer by exploiting and degrading their environments have brought green issues to the center of broad political movements such as Occupy in the United States, Cochabamba in Bolivia, *Indignados* in Spain, and the Gezi Park protests in Istanbul. They suggest another kind of globalization is possible, based on ecological rather than economic principles.

At the same time new intellectual currents have been influenced by environmentalism and have influenced ecocritical thinking. The *actor-network theory* associated with Bruno Latour (2005) makes a powerful philosophical and sociological case that humans *never* act alone, but are always caught up in networks that include both environmental features and technologies, which Latour calls "non-human actors." Taking off from Latour, a recent movement in philosophy, sometimes called *object-oriented ontology*, is shifting the traditional anthropocentrism to recognizing an ecosphere of what one leading figure calls simply "things" (Harman 2005) and others call *new materialism* (Barad 2007; Bennett, 2009). Repositioned in terms of environmentalism, these theories propose an alternative to the rigorous mutual exclusion of human and nonhuman situated at the foundation of Western philosophy: a new way of philosophizing the interconnectedness of everything as "ecological thought" (Morton 2012). The very ideas of "nature" and "environment" are under attack because they suggest a separation between us humans and them nonhumans that, the new philosophers argue, no longer exists, if indeed it ever did.

We have long understood that media *frames* the world in specific representational ways (Goffman 1974). For media studies, ecocriticism's evolving theories enable new frames of reference and the ability to reframe familiar media themes. From the care of animals on set to the environmental footprint of digital cameras (Maxwell and Miller 2012), the connections between material media and the resources from which they are made have become new grounds for analysis and critique (Bozak 2012). In addition, issues of race and class are being reinvestigated in terms of climate justice and the unequal burden of pollution. We have also long understood media as *flow* – the processes and means by which we communicate (Williams 1974). We now understand media as particular concentrations of flows of minerals and energy. We begin to understand human beings themselves as media through which other environmental forces pass. Finally, we have recently begun to think of media as *convergence* – the interlocking, overlapping presence of media across a variety of platforms, from traditional print to the social media forums of the Internet (Jenkins 2006). Now, based on ideas of the commons and of communication as the convergence of human and more-than-human, we look toward a new politics grounded in the interlocking presence of ecosystems. If politics is, as Aristotle argued, the debate over how we should live, then media, with which so many suggest we cannot live, are central to the politics of the twenty-first century. Ecomedia studies is then the complex work of deciphering which forms of media – texts in contexts – facilitate ecological discussion and which squash it, praise inaction, and "commonsensically" make invisible not only non-human but the majority of human agents from participation and refuse to discuss anything but wealth creation as the essence of how we should live.

The chapters that follow look at these debates from a variety of perspectives, typically focusing on a single medium and one or two individual examples. The case-study format is vital because it allows us to look not at the statistical probabilities of things occurring on a national and transnational level but at the very specific ways in which each unique instance actually occurs and matters. Since, as we have seen, nothing happens outside the vast connectedness of ecology, each instance also leads us to consider its radiating impacts across virtual and physical mediascapes. Ecocriticism implies making ethical judgments. Our authors have made theirs: you must then judge them. Among your criteria for judging them will be the question of how they live up to the demand that ecocriticism should create more room for more people and more life, especially those traditionally excluded by class, race, gender, sexuality, ethnicity, or species, to discuss our common future on Earth.

Section and chapter organization: frames, flow, and convergence

As an introduction to ecocritical exploration of a variety of media, the collection draws together an interdisciplinary group of scholars from across the globe. In our first section, *frames*, authors discuss traditional visual texts such as comics, film, and photography; in the second section, *flow*, they turn to broadcast media, such as radio and television, and media infrastructures we traditionally associate with such broadcasts but which also ground new media. Our last section, *convergence*, highlights the blurred terrain of new media such as multi-platform advertising, video games, the Internet, and digital renderings of scientific data. At the start of each section, overview chapters discuss the organizing concepts of frame, flow, and convergence, serving to link these familiar media studies ideas to ecocritical inquiry. Each section then includes several longer chapters that present extended analyses of a particular type of media, case studies of media texts, and discussions of scholarship currently shaping the field. Each chapter also includes a list of keywords, discussion questions, and a list of further reading to make the collection particularly useful as a textbook or reading group selection.

Carter Soles and Kiu-Wai Chu's opening section overview draws attention to how framing in photography, film, and comics (the media genres of this first section) share basic units of similarity, such as images, panels, and shots, but also promise unique distinctions in how physical time and space can be regulated and rendered. As the following chapters in the section then elaborate, each genre's frames speak to particular eco-discussions, but also provide openings for further theorizing, praxis, and transmedia, transdisciplinary conversations.

Thus, in "Beyond Nature Photography," H. Lewis Ulman analyzes how photography, whether understood as framing the history of human and nonhuman relationships through a transparent lens or as reflective mirror, raises concerns about the ethics of representation – from the "ecoporn" of advertisements to the "terrible beauty" in Edward Burtynsky's dramatic images of extractive industrial scenes. To demonstrate these issues, Ulman further presents a case study of the evolving prairie lands representations of US photographer Terry Evans. Next, in "Eco-nostalgia in Popular Turkish Cinema," Ekin Gündüz Özdemirci and Salma Monani frame their analysis of writer/director Semir Aslanyürek's 2001 film *Şellale* in terms of ecological nostalgia. In doing so, they invite Turkish cinema scholars to reframe Turkish cinema as ecocritically engaging and invite ecocinema scholars to reevaluate their current neglect of a rich and diverse national cinema. In the final chapter of this opening section, Veronica Vold examines concepts of environmental justice (EJ) and environmental racism in American comic strips. In "The Aesthetics of Environmental Equity in American Newspaper Strips," Vold juxtaposes African American artist Jackie Ormes's mid-twentieth-century *Torchy in Heartbeats* with two White-authored environmental comics of the time, *Mark Trail* and *Peanuts*, to draw attention to mainstream US culture's EJ blind spots. Vold explores the formal architecture of the comics and their content to highlight Ormes's EJ themes and recover its insightful racial and gendered critiques.

The second section of the collection opens with Stephen Rust's overview chapter, "Flow: An Ecocritical Perspective on Broadcast Media," which readies readers for the chapters on radio, television, and broadcast infrastructure by interrogating the concept of media flow. Rust argues that the fields of ecomedia studies and media ecology must converge if we are to fully understand both the textual and material implications of flow.

Sean Cubitt's chapter, "'I Took Off My Pants and Felt Free': Environmentalism in Countercultural Radio" reads the career of the eclectic US musician Captain Beefheart against the backdrop of the transition from AM pop to FM alternative rock radio in the United States and the rise of pirate and then commercial and public service pop radio in Europe during the 1960s and 1970s. As Cubitt traces the curious flow of Beefheart's work, he acknowledges its powerful environmental themes and its hardcore cult following but also critiques the individualistic contours of such music making, recognizing its problematic inability to drive collective ecopolitical change. In "New Zealand Reality Television: Hostile or Hospitable?" Sarina Pearson takes a postcolonial approach to examine how New Zealand settler–produced and Maori-produced reality television shows, when read together, do not simply reaffirm settler–Maori dichotomies but also interrupt prevalent discourses about settler–indigenous antipathy to flow together and problematically ally against more recent immigrants. The final chapter in this section, Lisa Parks's "Earth Observation and Signal Territories: U.S. Broadcast Infrastructure, Historical Network Maps, Google Earth, and Fieldwork," is a revised version of an article that first appeared in the *Canadian Journal of Communication* in 2013. Parks engages with three different modes of Earth observation – historical network maps, Google Earth interfaces, and fieldwork – to develop the concept of "signal territories" and elucidate a critical approach for studying US broadcast infrastructure. By highlighting physical infrastructures – technological hardware and processes in dispersed geographic locations – as important nodes in media flow, Parks explores what is at stake in understanding the ecological materiality of media systems from both afar and up close.

Anthony Lioi's overview chapter, "Bert versus the Black Phoenix: An Introduction to Convergence and Ecomedia," kicks off the final section of the collection by linking new media's convergence theory to ecocritical concerns. Given the most recent development in convergence theory, the notion of "spreadability," Lioi contends that a combination of formal and ethnographic methods will enable ecomedia studies to engage the productive value of new media environments without sacrificing a critique of their ecological structures and functions.

Highlighting convergence, Joseph Clark critically examines the evolution of advertising as it colonizes new media even as he points to productive eco-possibilities for resisting the totalizing narratives of commodification in his chapter "Selling with Gaia: Advertising and the Natural World." Shifting focus, though not the new media interface, in "Where the Wild Games Are: Ecologies in Latin American Video Games," co-authors Lauren Woolbright and Thaiane Oliveira consider video games produced or set in Mexico and Brazil, two of the world leaders in video game production. The authors frame their argument in terms of ecocultural dynamics, video game aesthetics, and technological convergence to explore how Mexican and Brazilian games point to untapped ecopotential in their depictions of, and gameplay with, the unique landscapes, cultures, and environmental concerns of these two complex nations. From Latin America and video games, we turn to Aimei Yang's chapter "New Media, Environmental NGOs and Online-Based Collective Actions in China." Yang contends that China's new media environment might have some of the strictest government censorship policies but is nonetheless a prominent site for civil society to operate environmental networks that can instigate political change.

In the collection's final chapter, "Earth Imaging: Photograph, Pixel, Program," Chris Russill takes us beyond terrestrial concerns and into the Earth's orbit to explore the implications of turning our media technologies back on the planet. In historically tracing several iconic images – the photographing of the whole Earth from space in the 1960s, the pixilation of these photos in the 1990s, and the programming of Google Earth between 2005 and 2015 – Russill helps us grasp at the telescoping convergence of science and technology in popular ecomedia and its long histories and asks us to critically evaluate its futures.

In all, such critical evaluation is the point of each of our chapters. Collectively, we hope the chapters not only present an introduction to a rich variety of ecomedia theory and practice, but also make room for additional dialogue that might soar beyond everyday common sense toward a more vigorously explored commons sense.

Conclusion: from common sense to commons sense – personal reflections

As editors, each of us has been conditioned in some way by our experiences with media, from our upbringings in the United States (Steve), India (Salma), and Great Britain (Sean), to our personal viewing and listening habits as young people and now adults and our current work with students in university classrooms. By way of conclusion, we wanted to share a few short stories that we feel may offer readers a bit of further insight on why our work with the contributors to this collection and building ecomedia studies into a viable field of academic inquiry has meant so much to us as individuals.

STEVE: When I was five years old, my parents took me to see *The Empire Strikes Back* at the local theater in our small town in the western US state of Idaho. The memory of waiting in line for hours with so many people before the film has always reminded me of how powerful our shared experiences of media can be. A child of the VCR generation, I watched the film over and over and over with my siblings and spent many hours in the forest just beyond our backyard trying to move sticks and stones with "the force."

On Saturday mornings, I often watched Marlon Perkins on *Wild Kingdom* rather than cartoons. Perkins taught me that although the world seemed utterly vast to a small-town kid, the exotic wild animals I so longed to see in person someday were already disappearing from the planet due to habitat destruction and poaching. Years later, when I watched the 1982 Canadian Broadcasting documentary *Cruel Camera* on the Internet, I was shocked to discover that much of Perkins's show had been staged using captive animals. Of course, being an ecocritic means confronting such truths without becoming so jaded that we simply give up, a fact my students help me remember all the time.

Many years after cheering on my childhood eco-heroes Luke Skywalker and Marlon Perkins, I was invited by Jon Lewis to serve as assistant editor of *Cinema Journal* while I completed my MA degree. In the three years that I worked for the flagship journal of the Society for Cinema and Media Studies (SCMS), I read hundreds of articles by leading professors and graduate students. Yet in all of that time, I cannot recall reading a single article – either published or rejected – that analyzed cinema and media from an ecocritical perspective. My mission as a scholar has been framed by that experience.

In many ways this project began back in 2009 when I met Salma at the Association for the Study of Literature and Environment (ASLE) conference in Victoria, BC. Salma and I both came away from that event with a clear sense that the study of media and the environment had finally begun to coalesce as a distinct field of study, as scholars from around the world were beginning to find each other's work and share ideas. Within a few weeks of the conference, we created EcomediaStudies.org, an online community dedicated to facilitating interdisciplinary and innovative approaches to the study of nonprint media as it applies to environmental discourse and action. One of my primary tasks has been maintaining the site's comprehensive bibliography of work in the field.

In 2010, I organized a series of panels on cinema and the environment for the SCMS conference in Los Angeles, where I met Sean, whose 2005 book *EcoMedia* remains one of the field's seminal texts. Salma, Sean, and I were convinced that the time was right for collections that would provide some much needed cohesion to this burgeoning field. For our first collaborative project, *Ecocinema Theory and Practice* (2013), we chose to highlight the many ways in which ecocriticism can be applied to the study of one particular media. Before that book was even finished, however, we had already started talking about this current collection because, after all, cinema is only one aspect of media's multifaceted relationship with ecology. Of course, we had no idea that we would be blessed with such an incredible array of talented contributors, whose collective efforts have made working on this collection far more fulfilling than I could have ever imagined.

SALMA: Other than our productive, previous collaboration on *Ecocinema Theory and Practice* (2013), two formative influences prompted me to coordinate this collection with Steve and Sean. While the first reaches back into my earliest memories of media experiences, the second is a more recent inspiration.

I spent the first nineteen years of my life in India before arriving in the United States as an international student on a scholarship for my undergraduate education. While individuals like Steve have early childhood memories of watching cartoons on color television sets as they ate sugary cereal on Saturday mornings, I don't. Television was government controlled. In 1980, when I was six, my family acquired our first television set (black and white, with a roof antennae prone to being the lookout post for passing feisty, festive monkeys).

Each evening around 5:30 pm, we'd wait with anticipation to see the screen turn from static to the enlarging, spiraling swirl of Doordarshan's logo. The signature montage's slow-paced and weirdly eerie soundtrack conveyed the solemnity of the government broadcast's usual fare of evening entertainment – news, a few classical music recitals, and more talking heads for a couple of hours before the spiraling swirl signaled a return to static. I joke about how my experience growing up with my Indian family put me consistently about five to ten years behind the media curve of my US peers.

(I hate to admit that my first LP45, which I purchased in 1981, was ABBA's 1976 *Dancing Queen*).

This media lag is something my sister's kids do not experience. Where a family of five, like mine in late-twentieth-century India, shared one rotary phone, one television, and one LP player, it's the norm for twenty-first-century middle-class Indians, like their counterparts in the US and across the world, to each have their own cell phone and televisions in different rooms, as well as personalized computers with video games, social media, and Internet at their fingertips. Reflecting on this changing mediascape motivated the global reach of this collection, as did a more recent influence – my attendance and subsequent work on film and media arts festivals that bring together artists from across the globe.

Through their programming, environmental festivals such as the Finger Lakes Environmental Film Festival (FLEFF) in upstate New York, the DC Environmental Film Festival, and the TiNai Ecocinema Film Festival (in India) and indigenous film festivals such as the Native Film and Video Festival hosted by the Smithsonian in New York and the ImagineNATIVE Film and Media Arts Festival (in Toronto, Canada) serve as vibrant gathering spaces that use media's power and interrogate its pitfalls to help reinscribe voice and vision to the traditionally disenfranchised, illuminating what is so often kept invisible in the everyday of neocolonial societies.

This coedited book is inspired by the spirit of such spaces. Like the interruption of feisty, festive monkeys on the television antennae of my youth, the vibe of a live celebratory festival in full swing provides an exhilarating and humbling experience. There's a magic in the media noise, in the dynamics of knowing that human and more-than-human are at play with each other, each influencing and shaping the other; how we engage the moment, with openness, wonder, and critical reflectiveness – i.e., with a sense of personal humility – might point to the promise of a collective way forward.

SEAN: I think the first book I ever read was a comic strip, in the style of boy's adventure comic annuals, called *Biggles and the Flight of the Condor*. My sister helped me, because at that stage I wasn't yet at school and couldn't read myself. From memory there were anacondas, a jungle, and a race for treasure at Machu Picchu. I couldn't swear that this was the start of my passion for nature. We grew up in rural Lincolnshire and spent long hours netting two- or three-inch-long sticklebacks in the River Slea and in winter chasing bats to try to catch them in torch beams. The hedgerows were full of robins' nests, and on long summer days we scrumped apples from the local orchards and plucked blackberries, fruit that seemed always to have been visited by the birds before we got to them.

In the living room was a large brown radiogram, its dial marked with names of stations from unknown places: Hilversum, Luxembourg. Years later I recorded a fragment of one of the children's radio shows, where Vernon Dalhart's *The Runaway Train* was cut off by an announcer's voice: "We have to stop the track there because otherwise we would have time only for one or two hymns." It was a different time. But it did include a wonderful BBC educational program on how to observe wildlife. I decided that when I grew up I would be a vet.

Time intervened. The cinema fascinated me, as it still does. Television was a late arrival. Books absorbed me: *Tarka the Otter*, for instance, which shed the anthropomorphism of other children's books, as did Jack London's *Call of the Wild*. The world seen from another viewpoint, soon to become a passion for science fiction's estrangement effects, somehow made the curious relation of representation to reality an emotional state, a hovering between worlds. This of all things was and remains to me the core of the environmental principle: to be both ourselves and other.

Discovering email and ftp in the late 1970s, working with video activists in the 1980s, witnessing the huge change brought by the arrival of the world wide web in the 1990s: the concept of media expanded, the links between them (and the older arts, music, and painting especially) became my profession as well as my passion. The immense commercialization of the Internet in the 2000s notwithstanding, the utopian potential of childhood and of art and activist media has always had for me the power, not to recapture lost innocence, but to create a new world, where we could indeed listen to the thoughts of animals, the stirrings of forests, the seismic voice of the planet as part of the immense dialogue of humanity with itself.

Ecocriticism comes as the most significant way to address the ancient cornerstones of aesthetics, of communication, and of politics, which I have come to understand as the question of how we should live. Ecocriticism asks the fundamental questions of Truth, Beauty, and the Good that children, in their groping manner, still reach for, before we teach them to aspire otherwise. It is not only what we fight against that matters, but what we struggle for, in our lives and those of our students.

Keywords

Actor-Network Theory
Common Sense
Commons Sense
Convergence
Digital Revolution
Ecocritics/Ecocriticism
Ecomedia Studies
Environmental Humanities

Environmental Studies
Flow
Frames
Global Environmental Crisis
Media
New Materialism
Object-Oriented Ontology
Slow Violence

Discussion questions

1 What is your personal level of familiarity with the topic of ecocriticism, and how do you think that will impact your ability to engage with the ideas in this book?

2 How are environmental issues reflected in the media you engage with on a daily basis both in obvious/direct ways (like with films such as *An Inconvenient Truth* or *Avatar*) and in more vague/indirect ways?

3 Why is the difference between Farrell's notions of common sense and commons sense so crucial to understanding the relationships between media, society, and the environment?

4 From your experience, what are some particular ways that you have witnessed media texts change the way you, your friends, and/or your family discuss and think about environmental topics such as weather, air and water pollution, endangered species, travel, and even space exploration?

5 Do the key concepts of frame, flow, and convergence make sense to you as a way to organize a collection of essays on media and the environment? What are some alternative ways that a collection such as this could be organized and why?

Works cited

Adamson, Joni, Mei Mei Evans, and Rachel Stein. 2002. *The Environmental Justice Reader: Politics, Poetics, and Pedagogy*. Tucson: University of Arizona Press.

Anderson, Alison. 1997. *Media, Culture, and the Environment*. London: UCL Press.

Barad, K. 2007. *Meeting the Universe Halfway: Quantum Physics and the Entanglement of Matter and Meaning*. Durham: Duke University Press.

Bennett, Jane. 2009. *Vibrant Matter: A Political Ecology of Things*. Durham: Duke University Press.

Boccaletti, Giulio, Markus Löffler, and Jeremy M. Oppenheim. 2008. "How IT Can Cut Carbon Emissions." *McKinsey Quarterly*, October. Accessed February 2, 2015. http://www.mckinseyquarterly.com/How_IT_can_cut_carbon_emissions_2221

Bozak, Nadia. 2012. *The Cinematic Footprint: Lights, Camera, Natural Resources*. New Brunswick, NJ: Rutgers University Press.

Buell, Lawrence. 1995. *The Environmental Imagination: Thoreau, Nature Writing, and the Formation of American Culture*. Cambridge, MA: Harvard University Press.

Callicott, J. Baird, and Michael P. Nelson. 1998. *The Great Wilderness Debate*. Athens, GA: University of Georgia Press.

Cronon, William. 1982. *Changes in the Land: Indians, Colonists, and the Ecology of New England*. New York: Hill and Wang.

Cubitt, Sean. 2005. *EcoMedia*. Amsterdam: Rodopi.

Dobrin, Sidney I., and Sean Morey, eds. 2009. *Ecosee: Image, Rhetoric, Nature*. Albany: State University of New York Press.

Farrell, James. 2010. *The Nature of College: How a New Understanding of Campus Life Can Change the World*. Minneapolis: Milkweed.

Goffman, Erving. 1974. *Frame Analysis: An Essay on the Organization of Experience*. Cambridge, MA: Harvard University Press.

Harman, Graham. 2005. *Guerrilla Metaphysics: Phenomenology and the Carpentry of Things*. Chicago: Open Court Press.

Ingram, David. 2010. *The Jukebox in the Garden: Ecocriticism and American Popular Music Since 1960*. Amsterdam: Rodopi.

Jenkins, Henry. 2006. *Convergence Culture: Where Old and New Media Collide*. New York: New York University Press.

Latour, Bruno. 2005. *Reassembling the Social: An Introduction to Actor-Network Theory*. Oxford: Oxford University Press.

Martinez-Allier, Joan. 2002. *The Environmentalism of the Poor*. Geneva: United Nations Research Institute for Social Development/World Summit on Sustainable Development. 30 August. Accessed Feb. 2, 2015. http://www.unrisd.org/unrisd/website/document.nsf/8b18431d756b708580256b6400399775/5eb03ffbdd19ea90c1257664004831bd/$FILE/MartinezAlier.pdf

Marx, Leo. 1964. *The Machine in the Garden: Technology and the Pastoral Ideal in America*. New York: Oxford University Press.

Maxwell, Richard, and Toby Miller. 2012. *Greening the Media*. Oxford: Oxford University Press.

Meister, Mark, and Phyllis M. Japp, eds. 2002. *Enviropop: Studies in Environmental Rhetoric and Popular Culture*. Westport, CT: Praeger Publishers.

Merchant, Carolyn. 1992. *Radical Ecology: The Search for a Livable World*. New York: Routledge.

Molloy, Claire. 2011. *Popular Media and Animals*. London: Palgrave Macmillan.

Morton, Timothy. 2012. *The Ecological Thought*. Cambridge MA: Harvard University Press.

Neuzil, Mark. 2008. *The Environment and the Press: From Adventure Writing to Advocacy*. Evanston, IL: Northwestern University Press.

Nixon, Rob. 2011. *Slow Violence and the Environmentalism of the Poor*. Cambridge, MA: Harvard University Press.

Pulitano, Elvira. 2012. *Indigenous Rights in the Age of the UN Declaration*. Cambridge, UK: University of Cambridge Press.

Rust, Stephen, Salma Monani, and Sean Cubitt. 2013. *Ecocinema Theory and Practice*. New York: AFI/Routledge.

Schama, Simon. 1995. *Landscape and Memory*. London: Harper Collins.

Seymour, Nicole. 2013. *Strange Natures: Futurity, Empathy, and the Queer Ecological Imagination*. Champaign, IL: University of Illinois Press.

Tuhiwai Smith, Linda. 2012. *Decolonizing Methodologies: Research and Indigenous Peoples*, 2nd ed. London: Zed Books.

Williams, Raymond. 1973. *The Country and the City*. Oxford: Oxford University Press.

———. 1974. *Television: Technology and Cultural Form*. London: Fontana.

Part I
Frames

Part

Frames

1 Overview

Framing visual texts for ecomedia studies

Carter Soles and Kiu-Wai Chu

Introduction

Framing, both aesthetic and ideological, is integral to the construction of visual images. Photography, film, and comics all rely upon framing to shape viewer/reader perceptions and to express a particular point of view via choices about visual perspective. As the essays in this section make clear, this concept of framing is of special importance to ecocritics, since matters of point of view and vision are so dramatically at stake in works grappling with environmental and interspecies issues. Framing, and the aesthetics of the image within a frame, shape how artists and their audiences perceive the environment.

Since the emergence of media and cultural studies in the 1960s and '70s, film and media texts have been analyzed through different conceptual frames such as gender, class, and race. Taking an environmental turn over the past decade, scholarship in media studies has increasingly placed a wider range of texts into ecocritical contexts. We should now ask of any text – be it a comic strip, a photograph, or a film – what does it tell us about the environment? How does it reflect humans' complex relationships with the more-than-human world? Every text can now be framed and read from an ecocritical perspective.

Ecocritical framing across media – photography, film, and comics

Photographer Edward Burtynsky suggests that photographing landscape involves "impos[ing] a rectangle or square over a chunk of reality, eliminating much more than it includes" (Campbell 2008, 47). With framing, certain aspects of the environment and its relationships with human beings are emphasized and magnified, while others are omitted or eliminated. Reality must be framed and turned partial in order to be represented. In cultural studies scholar John Berger's words, "all photographs have been taken out of a continuity," and with such discontinuity, photographs are by nature contradictory and ambiguous (Berger and Mohr 1995, 7, 85–92). These contradictions and ambiguities make photography both an aesthetic artefact that satisfies our visual and affective pleasures and, at the same time, a reflexive political tool that facilitates thinking about environmental issues.

In recent years, film, or moving image, began to engage in more systematic conceptualization and theorization in terms of "ecocinema" and "eco-films." In examining the ecocritical capacity of film, Paula Willoquet-Maricondi establishes a clear distinction between *environmentalist film* and *ecocinema*. To her, the former usually consists of a specific environmental or political agenda and tends to offer a pro-environment, pro-conservation, and pro-sustainability perspective which "affirms, rather than challenges, the culture's fundamental anthropocentric ethos" (2010, 47). "Ecocinema," on the other hand, covers a broader range of films that may cultivate our perceptions of ecological and environmental issues through various approaches. These eco-films range from lyrical and contemplative films that foster viewers' appreciation of nature's constituents, to cinema with overt activist potential that "inspires our care, inform[s], educate[s], and motivate[s] us to act on the knowledge they provide," often without asserting a single-sided environmentalist or political agenda to viewers (2010, 45).

Beyond these fairly specific definitions, different popular film genres adopt various cinematic styles and conventions that convey environmental and ecocritical ideologies. Certain fictional genres seem to open themselves more readily than others to ecocritical analysis, framing their ecological investments in ways more apparent to viewers and critics. Ecocritical work on science fiction (Brereton 2005), the Western (Murray and Heumann 2012; Carmichael 2006), and horror (Rust and Soles 2014) demonstrates that, for many ecocritics, analysis of popular Hollywood genres is crucial for understanding how these texts convey ecological ideas to the mass viewing public. Of course, as Andrew Hageman cautions us, these films are always embedded in consumer capitalist ideology and therefore contain many internal contradictions which require dialectical ideological critique to expose: "holding a film's constituted and constitutive ideologies together indicates its contradictions, which brings into view the determinate disorder of ecological crises we face within capitalism" (2013, 77). Yet Hageman sees such critique as ecocritically productive and encourages ecocritics to analyze all cinema "with an eye to form and content alike" (2013, 83–84).

Comics share certain formal characteristics with film and, since the early 2000s, provide the source material for most mainstream blockbuster cinema. Similarly to film editing, comics panels and the gutters that separate them offer an interesting model by which we may understand how gaps between panels (or shots) invite the reader (or viewer) into the text, supplying meaning by interpreting what takes place in the ellipses created by blank spaces between panels. Cuts and gutters invite *suture*, what comics theorist Scott McCloud calls *closure*, an act of interpretation in which the reader supplies that which exceeds the static frame, contributing meaning to an unfolding sequence of shots or panels; in essence, narrativizing time. As McCloud writes, comics in particular are "a medium where the audience is a willing and conscious collaborator and closure is the agent of change, time, and motion" (1994, 65). The potential for reader agency in comics has potent implications for how comics regulate time and space and, ultimately, how they generate meaning.

Kom Kunyosying explores comics form's potential to convey ecocritical messages, arguing that comics panels draw metonymic potential from their juxtaposition (2014, 570). Since comics panels always exist in relation to each other, "simultaneously still and sequential," they elide many of the reductive and anthropocentric traps of metaphor (2014, 570, 571). For Kunyosying, comics form is ecocritical because it resists metaphor, in which nature is reduced to symbols, instead promoting environmental consciousness by rejecting artificial hierarchies that consider the human as clean and exclusive from the ecological and animal.

Photographic frames, cinematic frames, and comics panels have much in common; they delimit visual space and regulate time in their respective media. In recent years, visual ecomedia studies sees an expansion in framing as essential to addressing contemporary environmental conditions in new ways. Such expansions can be seen in three particular aspects: *spatial, temporal,* and *speciesist.*

Framing of space and place

Contemporary photographers and artists such as Burtynsky, Chris Jordan, and Vik Muniz focus their lenses beyond pristine nature and towards deteriorated industrial landscapes and garbage dumps. Their works reveal how landscapes of ruins, garbage, and toxic waste, when being framed or digitally enhanced, can look aesthetically pleasing. When considering the meaning and impact of a photograph, it is important to take into account the context in which an image is shown or exhibited and how the viewer encounters it. Burtynsky, Jordan, and Muniz's works are often exhibited in art galleries and museums in magnified, giant proportions. These exhibits urge us to confront what we reject and disavow in real-life settings, and in turn to reassess our ecocritical responsibilities and awareness in the era of global environmental degradation.

With technological advancements, we are now able to frame images of spaces and places otherwise unseen by the human eye, such as the accumulated trash deep beneath the ocean, or in a different scale, the interiors of human organs in medical photography. Such imagery facilitates our understanding of interactions between human beings and the more-than-human world, as well as what Karen Barad describes as *intra-actions* within human and nonhuman bodies. In viewing such images, we are prompted to alter our sense of self as we reflect on the material and discursive practices that constitute a world of interconnectedness in its state of becoming (Barad 2007).

With a growing emphasis on transnational and global perspectives in perceiving the world, some ecocritics such as Ursula Heise advocate a shift from a sense of place to a sense of planet, which signifies a territorial expansion of framing not just in photography (for example, through the ubiquitous presence of satellite imagery) but also in ecocinema (Heise 2008). In the last fifteen years, ecocritical emphasis has significantly shifted from western wildlife cinema to various genres produced globally, resulting in a diverse range of transnational films that deprioritize place in order to "overcome some of the limitations of the binary between globalized and national forms of ecocinema" (Kääpä 2013, 37). From Godfrey Reggio and Ron Fricke's avant garde films (*The Qatsi Trilogy*, 1982, 1988, 2002; *Baraka*, 1992; and *Samsara*, 2011), to cross-regional documentaries (e.g., Jennifer Baichwal's *Manufactured Landscapes*, 2006, and Jia Zhangke's *Useless*, 2007), to coproduced fictional films (e.g., Neill Blomkamp's *District 9*, 2009, and Steven Soderbergh's *Contagion*, 2011), many transnational ecofilms offer deterritorialized, planetary perspectives that are in cohesion with Ursula Heise's concept of ecocosmopolitanism.

Comics may have certain formal advantages when it comes to conveying an ecocritical experience via framing and sequence. Comics use framing and the layout of panels to represent complex, fluid, and ultimately rewarding tensions – between images and text, between sequential panels and pages – to their readers. Comics theorist Thierry Groensteen broadly defines the comics medium as necessarily, yet not sufficiently, composed of images that are "multiple and correlated in some fashion," and he refines this definition by stating that "a page of comics is offered at first to a synthetic global vision, but that cannot be satisfactory. It demands to be traversed, crossed, glanced at, and analytically deciphered" (2009, 130). This traversing and crossing of the physical and visual territory of the comics page, while unique to how comics frame space, can be seen as analogous to Scott MacDonald's ecocinema experience, a conscious and thoughtful engagement with the text that both requires and generates a meditative, analytical frame of mind akin to what one finds in experiences of the natural world. However, the comics page may do this in an even more multilayered and complex, if less immersive, fashion than does cinema. Whereas, in film viewing, the viewer is always locked into the strict sequential revelation of frames as they are projected, Groensteen notes that the "moment-to-moment" style of reading encouraged by comics panels in sequence "does not take a lesser account of the totality of the panoptic field that constitutes the page (or double page), since the focal vision never ceases to be enriched by peripheral vision" (2009, 130). The experience might be likened to that of engaging photographs in an art gallery, where viewers can similarly be prompted to explore the individual shot within its broader context of other shots.

While to some extent the spatial dimensions of the cinematic frame may be approached in this holistic way, both focally and peripherally, the temporality of motion pictures – unless paused in home-video playback – limits this dual reading/viewing strategy in a way that comics and still photography do not. More control over temporality and chronology is ceded to the viewer of still images and the reader of comics than to the viewer of cinema.

Framing and time

Framing and time are of particular concern to ecocritics due to the need to consider nonhuman modes of reckoning **chronology**, i.e., geological time, "deep" time, slow cinema, etc. Gilles Deleuze notes that the cinematic frame "gives a common standard of measurement to things which do not have one [. . .] the frame ensures a deterritorialisation of the image" (1986, 14–15). Thus framing plays a key role not only in demarcating physical and visual space, but creates the basic units – shots, panels – by which time is rendered legible.

In the photographic series *Manufactured Landscapes* and *Water*, Burtynsky documents naturally scarred and human-destroyed physical environments in static shots, framing instants of the ever-transforming and -deteriorating landscapes in the contemporary world into timeless images. Supplementing the photo series are Jennifer Baichwal's films *Manufactured Landscapes* (2006) and *Watermark* (2013, codirected by Burtynsky). The two documentaries center on Burtynsky's development of his photographic projects and take viewers on cinematic journeys to places all over the world, from the demolished ruins of the Three Gorges Dam area along the Yangtze River in China, to the dried-up lands along Colorado River and the barren desert delta, to the Ganges River in India in which over 30 million pilgrims bathed. The moving images in the films supplement Burtynsky's static photos with stories of interviewees, which portray the landscapes with more personal, intimate moments that unfold with time.

In recent avant garde and art house films, the adjustment of cinematic temporality has been seen as an important development for ecocinema. For MacDonald, the ecocinema experience is created by the incorporation of long takes, an absence of nondiegetic sound (especially music), and a relative reduction of human subjectivity and point of view in favor of a *slow*, non- or loosely narrative cinema that represents "the inverse of the fundamentally hysterical approach of commercial media" which "models unbridled consumption of products and the unrestrained industrial exploitation of the environment" (2013, 19). MacDonald argues that viewing truly ecocinematic films of this type helps retrain viewer perception and "nurture a more environmentally progressive mindset" (2013, 20). Adrian Ivakhiv, on the other hand, sees *slow cinema* as a means of narrowing the gap between cinematic time and real time (or, in his term, ecological time), which facilitates the depictions of "enfoldment of objects or processes within other processes, all of which unfold according to their own durations" (Ivakhiv 2013, 304–05).

Comics provide the reader a high degree of control over how time is perceived, since the reader decides how quickly or slowly – and in which order – to proceed from panel to panel, page to page. The comics reader may read the words and scan the visual images quickly or may spend a great deal of time on one particular image or panel that is aesthetically pleasing or interesting. The reader can, in effect, create a kind of "slow cinema" effect, depending upon how he or she reads, and may manipulate the chronology of a comics work by reading panels and pages out of order. The deeper significance of these reading strategies are explored further in the next section.

Framing beyond anthropocentrism: expanding speciesist perspectives

By shifting subjectivities from human to nonhuman subjects, framing can be expanded away from *speciesism*, which, analogous to racism or sexism, focuses on prejudiced beliefs in human supremacy over nonhuman species (particularly animals). In theorizing ecocinema, Willoquet-Maricondi emphasizes the aspect of a reduced human subjectivity, which shifts viewers' perspective "from a narrow anthropocentric worldview to an earth-centered, or ecocentric, view in which the ecosphere [. . .] is taken as the 'center of *value* for humanity'" (2010, 45–46). Photography, comics, and films are able to reposition nonhuman beings (animals, plants, and nonliving objects) as a subject of concern. This can be as simple as attaining a lower angle shot from the ground level to depict perspective of a small animal in the wild or, in a film such as Michelangelo Frammartino's *Le Quattro Volte* (2010), shifting subjective focus from an old man to a newborn goat and from a majestic fir tree to ashes in the air. The film prompts viewers to cultivate a nonanthropocentric perspective in perceiving the world, reminding human viewers of our animality or vegetality, thus narrowing the distinctions among different players in the film and different species in the world.

In addition to visual images, written inscriptions or audio aspects add verbal effects that also facilitate framing of the environment. Soundscape in film often plays a crucial role in reflecting the relationships between human and nonhuman beings. Jennifer Ladino points out that in Castaign-Taylor and Barbash's documentary *Sweetgrass* (2009), the speciesist perspective and nonhuman agency are enhanced by the directors placing microphones on individual animals to record sounds produced by the sheep herd, resulting in a "'synaesthetic participation' for viewers, in which human and animal sound are constantly juxtaposed and . . . given equal weight" (Ladino 2013, 140). While sounds of nature remind human beings of our coexistence with the more-than-human world, electronic-processed sound effects featured in films with modern urban settings intensify the relation between image and sound, generating a negative aesthetics that characterizes contaminated urban landscapes. The opening sequence in Michelangelo Antonioni's *Red Desert* (1964) is about a woman and her young son in an Italian industrial area in the 1960s. Accompanying the bleak visual depiction of petrochemical plants in toxic fog is the background noise from the factory engines, which engulfs the frame for an extended fifteen minutes. Such sound effects enable viewers to share feelings of irritation, alienation, and anxiety experienced by the mentally and emotionally disturbed female protagonist who fails to adapt to the deteriorating urban environments in the modern technological age.

The dense layering of aural and visual codes in cinema finds its analogy in the dualistic, dialectical reading strategy demanded by comics. This strategy is elaborated by Charles Hatfield, who denotes several key tensions at play in comics, which impact how meaning is generated by the interactions between reader and text. Hatfield confirms Groensteen's notion that comics ask the reader to engage with the page layout as both "sequence and object" (2005, 48) and further delineates three additional tensions germane to comics paneling, "between *codes* of signification; between the *single image* and the *image-in-series;* [. . .] and, more broadly, between reading-as-*experience* and the text as a material *object*" (2005, 36).

Discussing the interplay between visual and verbal codes, between image and written text, Hatfield argues that "in comics word and image approach each other: words can be visually inflected, reading as pictures, while pictures can become as abstract and symbolic as words" (2005, 36–37). This tension or slippage between verbal and visual codes offers many possibilities for ecocriticism, particularly a destabilization of the boundary between the symbolic and the mimetic, even the human and the nonhuman, at the level of comics form. The flexibility between codes, the dynamic exchange between word and image, strongly affects how the comics' reader negotiates transitions between panels and the sense of closure that sequencing can produce. Thus, the negotiation of the panels, and the time-sequencing they map out spatially, is mitigated by this unique slippage or interaction between types of coding in comics.

Yet it is Hatfield's last tension, *between*, that may offer the most interest to ecocritics, focused as it is upon the materiality of comics. While printed photographs and comic panels possess such a materiality for the viewer, cinema is notoriously difficult to pin down in terms of its material referent, instead coming to us via a projected image seemingly stripped of its material form. Comics, especially when read in printed form (as opposed to, say, online) possess a material and sensual dimension that influences not just the design and packaging of a publication but also its style and technique (Hatfield 2005, 60). For example, in *Maus* Art Spiegelman deploys a technique in which "the page repeatedly refers to itself, as 'objects' overlap the panels, creating at once an illusion of volume and sense of intimacy (as if these found objects have been mounted in a diary or a scrapbook)" (2005,

64). This same technique is used several times in Charles Burns's *Black Hole* to depict various objects discovered in the woods in the comic's diegesis as if they were scattered across the pages of the comic itself. This self-reflexive attention to the materiality of comics and the objects they depict offers distinct advantages to authors and readers wishing to convey ecocritical messages and to engage readers in some form of materially grounded ecocritical experience.

Given the wide array of ecocritical possibilities that photography, film, and comics have to offer, framing is a capacious conceptual category, referring at once to the visual, the chronological, the spatial, and the ideological. In all three media, the frame directs what we see, though it is not inflexible, impermeable, or monolithic.

Box 1.1   Talk about it – frames as constraining or expanding ecological awareness?

To a great extent, all media forms are ambiguous and contradictory, for they convey partial and selective representations of reality. As a class, divide into groups, with each group taking charge of selecting examples from one of the media forms – photography, film, and comics. Conduct a textual analysis of what is in the frames of each example. Feel free to research the contexts that surround the frame. Share with your classmates: does what is represented exhibit ecocritical capacities in the present world, or, on the contrary, do these representations obscure or mask ecological destructions?

Humans are particularly visually oriented animals, and visual media play a powerful and prevalent role in shaping contemporary human culture. Analyzing the ways in which our visual texts frame the world for us, and specifically how they represent and suggest ecocritical ideologies, is a critical strategy that can be used to develop nonspeciesist ways of living and prospering on planet Earth. As you read the chapters in this section, keep in mind that one of the key goals of ecomedia studies is to advance interdisciplinary and multimedia analysis of all three kinds of visual media discussed here toward that greater philosophical end.

Keywords

Anthropocentrism
Chronology
Ecocinema
Environmental film
Framing

Intra-action
Slow cinema
Speciesism
Suture

Discussion questions

1 Consider the following modes of photography; how does each of their forms of exhibition and presentation convey ecocritical messages to different effects?

- Journalistic photos in newspapers and online media spaces
- Advertising and publicity images on outdoor billboards
- Art photography in museums and galleries
- Personal mobile photo snapshots

2 In a broad sense, cinema combines formal properties of still photography (photorealistic images) with some of the structures of comics (images ordered in sequence and accompanied by a verbal/aural component). Given their formal similarities *and* differences, what kinds of ecocritical messages might each of these three media be uniquely suited to convey?

3 This chapter considers space, time, and anthropocentrism as important ecocritical characteristics to be conscious of when viewing what occupies a frame and how this frame references the world beyond. Choose one of your favorite photographs, comics, or films. Conduct an ecocritical reading of it using these representational frames as starting points for analysis.

Further reading

Bozak, Nadia. 2012. *The Cinematic Footprint: Lights, Camera, Natural Resources.* New Brunswick, NJ, and London: Rutgers UP.

Braddock, Alan C., and Christoph Irmscher. 2009. *A Keener Perception: Ecocritical Studies in American Art History.* Tuscaloosa: The University of Alabama Press.

Cubitt, Sean. 2005. *EcoMedia.* Amsterdam: Rodopi.

Haraway, Donna J. 2003. *The Companion Species Manifesto: Dogs, People, and Significant Otherness.* Chicago: Prickly Paradigm Press.

Lim, Song Hwee. 2014. *Tsai Ming-liang and a Cinema of Slowness.* Honolulu: University of Hawai'i Press.

Wolfe, Cary. 2003. *Animal Rites: American Culture, the Discourse of Species, and Posthumanist Theory.* Chicago: The University of Chicago Press.

Works cited

Barad, Karen. 2007. *Meeting the Universe Halfway: Quantum Physics and the Entanglement of Matter and Meaning.* Durham, NC: Duke University Press.

Berger, John, and Jean Mohr. 1995. *Another Way of Telling.* New York: Vintage Books.

Brereton, Pat. 2005. *Hollywood Utopia: Ecology in Contemporary American Cinema.* Portland, OR: Intellect Books.

Campbell, Craig. 2008. "Residual Landscapes and the Everyday: An Interview with Edward Burtynsky." *Space and Culture* 11.1: 47.

Carmichael, Deborah A., ed. 2006. *The Landscape of Hollywood Westerns: Eco-criticism in an American Film Genre*. Salt Lake City: University of Utah Press.

Deleuze, Gilles. 1986. *Cinema 1: The Movement-Image*. Translated by Hugh Tomlinson and Barbara Habberjam. Minneapolis: University of Minnesota Press.

Groensteen, Thierry. 2009. "The Impossible Definition." In *A Comics Studies Reader,* edited by Jeet Heer and Kent Worcester, 124–31. Jackson, MI: University Press of Mississippi.

Hageman, Andrew. 2013. "Ecocinema and Ideology." In *Ecocinema Theory and Practice*, edited by Stephen Rust, Salma Monani, and Sean Cubitt, 63–86. New York and London: Routledge.

Hatfield, Charles. 2005. *Alternative Comics: An Emerging Literature*. Jackson, MI: University of Mississippi Press.

Heise, Ursula. 2008. *Sense of Place and Sense of Planet: The Environmental Imagination of the Global*. Oxford, UK: Oxford University Press.

Ivakhiv, Adrian J. 2013. *Ecologies of the Moving Image: Cinema, Affect, Nature*. Waterloo, Ontario: Wilfrid Laurier University Press.

Kääpä, Pietari. 2013. "Transnational Approaches to Ecocinema: Charting an Expansive Field." In *Transnational Ecocinema: Film Culture in an Era of Ecological Transformation*, edited by Tommy Gustafsson and Pietari Kääpä, 21–43. USA: Intellect.

Kunyosying, Kom. 2014. "Horror Comics Ecology: Metonymy and Iconicity in Charles Burns's *Black Hole*." *Interdisciplinary Studies in Literature and the Environment* 21.3: 562–574.

Ladino, Jennifer. 2013. "Working with Animals: Regarding Companion Species in Documentary Film." In *Ecocinema Theory and Practice*, edited by Stephen Rust, Salma Monani, and Sean Cubitt, 129–148. New York and London: Routledge.

MacDonald, Scott. 2013. "The Ecocinema Experience." In *Ecocinema Theory and Practice,* edited by Stephen Rust, Salma Monani, and Sean Cubitt, 17–41. New York and London: Routledge.

McCloud, Scott. 1994. *Understanding Comics*. New York: HarperPerennial.

Murray, Robin L., and Joseph K. Heumann. 2012. *Gunfight at the Eco-Corral: Western Cinema and the Environment*. Norman, OK: University of Oklahoma Press.

Rust, Stephen A., and Carter Soles, eds. 2014. "Ecohorror Special Cluster." *Interdisciplinary Studies in Literature and the Environment* 21.3: 509–587.

Willoquet-Maricondi, Paula. 2010. *Framing the World: Explorations in Ecocriticism and Film*. Charlottesville: University of Virginia Press.

2 Beyond nature photography
The possibilities and responsibilities of seeing

H. Lewis Ulman

Introduction

In her often-cited introduction to *The Ecocriticism Reader*, Cheryll Glotfelty (1996, xix) argues that "As a critical stance, [ecocriticism] has one foot in literature and the other on land." Adapted to visual media, Glotfelty's dictum might claim that as a critical gaze, ecocriticism has one eye on *semblance* and the other on *substance*, on mediation and matter. Such a visual gaze results in a stereoscopic view that reveals, in Sean Cubitt's (2005) terms, how mediation (*technê*) repeatedly breaks apart and (re)joins the domains of human culture (*polis*) and its encompassing and consubstantial natural environment (*physis*). Though *technê* belongs to a complex constellation of concepts in Greek philosophy, we can usefully define the term as a coherent set of principles for making or producing something. For instance, in *On Rhetoric* Aristotle (1991) argues that an analysis of the available means of persuasion in public speeches about civic matters constitutes the *technê* of rhetoric. Though its implications extend widely, Cubitt's view of mediation involves no mystery: in the case of photography, mediation requires a representing subjectivity – the photographer; an object of representation such as a landscape, plant, or animal; and a medium of representation such as a digital photograph. The act of making a photograph separates its subject visually and temporally from its surroundings, translates it into a different physical form (a photographic negative or digital file), and rejoins it with other photographic representations that share features such as genre, medium, style, subject, or interpretive lens – presumably redefining to some degree viewers' relationships with and capacity to experience the object(s) depicted in the photograph by influencing how we expect a landscape or animal or wildflower to appear.

The phrase "photographic memory" refers to richly detailed, accurate recollections. We describe detailed, seemingly objective representations as "photorealistic." Yet even a passing familiarity with the process of making a photographic image and the processing of photographic negatives or manipulation of digital images alerts us to the possibility, if not the inevitability, of distortion – or worse. For instance, Lydia Millet warns about the seductions of what she terms *ecoporn*: "picture-book nature, scenic and sublime, praiseworthy but not battle-worthy. Tarted up into perfectly circumscribed simulations of the wild, these props of mainstream environmentalism serve as surrogates for real engagement with wilderness, the way porn models serve as surrogates for real women" (2004, 147). As I compose this essay, my Facebook timeline contains two subsequent entries that, in their contrasting styles, illustrate Millet's point. The first depicts a unique nighttime image of a great horned owl photographed in flight. The accompanying text in *Audubon Magazine* tells of the photographer's efforts over three nights, after hearing the "subtle hoots of a pair of great horned owls," to capture the image before getting his "reward," which the story describes as a "mid-air shot, with the owl veiling its face with its massive, dappled wing. Still visible: its spherical eyes, casting a moon-like pallor over the picture" (Saha 2014). Making this image required the photographer to shoot from a blind and, almost certainly (the text doesn't provide other technical details), to use a flash to capture the image at night and freeze the owl's motion. The next item on my timeline, from Green Columbus (2014), includes a prosaic snapshot featuring two young women preparing beds for planting along a city street as part of a citywide volunteer effort celebrating Earth Day. They are dressed and equipped for yard work – headbands, sweaters, jeans, and running shoes, shovels in hand. The image could easily have been made with a cell phone or simple point-and-shoot camera.

Box 2.1   Nature photography as ecoporn?

You may have encountered nature photographs in calendars, coffee-table books, and glossy magazines that share the "scenic and sublime" aesthetic labeled by Lydia Millet (2004, 147) as ecoporn when they "serve as surrogates for real engagement with wilderness." Like Simmons Buntin's photography teacher, Millet challenges us to question visual clichés that constrain our engagement with environments. It's not easy. Camping and canoeing on a remote Vermont lake as I write this essay, I can't resist taking photos of a dramatic sunset reflected in the water or storm clouds looming over the mountains, even though I know that we have all seen hundreds of such images. Have I succumbed to ecoporn? Or is actually hiking, camping, and canoeing in the Green Mountain National Forest an antidote to ecoporn's aesthetic of the "scenic and sublime"? If not, what might constitute a "battle-worthy" image? Choose an environment or issue about which you care deeply, and describe what might constitute a battle-worthy image related to it. How would you present that image to others?

While I would hesitate to call the photo of the owl and the accompanying text "ecoporn" – the phrase suggests, albeit for rhetorical effect, a too-easy mapping between rather different domains of representation – the photo and associated text embody elements of Millet's definition, both because of how they present their subject and what they omit from our view and consideration. For instance, the owl is flying level across the photographer's line of sight, its body is viewed along its long axis, and its wings are caught in mid-beat by the photographer's flash. Rather than "veiling its face" with its wing, the owl appears simply to look to its side – toward the photographer – as it flies along, perhaps assessing a potential threat. The look is not coy but cautious. In addition, the description does not reveal the time of year in which the image was made, which might indicate whether the pair of owls were nesting, a time when photography might disturb their mating behavior. By contrast, the photo depicting the Green Columbus event draws little attention to the details or circumstances of its making, deploying a documentary style to encourage us to emulate the volunteers at the event. All photographs, whether or not they draw attention to their technological mediation, frame both substance and semblance, suggesting where – and from where, and how, and why, and to what effect – we might direct our gaze and our attention.

Ecoporn and publicity photos for environmental volunteer initiatives represent just two points on a spectrum of photographic genres of potential interest to ecocritics. Other genres might include advertising, journalism, documentary photo essays, tourist/amateur snapshots, and fine art photography. But *nature photography* constitutes perhaps the most familiar – and general – genre designation that readers are likely to associate with ecocriticism. Nature photography, like any artistic genre, is easier to stereotype than to define, and it is perhaps more interesting at its fuzzy boundaries than in its easily recognized conventions – attractive images of plants, animals, and landscapes, typically devoid of (or deemphasizing) human presence. For instance, of the ten photographs randomly chosen from members' portfolios to serve as the Daily Sampler displayed at the top of the pages of the North American Nature Photography Association's (NANPA) website for May 7, 2014, none contain an image of a human, and only one depicts a human-built structure (a fence line running across a field; the latter is, of course, also a human construction).

Contemporary ecocriticism recognizes that nature (*physis*) encompasses more than pristine wilderness or, indeed, nonhuman nature, extending its purview to representations of urban settings and other built environments (Barlett 2005; Bennett and Teague 1999; Bosselaar 2000; Dixon 2002; Loftus 2012; Pyle 1993). From that broader perspective, nature photography, given that it always involves human perception and a mediating human technology, is perhaps best defined as a photographic reflection on the relationship between the human and nonhuman realms of the natural world. So defined, nature photography includes images of humans and the human-built world. Just as Karla Armbruster and Kathleen Wallace's groundbreaking collection, *Beyond Nature Writing* (2001), argued that literary ecocriticism should not be bound by its historical emphasis on nonfiction nature writing, "Beyond Nature Photography" argues that ecocriticism must engage a wide range of photographic genres, styles, and purposes that help shape our understanding of our places in, and responsibilities to, our environments. Moreover, if it is to provide insight into the nature of photography's mediation, ecocritical analysis must engage with the *technê* of photography, just as it engages with the techniques of fiction, poetry, or nonfiction prose. For instance, to return to the images of the owl in *Audubon Magazine* and the volunteers on the Green Columbus site, we might note that the image of the owl not only draws our attention to an aspect of an owl's flight few of us will ever witness with such clarity, but it also draws attention to the photographic mediation, since most viewers will recognize that creating the image required great skill and special equipment. By contrast, the image of the Green Columbus volunteers draws little attention to the mediation – it appears to be a casual snapshot – yet it serves its purpose in part because it is well focused, lit, composed, and timed. The two figures in the foreground are poised in the act of turning the soil, and the other figures in the background give a sense of wider participation in the event. Even when *technê* seems "artless," to understand how photographers and photographs mediate our experience of place, we need to consider a full range of photographic *technê*, including choice of subject, framing, point of view, camera placement and angle, color, light, timing, focus, depth of field, metadata, documentary context, and medium of presentation.

In an essay responding to a volume of Emmet Gowin's aerial landscape photographs, Terry Tempest Williams asks questions that identify a central tension in any ecocritical approach to photography: "Do we view each photograph as a work of art and simply enjoy the pleasure of form and texture as its own aesthetic statement? Earth becomes the artist's canvas. Or do we see this portfolio of images as a haunting documentation of place, how we have altered the land with our industrial and technological might from agriculture to recreation to national security? Art becomes revelation" (2002, 126). We might ask further, do we necessarily experience photographs as aesthetic *and* discursive objects – artifacts whose creation inevitably imbues them with aesthetic sensibilities and discursive arguments. Viewing and creating photographs in a manner mindful of these three dimensions of the medium – aesthetic, discursive, and technical – constitutes the core of what we might call the *rhetoric of nature photography*. To explore these issues, "Beyond Nature Photography" first outlines an ecocritical approach to the *technê* of photography in more detail, then examines the photographic oeuvre of Terry Evans, touching briefly on the work of other photographers whose work similarly frames our relationship to the nonhuman world.

Photographic *technê*

The familiar wilderness and conservation injunction to "take only pictures, leave only footprints" encourages visitors to be mindful of their immediate impacts on landscapes and ecosystems. We understand that the phrase highlights our responsibilities to nonhuman life by asking us not to disturb environments on which other life forms depend and our responsibilities to other humans by asking us to leave environments intact for others' enjoyment and study. Of course, the phrase cannot serve as an all-purpose mantra for responsible environmental citizenship. I would like to focus here on what the phrase suggests about photography from the perspective of ecocriticism. First, the phrase reflects our cultural and material moment by what it suggests about our most common means of recording experience, especially experience of the "outdoors." We are enjoined to "take only *pictures*" (or, in common variations, "photos" or "photographs"). I can't recall ever being directed to "take only *field notes or sketches*," though surely people still keep trail journals and sketch or paint *en plein air*. Second, and more germane to this essay, the phrase metaphorically aligns photography with extraction rather than creation – presumably to offer a nondestructive alternative to removing "trophies" from public lands. We are asked to "*take* only pictures" rather than to "*make* only pictures," thereby eliding the *technê* of photography and suggesting that it merely records rather than shapes our experience (by comparison, consider how strange it would sound to suggest that we "*take* only oil paintings").

Thus, ecocriticism must attend to two dimensions of photography. First, like other media, photography is a material, embodied practice, and ecocritics might therefore attend to the effects of a photographer's presence and equipment on the environment in which a photograph is made. Second, photography involves a *technê*, an art of making which is, as earlier defined, grounded in formal techniques and aimed at shaping and communicating arguments, and ecocritics must ask how and to what effect a photograph has been made and presented to its audience.

In a recent essay, "Photographing the Resplendent Trees," Simmons Buntin (2011) provides an evocative practitioner's account of photographic *technê*. The essay explores the nature of photographic clichés – especially those of landscape photography – and Buntin's efforts to avoid clichés in his own landscape photography while coming to terms with their appeal. Buntin's photography instructor had cautioned him to avoid the clichés that characterized some of his work. Buntin ruminates about the process by which original photographic work can become a cliché through a process of wide distribution, which makes the image commonplace, and mimicry, which yields only the stereotypical, however pleasing for particular audiences and effective for particular purposes (2011, 182). His own journey away from cliché leads through *technê* as much as through sensibility. He structures his essay according to a list of "The Visual Elements of Photography" that he credits to the Amon Carter Museum in Fort Worth, Texas, arranging sections under the headings texture, focus, color, framing and composition, light quality, and angle of view. In the section entitled "Light Quality," he writes, "I found the most success where I turned the subject upon itself by mixing my choice of lenses. Instead of the wide-angle lens that would capture the mountain's breadth, I mounted a telephoto lens to hone in on a cliff washed with the contrast of yellow ash and emerald pine" (191). Buntin notes that nonphotographer friends sometimes ask whether the *technê* of photography "distorts" his experience of place. He responds that "the camera instead enables me to see much more of the landscape and, depending on the lens and other factors, to view the landscape from multiple perspectives" (186). Working with the camera slows him down, shifts his perspective, and encourages careful inspection and reflection. Moreover, Buntin notes that the resulting image file (like the photographic negative, we should note) provides an opportunity to "re-see" the place in the act of editing – a further mediation that contributes to the creation of "an image that contains not just the framed elements of the particular landscape, but also the complexities, histories, and emotion of the place and, to no small degree, the photographer" (187). Unstated but implicit in Buntin's account are the myriad ways in which our "unaided" perceptions are still mediated by our senses and our sensibilities. The camera, no less than our eyes and minds, is both a lens and a mirror.

Box 2.2   Talk about it: making media

Viewing and thinking critically about the media we encounter every day constitutes an important approach to ecomedia studies. However, ecomedia studies also encompasses *making* media – using the *technê* of media to explore our relationship to our environments. Such exploration doesn't necessarily require advanced technical skills or elaborate equipment.

Try this experiment: In an environment or setting you know well, frame an image that represents that environment to you using the viewfinder of a camera or just a rectangle formed by your thumbs and forefingers. Now vary your framing by choosing a different subject or changing your composition (e.g., including more or less of the scene in the frame, choosing a different perspective). How do changes in your framing affect your interpretation of the environment? Repeat the experiment in an unfamiliar environment.

Share your results with your classmates, who have also conducted the same experiment.

Terry Evans: a case study in landscape photography

In a series of books and exhibits published and presented since 1986, Terry Evans has challenged audiences to see intricate relationships among the natural history, cultural history, economics, and aesthetics of North America's Great Plains prairie biome. Her photographs document a wide range of human relationships to that landscape – exploration, inhabitation, alteration, cultivation, exploitation, appreciation, study, preservation, and restoration – and engage our sense of history, of place, and of our ecological relationship to the prairie and the nonhuman species with which we share that landscape.

Ecocriticism – and ecomedia studies in particular – provides a valuable lens through which to view Terry Evans's work. Through its complex reevaluation of how we construct our place in nature, Evans's photography helps keep our perceptions in step with the expanding cultural debate over the environment. Just as critics in the field of literature and environment studies expanded their approach from exaltation of wild places to a recognition of the reciprocal relationships between culture and nature in cities, from the need to pay attention to inhabitation as well as preservation, Evans's photographic projects have expanded our gaze and imagination to a more capacious sense of our engagement with environments. In addition, because Evans's work has appeared widely in both books and exhibits, her oeuvre reminds us that photographs we typically view stand at the end of a complex series of mediations, including the photograph recorded on film or a digital sensor; developing of film or editing of digital files; printing and mounting; composing of accompanying materials such as gallery catalogues, labels, introductory essays, and captions; and the design of books and exhibit spaces.

Introducing her first book of prairie photography, *Prairie: Images of Ground and Sky*, Evans (1986, 14–15) recounts how she came to photograph the prairie: "For years I had photographed people and assumed that anything I needed to learn could come from being in and observing human relationships. When some friends asked me to photograph some survey work they were doing on a nearby prairie, I agreed out of friendship, not out of interest in the prairie. One day on the prairie, while my friends worked, I wandered around looking, and suddenly I began to see the ground. The realization came that I could stand in one spot and look at the ground for at least an hour and still not see everything happening at my feet. I started to photograph the prairie ground." Eventually, of course, Evans looks up, and discovers the topography of the prairie. She takes advantage of slanting light to highlight the subtle undulations of the land. Occasionally, the skies over the prairie capture Evans' gaze entirely, and in other photographs she looks beneath the surface of prairie soil at the roots that bind the prairie, "holding the soil firm." Still other photos dramatize the role of fire in prairie ecology and land management.

As is commonly the case in books of fine art photography, the images in *Prairie* work in concert with words, including short introductions by Wes Jackson, Gregory Bateson, and Terry Evans; an appendix listing common prairie plants; quotes appearing opposite or alongside plates; and captions for each of the images. Jackson provides an overview of prairie ecology, contrasting its complex polyculture to the monoculture of agricultural fields (1986, 9–11). Bateson addresses Evans's photography more directly, praising her "synthesis between a scientific and an aesthetic understanding of nature," her attempt "to combine rigorous photography with love of the prairie" and "scientific rigor with imagination" (1986, 12). Evans's introduction complements and confirms Bateson's assessment of her work but provides more detail about her aesthetic engagement with the prairie landscape. While she mentions learning the names of flowers and grasses and other facts about the prairie ecosystem, Evans's essay focuses on visual, conceptual, and ecological patterns – complex, chaotic, cyclical, and spiral patterns that contrasted with the straight lines of monoculture fields. In the course of coming to terms with that complexity, she tells us, she realized that the "flat planar structure" of her photographs of the ground resembled the perspective common in pre-Renaissance art, which carried "more symbolism about the experience of reality than lens-like expressions" in part because "the form itself expressed a spatial awareness that went beyond the world of appearances" (1986, 14). In Evans's case, that awareness encompassed questions about "the nature of form in visual expression, the shape of space, the nature of the sacred, agriculture, the significant of learning the plants" and confronted her with "metaphors for human community about living with diversity and deep roots and a sense of place" (Evans 1986, 15). How does photography play a role in such explorations? Let's dwell for a moment on a single image.

The first full-page plate in *Prairie* frames a swirling profusion of prairie grasses intertwined with flowering plants. To the trained eye, the caption tells us, the photograph shows "Daisy fleabane, asters, mixed prairie grasses, and cheat grass" growing in Fent's Prairie near Salina, Kansas (Evans 1986, 17). To the untrained eye, the photograph bounds the chaos of tangled grasses in a square frame, highlighting the contrast between the rectilinear borders of the images and the chaotic, swirling leaves of grass. The contrast between the light tops of the leaves and their darker, lower portions and patches of soil visible through the leaves gives a sense of depth to the ground cover, but the perspective – pointing the camera straight down at a flat surface uniformly covered with grasses and forbs – abstracts the scene, removing any visual reference that might provide a sense of scale. The Preface tells us that Evans shot most of the images in the book with a 50mm or 60mm lens on a Hasselblad 500/CM, a medium-format camera, and the square format of the images suggests that Evans created 6cm × 6cm negatives. If she positioned her camera, fitted with a 50mm lens, approximately four feet above the ground (in the Preface to *The Inhabited Prairie*, Evans

[1998] mentions that she photographed the "untouched native prairie ... at waist-high distance") the image represents a square about 4.75 ft. on a side, or a bit over 22 square feet. Of course, we aren't told exactly how the image was made, and such calculations are in any case far less important than realizing that the image making in this instance *subtracts* references to relative size – unless we are already familiar with the typical size of daisy fleabane and cheat grass – that would be present in our visual field were we standing where Evans stood when she made the image. Other subtractions from our normal visual field – beyond the obvious facts that still photography can *evoke* but not *embody* smell, taste, texture, and movement – contribute to the image's effect. The black-and-white print subtracts color, and presenting the image on a bare, white page and reducing the size of the area depicted to fit on that page removes the presence of the larger prairie in our peripheral vision. Our eyes may still move around the image, exploring the variation that constitutes the deceptively homogeneous whole, but the image isolates the pattern of the grasses and forbs, as if on a laboratory slide, for our inspection.

Many other images in the book, in both black and white and color, explore this visual trope, emphasizing the fundamental role of grasses and forbs in the prairie ecosystem. Eventually, of course, Evans looks up – or down, in some aerial photographs – and turns her lens on the topography of the prairie. Here again, she employs her medium to shape our perception and conception of the landscape. In many images, she exploits the shadows produced by slanting morning or evening light to emphasize the topography of the prairie, putting the lie to the perception that the plains are uniformly flat, just as her photographs of grasses and forbs put the lie to the notion that the landscape is plain. Several other images resist the conventional practice of placing horizon lines in the top or bottom third of a frame, instead placing the horizon in the middle of the square frame, highlighting the broad views of ground and sky that characterize the prairie and inspired the title of the book. Still other images fill the frame with clouds and sky, mimicking the planar views of grasses and forbs and, thus, uniting ground and sky.

One more shift in perspective adds depth to Evans's ecological exploration of the prairie. The final image in the book depicts an embankment – we aren't told, nor does the framing reveal, how it was formed – that reveals the deep roots of prairie grasses. Text on the opposite page informs us that 85% of the biomass of the prairie exists below ground.

Most important in the context of Evans's development as a photographer, however, is the fact that no humans or built objects appear anywhere in the book. Of course, we know that we are looking at land with a history of human use, and the captions tell us that most of the photographs depict privately owned land or land set aside as nature preserves, but only a series of four images near the end of the book include explicit evidence of human management – controlled "burns" of prairie. Interestingly, the two short epigraphs that introduce this set of images refer to the (presumably) naturally occurring fires that were an important part of the prairie ecosystem, keeping encroaching woody plants at bay and rejuvenating the prairie grasses and forbs. Humans have been managing prairie landscapes with "burns" for thousands of years, and these images provide the only explicit visual evocation in *Prairie: Ground and Sky* of human presence.

In the Preface to her next book, *The Inhabited Prairie* (1998), Evans tells us how she came to search out patterns of human inhabitation of the prairie:

> I remembered an aerial view of mine of the unploughed Konza Prairie, near Manhattan, Kansas, in which the prairie hills looked like a woman's breast. Suddenly, I realized that the inhabited prairie was part of the body of prairie and that I could not understand prairie if I didn't look at the whole of it. . . . I began to photograph the rest of the prairie.
>
> (ix)

Although Evans focuses here on a dramatic shift in the *subject* of her photography, she also reveals important continuities in the *subjectivity* and *mediation* of the images in *The Inhabited Prairie*. Her trope of the "body" of the prairie explicitly connects these new images to those in *Prairie: Images of Ground and Sky* in a manner reminiscent of what Terry Tempest Williams (1994) has called "the erotics of place." Evans also highlights the strong compositional ties between *Prairie: Images of Ground and Sky* and *The Inhabited Prairie*: the images are still square format, presumably from medium format, 6cm × 6cm film negatives; unbroken horizon lines feature in several images; many images highlight pattern; and many of the images, both aerial photos and ones made on the ground, employ a planar perspective looking directly down on the subject and slanting light that highlights modulations and small structures in the landscape. For all these compositional ties, Evans presents the photos in *The Inhabited Prairie* differently: all are black-and-white prints; captions identify the subject and date on which the photo was taken, but no epigraphs complement individual photos or groups of photos. All the same, text informs our reception of the images. Donald Worster's Introduction employs the history of the U.S. Rectangular Land Survey – the grid – as a structure for an overview of human uses of the prairie (1998, ix), and Evans notes in her Preface that she and her pilots "flew high enough to see the grid but low enough to see a deer wandering across a bombing target, totally at home on the weapons range." The text alerts us to the presence of both land and inhabitation in the images.

The human presences in Evans's photographs range from an image of a car and pond nearly indiscernible in a vast prairiescape west of Minneapolis to human structures that overwhelm the landscape, such as a stretch of I-35 near Salinas, Kansas. Embedded in the patterns she viewed from 700 to 1,000 feet above the prairie and on the ground, she also saw stories of human habitation that broadened her historical and environmental understanding of the effects of human inhabitation on the prairie. Expecting to see evidence only of abuse, she read a more complicated narrative: "Other stories revealed by the facts of the landscape also changed my preconceptions. I found that I was no longer looking for abuse of the prairie. Instead, I was simply trying to read its stories from the facts of the landscape. . . . The prairie contains in her breast many stories of use and misuse, care and neglect" (Evans 1998, ix–x). Her subjects include farms, weapons ranges, natural gas storage facilities, landfills, grain elevators, an abandoned missile launch pad – and nature preserves. As we saw in Simmons Buntin's essay, it is a commonplace of photographic practice to explore various perspectives on a subject by altering compositional elements. In *The Inhabited Prairie* (1998), such variety lends nuance to her treatment of a new dimension of the prairie.

In *Disarming the Prairie*, published the same year as *The Inhabited Prairie*, Evans shifts her focus from the many forms of human inhabitation to a specific effort to restore land that has previously been dedicated to – and often harmed by – human uses. Focusing on the restoration of the Joliet National Arsenal as the Midewin National Tallgrass Prairie Park – the nation's first national prairie park – Evans captures a moment of transition on land still marked by evidence of its past use in the "preparation for three wars: World War II, the Korean War, and the Vietnam War" (Hiss 1998, 11). In her Introduction, she tells us that "[t]his is a book of hope, about a place on the verge of restoration, a place that has been used solely for human purposes now given back to nature with human care" (1998, ix). The forty-nine images in *Disarming the Prairie* (counting a triptych as one image) certainly bear a family resemblance to those in Evans's other books – they appear to be printed from square-format negatives; ten are aerial images of ammunition storage bunkers, narrow-gauge railroad tracks, and decaying dynamite factories, images that do not for the most part contain horizon lines; and two – of a red-winged blackbird's nest and the jawbone of a deer – employ the planar close-up view of the ground that Evans used to such strong effect in *Prairie: Images of Ground and Sky*. However, the images are also starkly different from those in her other books. For instance, while all of the images in *The Inhabited Prairie* are black and white, all of the images in *Disarming the Prairie* are in color, echoing Evans's evocation of spring and rebirth in her Preface: "When I returned [to the prairie in the spring], green was beginning to cover the stark gray outlines of abandonment. Lime green leaves on burr oaks, yellow haze on sugar maples, Virginia bluebells unfolding – vivid color brought the land alive again. Nature had reengaged this military landscape" (Evans 1998). And as Tony Hiss notes in his Introduction, "we see human traces – everywhere – but no human faces" (1998, 17). Evans's strategy for registering the subtraction of humans from this landscape often involves compositional approaches uncommon or wholly absent in her other landscape work to this point: focusing on human-scale scenes in which humans are even more conspicuously absent than they are in *Prairie: Images of Ground and Sky*. At a distance of a few feet, as if we were about to occupy the scene, she shows us a sink in a crumbling furnace room; a dust-covered chair at a desk containing a dust-covered rotary phone; a sign so obscured by rust that we have the sensation of leaning in to read it; three filing cabinets in an office building destroyed by fire, the bottom drawer open as if waiting for someone to refile some papers; a guard house door through which we can imagine workers passing to present their IDs. Through effective choices of subject, composition, framing, point of view, color, narrative, and documentary context, Evans speaks as eloquently through what circumstances and art subtract from the scene as she does by what she presents.

In an exhibit entitled *From Prairie to Field*, which debuted in 2002 at The Field Museum in Chicago and has since traveled to many other venues, Evans's photography of the prairie takes yet another conceptual and aesthetic turn. Employing a 4×5 large-format view camera and studio lights, Evans photographed botanical and zoological specimens preserved in The Field Museum's collection. In the exhibit catalogue, Evans connects the exhibit to her earlier images of the prairie, noting that they provide "counterpoint to the aerial surveys and to [her] earliest work, in which [she] studied the wild interwoven patterns of complexity in undisturbed prairie. This work is about human recognition of that complexity" (The Field Museum, 2002), and indeed, the images depict animal and plant specimens collected over the past 150 years by scientists attempting to document and understand natural history. The photographs, of course, serve a somewhat different purpose. Evans writes, "These prints are a re-presenting, if you will, of the specimens. I want to hold them up to the viewer as if to say, 'Look here! Do you see the beauty here? Do you see also what else is here, the questions about immortality and loss and beauty?'" These questions arise from what the acts of collection and photography have subtracted from the subject – the behavior of the living plants and animals, the time and habitats in which they lived, and so on. And as in her earlier photographs of the prairie, Evans pursues her artistic goals as much by what she subtracts from the subject as by what she emphasizes. As she explains, she does not present the specimens *in situ*. Rather, she has removed them from their drawers and cabinets, arranged them, and illuminated them with studio lights (see Figure 2.1)

In a photo of bull snake specimens, for example, Evans adds drama by rotating the jar so that we see two snakes' heads facing one another, and the studio lighting and arrangement isolates the jar from its curatorial context, even as the snake specimens have been isolated from their natural habitat. Through carefully controlled visual emphasis, Evans's photographs probe the minds of the collectors and provoke the imagination of viewers. Often, the photographs entail almost mathematical patterns that, by extrapolation, suggest the multitude of specimens in the collection – over 22 million – the innumerable animals and plants they represent, and the recognition by the collector of the immense variety of the natural world. In a drawer full of cardinal specimens, for instance, we recognize the complex morphological

Figure 2.1 Terry Evans at the Field Museum in Chicago.
Source: Courtesy of Gretchen Baker, Director of the Field Museum.

variation among individuals belonging to a single species, juxtaposed with the taxonomic complexity of human attempts to understand variation throughout the natural world systematically (see Figure 2.2). Evans focuses our attention on the specimens *and* the "hand of the collector," from "the flowing script on the herbarium sheets" to the careful mounting of specimens.

Layers of mediation complicate Evans's presentation of her subject. In the case of *From Prairie to Field*, we must account for three media: (1) the photographs themselves (i.e., the images captured on film, which are *not* presented for our inspection), (2) the prints we view in the exhibit, and (3) the exhibit space – all of which profoundly shape what we see and how we respond. The exhibit prints in *From Prairie to Field* differ from the prints we encounter in books of photography. They were made with Iris inkjet

Figure 2.2 "Cardinals" by Terry Evans.
Source: Courtesy of Terry Evans.

printers – also referred to as Iris giclée. Preparing an Iris giclée print involves scanning an original medium – in this case presumably color negatives – digitally editing the scanned image, then printing on a large drum printer (Hunter Editions 2014). The resulting prints – all in color and often life-size or larger in exhibits of *From Prairie to Field* – are indeed striking. I have watched visitors walk up to an Evans print in a museum gallery, lean in close, squint, and try to determine whether they are looking at a mounted

specimen – or an image of a specimen. In the preface to the exhibit catalogue, Evans (The Field Museum 2002) reflects on the relationship between
these highly detailed prints and the thousands of physical specimens she
sorted through at The Field Museum:

> The dried leaves, the feathers, the fur, the glass, and the labels of
> the specimens contain a tactile sensuousness that I want to commu-
> nicate. . . . It is important to me to present the specimens in a way
> that shows the viewer something close to my own experience of see-
> ing them. However, the finished print, in an odd way, sometimes looks
> more like the specimen than the specimen itself. This is perhaps because
> these highly detailed images move all the visual information to a two-
> dimensional surface.

Evans alerts us to an important characteristic of these photographs, but I
also suspect that something more is happening than the reduction of visual
information from three dimensions to two. Rather, as we have noted, *all*
of the information available to someone handling and working with the
specimens – visual, tactile, auditory, olfactory – is reduced to framed, two-
dimensional visual information, and the immediate context is shifted from
scientific study (collection, measurement, classification, and so on) to aesthetic gaze.

Through strategic acts of subtraction and emphasis, Evans's photographs
invite us to inspect elements of the specimens differently than we might if we
encountered them as researchers in the storage rooms of The Field Museum.
And therein lies a difficulty for many viewers, who encounter an unexpected
lifelessness in the images that they might expect in a natural history museum.
During one visit to *From Prairie to Field*, I heard comments like these from
visitors young and old: "Dead birds in an art museum!"; "These are all dead
birds!"; "Dead birds, dead animals, dead insects, dead foliage"; "They're
all dead!" I have overheard other visitors pose questions about loss, though
because they apparently missed the explanatory text, their questions are
probably not exactly the ones Terry Evans has in mind: "What did he do,
put them to death and then photograph them?" and "You mean they had to
kill all these before they took pictures of them?" By contrast, other viewers
are awed by the fine detail of the prints. I overheard one visitor reflect that
"Someday they will probably use these in scientific research." The photograph seemed most present to this viewer as a specimen of the specimens at
The Field Museum rather than as sad reminders of living individuals. More
often, however, viewers seemed to see in the photographs something akin to
the "terrible beauty" often associated with the haunting images of landfills,
mines, and tailings ponds in Edward Burtynsky's (Pauli et al. 2003) *Manufactured Landscapes* and Emmet Gowin's (2002) aerial images of altered
landscapes in *Changing the Earth: Aerial Photographs*. They are, in short,
aesthetically powerful, and therefore all the more compelling, reminders of

our effects on the ecosystems that sustain us and the other species with which we share the land.

Space permits only a brief mention of other projects that extend Terry Evans's examination of our footprint on the prairie. Although the editors of *Heartland: The Photographs of Terry Evans* (Davis, Aspinwall, and Watson 2012) place images from *Revealing Chicago* (Evans 2005) in a section entitled "Beyond the Prairie," the project reveals close ties – artistic, geographic, and environmental – to her earlier work. The aerial color photographs in *Revealing Chicago* echo the perspective that first inspired Evans to explore human inhabitation of the prairie, and her sensibility to place – and placement – remains strong. Just as William Cronon's (1991) study of Chicago and its relationship to its surrounding landscape in *Nature's Metropolis* invites a reconsideration of urban nature, Terry Evans's photographs of Chicago expands our visual understanding of how a city is situated by drawing our gaze inexorably from the lakeshore and downtown to the suburbs, farmland, and, finally, to the "open space" beyond in which she revisits efforts at preserving the prairie, such as the Medewin. Her more recent study of the oil boom in North Dakota moves farther west, but remains a study of our footprint on the prairie. The forty-two images on her website (Evans 2014) representing the project contain some familiar compositions – aerial shots of disturbed landscapes; a sardonic, human-scale shot of a boarded-up "bank from an earlier boom" – but sixteen of the photos, nearly 40%, are head shots, some identified by captions as portraits of a rancher, farmer roustabout, driller, Native American, contractor, pit hand, and water hauler. Though these tightly cropped portraits can't tell us the individuals' stories, they remind us that each person has a story, one interpolated in the land and the debate just as their faces are embedded among Evans's images of a marked landscape. By subtracting context from the portraits, Evans in effect places all of the individuals in the same landscape – the one we all share – at the same time eliding some of their different relationships to that landscape.

Box 2.3   Alternative approaches

This case study explores ecocritical issues generally applicable to photography by examining one photographer's work, but other approaches can yield different insights. Consider, for instance, how genre relates to environmental issues. What might we learn from advertising images, tourist photos, photojournalism spreads, scientific illustrations, activists' exposés, and so on. Similarly, we perhaps focus too easily on a narrow range of subjects – plants, animals, and landscapes, whether in urban, rural, or wild places. What might an ecocritical approach to interior architectural photography (focusing on the places in which humans spend most of our time), portraiture, or product photography tell us about our relationship to extractive technologies or our waste stream? Finally, how might different photographic technologies affect the ways we view and imagine our environments? Cell phones offer nearly ubiquitous and continuous opportunities to capture and manipulate images. Wearable, mountable cameras such as the GoPro offer new perspectives and options for camera placement. How do unique or emerging technologies – or new uses of common technologies – change the way we imagine our environments?

Photography necessarily mediates what it depicts as much through exclusion as inclusion, constructing narratives and posing questions by inviting us to reflect on what it temporally or spatially crops out of an image as much as what it includes and emphasizes. Throughout a series of linked projects spanning her career, Terry Evans has engaged viewers with an evolving exploration of human and nonhuman presences and absences on the North American prairies, asking critical questions about our relationship to that landscape. Other photographers show us the imprint of humans on the landscape (e.g., Edward Burtynsky and Emmet Gowin), and all face the dilemma that environmental photography must engage and confront the viewer through images that draw our gaze and challenge our understanding. However, I know of no other photographer whose work traces an arc of discovery that holds so much promise for ecocriticism and ecomedia studies as that of Terry Evans, who repeatedly asks us to reconsider the possibilities and responsibilities of seeing.

Keywords

Ecoporn	Rhetoric of nature photography
Erotics of place	Semblance
Physis	Substance
Polis	Technê

Discussion questions

1   Choose a photograph taken in an environment with which you are familiar. What elements of the environment have been subtracted from the image or deemphasized through its choice of subject, camera placement, point of view, timing, and composition? What story about the environment does that framing tell? What persons or groups might closely associate with that story? What stories does it omit? What persons or groups might closely associate with *those* stories?

2   Find a photograph of a landscape that you consider beautiful. What qualities of the image constitute its beauty? What do those aesthetic qualities tell you about how we value landscapes? Do those qualities – and the presentation of them in the image – bear any resemblance to pornography?

3   Check out one of the books of landscape photography mentioned in this chapter, or visit an exhibit of landscape photography. How do the images and the text (e.g., captions, notes, and introductory essays) relate to one another? What does their relationship suggest in general about the ways that images and text mediate our experience of landscape and environmental issues?

4   Choose an environmental issue that directly affects you and your friends and family. Ask several people to describe in as much detail as possible a photograph that they imagine would draw others' attention to the issue. Do their choices of subject and representation focus on understanding and appreciating environments or critically examining humans' effects on their environments – or both? What do their choices reveal about the issue?

5   Choose an image of a person or group in any environment that interests you (rural, urban, or wilderness). Defining *difference* as widely as possible (e.g., consider differences in age, gender, race, ethnicity, socioeconomic class, ability), discuss the following questions: Would you be surprised to find different people (e.g., different in some way than the people in the photograph) depicted in the environment? In what sorts of environments are you used to seeing different groups of people depicted? What relationships between cultural difference and environment do those images suggest, create, or sustain?

Further reading

Adams, Robert. 1994. *Why People Photograph: Selected Essays and Reviews*. New York: Aperture.

Baillargeon, Claude, Robert Francis Kennedy, Maia-Mari Sutnik, and Meadow Brook Art Gallery. 2005. *Imaging a Shattering Earth: Contemporary Photography and the Environmental Debate*. Rochester, MI, and Toronto, ON: Meadow Brook Art Gallery.

Barthes, Roland. 1981. *Camera Lucida: Reflections on Photography*, 1st American ed. New York: Hill and Wang.

Beckman, Karen Redrobe, and Liliane Weissberg. 2013. *On Writing with Photography*. Minneapolis and London: University of Minnesota Press.

Leopold, Aldo. 1949. *A Sand County Almanac, and Sketches Here and There*. Charles W. Schwartz. New York: Oxford.

Robinson, Mike, and David Picard. 2009. *The Framed World: Tourism, Tourists and Photography*. New Directions in Tourism Analysis. Farnham, England; Burlington, VT: Ashgate.

Sontag, Susan. 1990. *On Photography*. New York: Anchor Books.

Works cited

Aristotle. 1991. *On Rhetoric: A Theory of Civil Discourse*. Translated by George A. Kennedy. New York: Oxford University Press.

Armbruster, Karla, and Kathleen R. Wallace. 2001. *Beyond Nature Writing: Expanding the Boundaries of Ecocriticism*, Under the Sign of Nature. Charlottesville: University Press of Virginia.

Barlett, Peggy F., ed. 2005. *Urban Place: Reconnecting with the Natural World*, Urban and Industrial Environments. Cambridge, MA: MIT Press.

Bateson, Gregory. 1986. "The Prairie Seen Whole." In *Prairie: Images of Ground and Sky*, by Terry Evans, 12. Lawrence, KS: University Press of Kansas.

Bennett, Michael, and David W. Teague. 1999. *The Nature of Cities: Ecocriticism and Urban Environments*. Tucson: University of Arizona Press.

Bosselaar, Laure-Anne. 2000. *Urban Nature: Poems about Wildlife in the City*. 1st ed. Minneapolis: Milkweed Editions.

Buntin, Simmons B. 2011. "Photographing the Resplendent Trees." *Interdisciplinary Studies in Literature & Environment* 18.1: 179–196.

Cronon, William. 1991. *Nature's Metropolis: Chicago and the Great West*. New York: W. W. Norton.

Cubitt, Sean. 2005. *Ecomedia*. Contemporary Cinema. Amsterdam and New York: Rodopi.

Davis, Keith F., Jane Lee Aspinwall, and April M. Watson. 2012. *Heartland: The Photographs of Terry Evans*. Kansas City, MO; New Haven, CT; London: Hall Family Foundation in association with the Nelson-Atkins Museum of Art; Yale University Press.

Dixon, Terrell. 2002. *City Wilds: Essays and Stories about Urban Nature*. Athens, GA: University of Georgia Press.

Evans, Terry. 1986. *Prairie: Images of Ground and Sky*. Lawrence, KS: University Press of Kansas.

———. 1998. *Disarming the Prairie*. Baltimore: The Johns Hopkins University Press.

———. 2005. *Revealing Chicago: An Aerial Portrait*. New York: H. N. Abrams.

———. 2014. "Terry Evans Photography," under "North Dakota Oil Boom." Accessed May 7. http://www.terryevansphotography.com

Evans, Terry, and Donald Worster. 1998. *The Inhabited Prairie*. Lawrence, KS: University Press of Kansas.

The Field Museum. 2002. "From Prairie to Field: Photographs by Terry Evans." Chicago: The Field Museum.

Glotfelty, Cheryll. 1996. Introduction to *The Ecocriticism Reader: Landmarks in Literary Ecology*, edited by Cheryll Glotfelty and Harold Fromm, xv–xxxiv. Athens, GA: University of Georgia Press.

Gowin, Emmet. 2002. *Changing the Earth: Aerial Photographs*. New Haven, CT: Yale University Art Gallery in association with the Corcoran Gallery of Art and Yale University Press.

Green Columbus. 2014. *It's Called Gratitude*. Accessed May 17. http://www.green cbus.org/CampaignProcess.aspx?A=View&Data=BEQ19OtAHdeYjgP8BBNQlA %3D%3D

Hiss, Tony. 1998. "Turning Bullets into Birds." In *Disarming the Prairie*, by Terry Evans, 1–17. Baltimore: The Johns Hopkins University Press.

Hunter Editions. 2014. "What Is Digital Printmaking?" Accessed June 1. http://www.huntereditions.com/html/digital-print-faq.html#3

Jackson, Wes. 1986. "Living Nets in a New Prairie Sea." In *Prairie: Images of Ground and Sky*, by Terry Evans, 9–11. Lawrence, KS: University Press of Kansas.

Loftus, Alex. 2012. *Everyday Environmentalism: Creating an Urban Political Ecology*. Minneapolis: University of Minnesota Press.

Millet, Lydia. 2004. "Die, Baby Harp Seal!" In *Naked: Writers Uncover the Way We Live on Earth*, edited by Susan Zakin, 146–150. New York: Four Walls Eight Windows.

NANPA (The North American Nature Photography Association). 2014. Accessed May 7. http://www.nanpa.org/index.php

Pauli, Lori, Kenneth Baker, Michael Torosian, Mark Haworth-Booth, Edward Burtynsky, Art Gallery of Ontario, National Gallery of Canada, and Brooklyn Museum of Art. 2003. *Manufactured Landscapes: The Photographs of Edward Burtynsky*. Ottawa: National Gallery of Canada in association with Yale University Press.

Pyle, Robert Michael. 1993. *The Thunder Tree: Lessons from an Urban Wildland*. New York: Houghton Mifflin.

Saha, Purbita. 2014. "Photo of the Day: Great Horned Owl." *Audubon Magazine*. Accessed May 7. http://mag.audubon.org/articles/birds/photo-day-great-horned-owl

Williams, Terry Tempest. 1994. "Yosemite: The Erotics of Place." In *An Unspoken Hunger: Stories from the Field*, 81–87. New York: Pantheon Books.

———. 2002. "The Earth Stares Back." In *Changing the Earth: Aerial Photographs*, by Emmet Gowin, 125–131. New Haven, CT: Yale University Art Gallery in association with the Corcoran Gallery of Art and Yale University Press.

Worster, Donald. 1998. "A Tapestry of Change: Nature and Culture on the Prairie." In *The Inhabited Prairie*, by Terry Evans, xi–xvii. Lawrence, KS: University Press of Kansas.

3 Eco-nostalgia in popular Turkish cinema

Ekin Gündüz Özdemirci and Salma Monani

Introduction

In the opening of the 2001 Turkish film *Şellale* (Semih Aslanyürek), a close-up shot captures the green-white luminescence of falling water, and we hear the voiceover of Cemal's (the protagonist) mother advising her daughter, Şehra, to tell her dreams to the flowing water. As the camera tracks down the length of a waterfall, we hear Şehra describe how happy she was in her dream. The camera then pulls back into a long shot to reveal the base of the waterfall, ringed by women. The gentle and haunting notes of a ney, a traditional Turkish reed instrument, fill the soundscape. There is no diagetic sound, yet it is apparent from their gestures and expressions that the women are talking to the flowing water, as if to an intimate friend; all seem animated and sincere.

The dream-like quality is enhanced as the opening scene cuts, along with a tenser tonal shift in music, to sepia shots of a naked Cemal running through deserted streets and alleyways. Then we find Cemal suddenly in a space where the camera pans across ruins overgrown by weeds and littered with untidy reels of film. When Cemal holds up a strip of film, we see that the film is of the women at the waterfall. Then Cemal finds himself naked on a stage before a cheering audience of blind men. We realize that we are in his dream as the film cuts back to color. Through Cemal's voiceover we learn that he is an artist, unable to paint. As he speaks, he evokes his mother's wisdom of telling dreams to the waterfall: "I want to go back, Mother, to tell my dreams to the waterfall, to the inner corner of Daphne's eyes." As the opening credits appear on screen, we see mountain landscapes, industrial skylines, agricultural flat lands, and country roads roll by as if seen from a moving vehicle. Passing them, we arrive with Cemal in his childhood home, the town of Antakya, which lies in the rural belt of southern Anatolia.

The juxtaposition of the peaceful waterfall scene in color with the anxious, sepia-toned dreamscape of Cemal running naked in the streets alerts viewers to the film's central theme, Cemal's negotiations of past with present. Cemal's mother represents his idealized childhood memories and the comfort of home. In contrast, his nakedness, the deserted streets, and the overgrown ruins symbolize the troubles of his present. Because Cemal's story is foregrounded against Turkey's political history of the 1960s, many might also recognize the film as an example of popular New Turkish Cinema. Scholars such as Asuman Suner write that such films often use a nostalgic approach to the past to help Turkish viewers collectively engage with the country's last fifty years of turbulent sociopolitical changes (Suner 2010). In this chapter, we join current scholarly discussion on Turkish cinema to conversations in ecocinema studies by viewing *Şellale* as an example of Turkish film in which nostalgia takes on ecological import. Because their explicit focus is not on environmental protection, films like *Şellale* have not been theoretized as examples of Turkish ecocinema; however, they lend themselves quite readily to ecocritical readings. *Şellale*'s opening sequence foregrounds such readings through its juxtaposition of natural elements (the waterfall, the weeds, Cemal's naked body, the landscapes of mountains and flatlands) and cultural elements (the women's dream-telling, the film strips and reels, and the moving vehicle that carries us through the varied landscapes).

To better situate *Şellale*'s ecocritical potential, we will first discuss the broad purview of **ecocinema studies**. Second, by highlighting eco-film critics' interests in cinematic appeals to emotion, we will explore the idea of nostalgia as a complex emotion that speaks to ecological sensibilities. Third, we will apply our understanding of **eco-nostalgia** to *Şellale* to consider what such a reading might lend to our understandings of Turkey's national and transnational environmental discourse. Finally, we will summarize how such readings enrich our engagement with both Turkish cinema and ecocinema studies.

Ecocinema studies as primer

In the past few years, ecocinema studies has exploded as a vibrant field of interdisciplinary inquiry. In doing so, the field has shifted its focus to *all* films, not just ones that intend an environmental message (Rust, Monani, and Cubitt 2013; Pick and Narraway 2013). Because cinema's stories can influence the way we view and interact with the world (Leiserowitz 2004; Kääpä 2013), and because filmmaking is a resource-intensive activity (Maxwell and Miller 2012; Bozak 2012), such an inclusive understanding of *all* cinema as environmentally grounded, and thus a suitable subject for ecocritical analysis, seems relatively easy to grasp. That said, ecocinema scholars have approached the definition of **ecocinema** in various ways (MacDonald 2004; Willoquet-Marcondi 2010; Ivakhiv 2008; Ingram 2013). As a number of eco-film critics suggest, such definitions are dependent both on the film (its production, distribution, and intended messaging or **encoding**) and on its audiences (their sociocultural, political, and material contexts), as well as in how these two entities encounter each other. For example, Chris Tong writes:

> When we discuss a film, we discuss a film in relation to viewers . . . For any discussion to take place, the film must have meant something to

somebody. In fact, we often view the same film and arrive at different interpretations.

(2013, 118)

In recognizing the audience, Tong tweaks a definition of ecocinema that was proposed by Sheldon Lu and Jiayan Mi in their edited collection *Chinese Ecocinema in the Age of Environmental Challenge* (2009). Whereas Lu and Mi describe ecocinema as "cinema with an ecological consciousness" (2009, 2), Tong suggests that ecocinema is "cinema *viewed* from an ecological perspective" (2013, 118). Such a definition helps explain why many eco-film critics *decode* ecological potential in films that don't explicitly encode such meanings, such as westerns (e.g., Carmichael 2006; Murray and Heumann 2012), road movies (e.g., Brereton 2006) or science fiction (e.g., Taylor 2013) to reveal myriad environmental themes.

Along with attention to varied media and genres, eco-film critics have also theorized such ecological encounters in multiple ways, drawing on ideas such as critical race theory (e.g., Monani, Chiu, and Arreglo 2011), queer theory (e.g., Seymour, 2013), Marxist dialectics (e.g., Hageman 2013; Cubitt 2005), postcolonial, cosmopolitan, and transnational understandings (e.g., Kääpä and Gustafsson 2013), and ecophilosophy, which presents a comprehensive exploration of perceptual, social, and material relations (e.g., Ivakhiv 2013).

In this emerging dialogue, some of the most exciting recent scholarship is the attention eco-film critics give to the role *affect* and *emotion* play in cinema's ecological potential. While affect is the immediate, visceral bodily response we have as we watch a film, emotions illuminate our cognitive awareness of such responses. Eco-film critics, like those represented in Alexa Weik von Mossner's edited collection *Moving Environments: Affect, Emotion, Ecology, and Film* (2014), draw on humanistic, social, and scientific disciplines (such as film studies, psychology, and the cognitive sciences) to point to complex ways in which films (through their audiovisual presentations and narrative triggers) work to manipulate audiences' affect and emotion, as well as the ways and reasons why audiences resist, or succumb to, such manipulations.

Şellale employs *nostalgia* as an emotional hook to capture its viewers. But, before examining *Şellale* closely, let's consider the idea of *eco-nostalgia* to better recognize how an emotion can be ecologically pertinent and what this means for viewers of cinema.

Eco-nostalgia: nostalgia, the pastoral, and cinema

Nostalgia is described as a complex emotion that involves past-oriented cognitive and affective signatures – the mind's way of remembering through visceral engagement with feelings generated by real or virtual triggers of sight, sound, or other bodily sensations (Hepper et al. 2012). Deriving from the Greek words *nostos* ("return home") and *algos* ("longing"), nostalgia engages emotions such as affection and sadness to evoke the loss of a past time, place, or situation. Cultural studies scholar Svetlana Boym defines the time and place that nostalgia evokes as an "ideal home" (2001).

Nostalgia becomes particularly interesting when we recognize that our feelings for an ideal past are often about how we engage with the present (Hepper et al. 2012, 5). As Liu Wai Yeung writes, nostalgia is about a present sense of "identity along with its affiliated concepts such as belonging, memory, mode of living, recognition and culture" (2004, 17). In this entanglement of what nostalgia stands for and evokes, scholars also recognize ecological valences. Let us consider at least two ways in which nostalgia transmutes to *eco-nostalgia* – through bodily experience and through semiotics (etymologically and narratively).

At the bodily level, nostalgia is both abstract and yet affectively embodied. Materiality, a key concern for ecocritics, is apparent when we experience nostalgia, whether through a particular visceral trigger – e.g., through smelling, tasting, hearing or other bodily sensations – or through the *felt* emotions nostalgia evokes. Thus, bodily we feel the pain of sadness or the joy of remembrance. In being embodied, nostalgia is not an abstract emotion but a tangible sensation that reminds us of our own physicality. Through nostalgia, we are nature as much as we are culture. All nostalgia in this sense is eco-nostalgia as it is ecologically bound. However, we can also think of eco-nostalgia in terms of semiotics, which can narrow its meaning to evoking natural environments that surround us.

At the etymological level, the idea of nostalgia as deriving from the idea of home resonates with the idea of ecology. "Eco" derives from the Greek *oikos*, meaning "house," and while scientists consider ecology the study (*logos*) of our earthly house, environmental humanists have considered nature as "our widest home" (Howarth 1996, 69). Semiotic expressions like "Mother Nature" reiterate this alliance of nature as caregiver. Such expressions often extend across cultures. More importantly, as recent works like the edited collection *Ecologies of Affect: Placing Nostalgia, Desire and Hope* (Davidson, Park, and Shields 2011) suggest, our language helps shape not only our mental ideas of particular spaces but also the actual places themselves. For example, Svetlana Boym describes how in the mid-nineteenth century, European and colonial bourgeois added herbariums, greenhouses, and aquariums to transform their urban home spaces and express and satisfy feelings for *pastoral nostalgia* at a time of rapid urbanization (2001, 16).

Relatedly, the pastoral nostalgia that Boym refers to is useful as it spotlights how our language of nostalgia forms narratives that are ecologically salient. Highlighting the countryside as the site of nostalgia, the pastoral narrative usually encapsulates a thematic longing for a closer relationship with the natural environment. As ecocritic Terry Gifford writes, this relationship is predicated on the basis that a harmonious relationship with the natural environment will encourage a person's inner nature to also flourish (2014, 18). In effect, the pastoral narrative is one of eco-nostalgia. It is also one that most of us can recognize as reflecting a post-industrial longing for a simpler, less hurried way of life.

Box 3.1 Talk about it: the pastoral narrative as eco-nostalgia

The earliest known written pastoral text is Theocritus's third-century *Idylls*, from which the word "idyllic" comes. In remembering the Sicilian shepherd's song competitions from his youth, Theocritus imbued pastoralism with a sense of nostalgia for the rural life (Gifford 2014; Garrard 2004).

In the mid-nineteenth century, as industrialization swept across the United States, Henry David Thoreau extolled the pastoral narrative through publications such as *Walden* (1854), which described his experiment in deliberate and simple living in the woods of Concord, Massachusetts. Leo Marx's *The Machine in the Garden: Technology and the Pastoral Ideal in America* (1964) and Laurence Buell's *The Environmental Imagination: Thoreau, Nature Writing, and the Formation of American Culture* (1995) are examples of ecocritical work that engage with Thoreau's pastoral ideas.

Even more recently, at the turn of the twenty-first century, Al Gore used the pastoral narrative as eco-nostalgia in his famous climate change documentary, *An Inconvenient Truth*. In describing the scenes that highlight his memories of his rural home, eco-film critics Robin Murray and Joseph Huemann suggest that the film's arguments to address climate change rest on shared *eco-memory* rather than future predictions (2009, 197).

While the pastoral is one way to explore eco-nostalgia, have you experienced a longing for a different kind of nature? For example, that of a city? Or a wilderness area? Or your childhood pet? If so, provide examples you can share with your classmates.

Cinema often evokes the pastoral narrative to help viewers engage with particular protagonists and plotlines. In movies ranging from Hollywood film adaptations of classic Greek tales such as the *Odyssey* to New Turkish Cinema like *Şellale*, rural landscapes are often depicted as idealized places of tranquility and calm, spaces that stand in contrast to the chaotic discomfort of the present. As protagonists remember their past and seek to return to such spaces, pastoral narratives take on a classic "pastoral momentum of retreat and return" (Gifford 2014, 18). They are literally a story's sites of "home longing." However, because many narratives engage a *sentimental pastoral* that feeds into a romantic and simplistic nostalgia for an uncomplicated idyllic past (Gifford 2014, 24), many eco-scholars also highlight the problems of such depictions. An early example of an *antipastoral* critique is Raymond Williams' 1973 *The Country and the City*, which exposes how such narratives perpetuate ahistoric and blinkered erasures of complex socioecological relations.

One might argue that sentimental pastoral narratives lend themselves to Boym's notion of *restorative nostalgia*, which is concerned primarily with preserving a glorified and mythicized past (Boym 2001, 41–55). According to Boym, restorative nostalgia assumes that a particular memory of the past is reality: "Restorative nostalgia does not think of itself as nostalgia, but rather as truth and tradition." Such nostalgia aims to repaint the past in its original form. In contrast, viewers who recognize the "ambivalences of human longing and belonging" and who do not "shy away from the contradictions of modernity" are able to engage in what Boym calls *reflective nostalgia*. This type of nostalgia is aware of the gap between memory and reality and lends itself more easily than restorative nostalgia to Gifford's notion of a *complex pastoral.*

The complex pastoral "is aware of the dangers of idealized escapism while seeking some form of accommodation between humans and nature" (Gifford 2014, 26). Despite the sentimental pastoral's focus on a romanticized idyllic place, it can also engage a reflective nostalgia, because longing for the ideal home does not preclude an understanding of the gap between memory and the present. As Boym writes, reflective nostalgia "reveals that longing and critical thinking are not opposed to one another, just as affective memories do not absolve one from compassion, judgment, or critical reflection" (2011). As long as the idea of a simplified rural past is recognized as such, it can engage a reflective nostalgia. In doing so, it can in Boym's words "be ironic and humorous" as opposed to restorative nostalgia "that takes itself dead seriously" (2011).

While viewers can be self-reflexive in engaging with the pastoral narrative as complex or sentimental, and with eco-nostalgia as reflective rather than restorative, do cinematic texts also help frame these engagements? If so, how? What might we learn about real-world ecologies through such engagements with cinematic eco-nostalgia and the pastoral? To answer these questions, let's turn back to our example of popular Turkish cinema, *Şellale*. By placing the film in its extrafilmic context (the tradition of New Turkish Cinema and the sociocultural and ecopolitical concerns of Turkey), we can explore whether and how the film text invites its viewers to reflect on and engage with the ecological conditions of their time.

Eco-nostalgia in *Şellale*

Released in 2001, *Şellale* is a melodramatic comedy that enjoyed box office success in Turkish theaters and fits within the wave of *New Turkish Cinema*, a period of filmmaking that began in the mid-1990s. As Asuman Suner writes

in *New Turkish Cinema: Belonging, Identity and Longing* (2010), New Turkish Cinema arose after a "period of grave recession and crisis" (2010, 26).
The 1990s had shrunk the national economy and devastated the film industry,
which had languished since a 1980s military coup destabilized Turkey's fragile
democratic apparatus. In the mid-1990s, as Turkey limped to democratic rein-
statement, the Turkish film industry began to revive, and by the early 2000s
two strands of film – popular film, like *Şellale*, and art film, which gained international repute at film festivals – marked the start of New Turkish Cinema.

In making sense of this period of filmmaking, Suner and others point to
some common film characteristics. One of these is the pastoral narrative.
Many Turkish critics describe such films as **rural** or **homeland** movies. Turkish art critic Cem Erciyes uses the term **back to rural** movies and states that
urban directors in New Turkish Cinema headed into the provinces to recreate
and share stories about their childhood experiences (Erciyes 2011). Suner cat-
egorizes *Şellale* as one amongst many popular Turkish films that nostalgically
look to the provinces as the "felicitous space" of childhood innocence (2010,
26). By locating Cemal's nostalgic childhood memories at the juncture of the
1960s military coup, *Şellale* represents a critical rupture between an idealized,
national past – "a collective childhood" – and the less-than-perfect present
(27). While Suner and other Turkish film scholars have highlighted the pastoral narrative as nostalgically configured and thus an important marker to
Turkey's contemporary sense of nationhood and identity, they have not necessarily explored the environmental potentials and problems of such nostalgia.

Şellale's plot revolves around Cemal's desire to rediscover and restore the
creative capacity that fires his artistic work. Disturbed by dreams such as
the one from the opening scene, Cemal feels vulnerable and unable to paint.
To counter his anxiety, Cemal decides to return to his childhood home in
rural Antakya to recreate a sense of individual well-being. Other than two
short scenes that place Cemal in the present and bookend the narrative, the
film locates itself in Cemal's memories of his childhood. Central to these
memories are Cemal's recollections of the town's waterfall, where dream-
telling served as a cathartic release for the community.

In foregrounding water, a distinctly natural element, as the source of
Cemal's nostalgia and inspiration, *Şellale* symbolically evokes eco-nostalgia.
Borrowing from traditional Turkish dream-telling lore, *Şellale* presents
flowing water as the thread that connects past to present to future: it is
through the sustainable flow of a renewable resource that dream interpretation might help one understand the past and/or predict the future. Thus
Şellale evokes an idealized sense of cooperatively and respectfully coexisting
with nature. From the opening scenes of peaceful harmony, to the start of
the climax that results in the waterfall being dammed, to the ending scenes
where we are back in the present and the waterfall is flowing vigorously
again, we can trace not only a tale of nostalgia, but one of eco-nostalgia.

Eco-nostalgia, like the gentle, plaintive music that is *Şellale*'s primary sound
track, permeates the film's affective and emotional registers. In recreating
Cemal's childhood memories, *Şellale* paints a fond portrayal of rural town life

Figure 3.1 *Şellale* poster.
Source: Courtesy of Ezel Akay and Yalçın Kılıç, Producers, IFR.

that balances nature with human activity. This balance manifests in simple activities, such as women milling wheat or washing clothes by the waterfall or Cemal freeing chickens from a coop, and in the town's design, which includes stone courtyards under leafy trees and surrounding golden wheat fields.

A key scene shows Cemal and his sister in a flour mill. Bathed in soft yellow light, with rustic mud floor and stone grinding wheel, the mill is the background for this exchange between Cemal and Şehra, his sister:

Şehra: The wheat spilled on the floor. Shall we collect and plant it in our garden?
Cemal: It's better to give it to the beggars.
Şehra: But they would want flour, not the wheat.
Cemal: This will be flour if we grind it.
Şehra: How will you turn the mill?
Cemal: Not me, the water will turn it.
Şehra: So is the water more powerful than people?
Cemal: Of course it is. Otherwise, would we tell our dreams to the waterfall?

Through such instances and its central focus on a respectful relation between local people and the waterfall, *Şellale* manifests ecological qualities such as cooperation and goodwill in its depictions of rural life.

The film constructs a narrative of returning home as parallel to a narrative of returning to nature. This is most obvious at the end of the film, when we return to the opening scene of local women telling their dreams to the waterfall. Here, as Cemal's mother turns to the camera, the image freezes, transforming into a painting. As the camera pulls back to a long shot, we are back in the present. Cemal sits thoughtfully beside his easel in front of the waterfall. We understand at this moment that recounting his childhood memories here at the waterfall has inspired Cemal to restart painting.

In these final moments, we see a burst from the waterfall, as if the dam that held it back has been breached. As the camera pulls back further, we see Cemal's joy, his own release, as he walks, arms outstretched, face upturned into the waterfall, whose height dwarfs him and whose spray envelopes him. The music that was heard at the start of the film and throughout its course fills the soundscape and echoes the haunting, dream-like quality of the film's start. The film does not reveal whether the waterfall's recovered flow is just a part of Cemal's imagination. Even so, the event embraces an ecological message – one that not only gives nature the dominant presence but also, in Cemal's embrace of the water, seems to be about "some form of accommodation between human and nature" (Gifford 2014, 26).

At the same time, because *Şellale* is framed as a lighthearted melodrama, even as its ending is uplifting, its narrative tells a story of loss and recovery that weaves together risks to human *and* nature alike. Specifically, the waterfall's original vibrancy and recovered flow bracket an event that results in its damming. Though portrayed comically, the damming scene is a crucial moment in the film. In this scene, a national government representative and a local committee stand in front of the waterfall and present the dam to the villagers as a part of the industrialization initiatives that will improve the town's living conditions. The representative starts his speech by praising God, the United States, and the deputy standing next to him. As he speaks the camera pokes fun at him, angling a close-up view of his behind, and we see his discomfort in pants that obviously don't fit right. The ceremony involves dynamiting rocks upstream to block the flow of water. At the waterfall, the group hears the blast and observes the decreased flow in the waterfall. In the ensuing silence, they all look at the deputy, the head of local hierarchy, who only says: "Oh gosh." The words foreshadow the collective realization of the enormity of the change. Shortly afterwards, in a scene between Cemal and Şehra that is set before the waterfall (see Figure 3.2), Şehra becomes upset as she realizes that her dream-tellings will be affected by the waterfall's new state. She asks morosely, "What would happen to us if we don't dream?" Cemal answers: "You can never tell. Maybe we would die."

The damming and this conversation mark the film's turn from comedy to drama. In the scenes that follow, Cemal's father is imprisoned and Şehra is injured and dies. In using the damming as the catalyst for these events, *Şellale* ties its viewers' emotional responses towards its characters to the fate of nature within the film, and thus evokes an ecological commentary that transcends the boundaries of Cemal's imagination and points to national and transnational ecopolitics.

Figure 3.2 Still from *Şellale*: Cemal and Şehra under the waterfall.
Source: Courtesy of Ezel Akay and Yalçın Kılıç, Producers, IFR.

Şellale highlights a period in Turkish history (the 1960s) characterized by immense social and environmental change, partly driven by Turkey's push to modernize and industrialize. These changes started in the 1950s as those in national power aggressively pursued Turkey's "westernization" agenda. Industrialization was a primary cause for urban migration and also involved rural development projects that were not always beneficial to local populations. *Şellale* alludes to the problems of rural development where outsiders (specifically the federal government and Americans) impose on locals with promises of modernization but without attention to modernization's downsides. The damming draws attention to the threats rural communities faced at the time and continue to face due to Turkey's continued instability in economic progress.

Box 3.2   A snapshot of Turkey's economic development policies as environmental threat

Turkey's foreign-dependent economic policy since the 1950s has affected the country's environment. Because urban areas have been the center of industrialization and tariffs did not protect domestic rural production against imports, many people abandoned their rural lives and migrated to the cities in search of work. In Istanbul, the population increased from 1.3 million to 1.5 million between 1955 and 1960 (Keyder 1999, 208). Rapid urban growth included poorly managed shantytowns and damaged existing historical infrastructure and ecological resources.

Recent environmental protests towards urban historical locations such as Emek Cinema being razed to develop shopping areas, or the disruption of the sole forest near Istanbul for a bridge project, speak to continuing conflicts between economics and the environment. The project to destroy Gezi Park, the green area of the city center, is perhaps the most internationally famous example of such tensions. Environmental demands were part of a much larger, interwoven protest for sociopolitical change in June 2013. Even if Gezi Park is saved, the discourse of economic progress continues to threaten understandings of Turkey's environment.

For a better understanding of Gezi Park manifestations, see the documentaries *The Beginning* (Serkan Koç, 2013) and *Gözdağı* (Can Dündar, 2014).

Further reading on the urbanization and modernization process of Turkey: Göktürk, Deniz, Levent Soysal, and İpek Türeli, eds. 2010. *Orienting Istanbul: Cultural Capital of Europe?* New York: Routledge; Karpat, Kemal H. 1976. *The Gecekondu: Rural Migration and Urbanization.* Cambridge, UK: Cambridge University Press; Keyder, Çağlar, ed. 1999. *Istanbul: Between the Global and the Local.* Lanham, MD: Rowman & Littlefield.

Şellale also touches on the destructive effects of global food politics on local production, a cause of increased urban migration. The barber, Selim, portrayed as clearly anti-imperialist, criticizes the American dried milk that is distributed free of charge in Turkish schools as part of the Marshall Plan and warns Cemal not to drink the "unreliable milk." Selim says that invasions are made by unreliable food instead of weapons; according to him dependence on imported food instead of local systems causes a loss in independence.

Drawing attention to the disruption of a local, sustainable way of life, Cemal's longing for his pre-dam past configures the natural environment as co-victim in this narrative of loss. But through his fond memories of the past, nature also figures as a mediator in Cemal's process of recovery, and, as the final scene suggests, engenders its own restoration.

Because Cemal's pre-dam memories show a rural existence in tune with nature's rhythms, *Şellale* can be criticized for generating a *sentimental pastoral* that is romantic and idyllic despite external threats. Scholars such as Suner see this sentimentality as a way that popular Turkish films avoid a complicated past, instead feeding simplistic longings for a "lost paradise" (Suner 2010, 37). Suner further suggests that the film's conflicts are simplistically portrayed as "before/after" or "insider/outsider" (local villagers versus external forces like the government or the United States).

As Suner acknowledges, however, *Şellale* does escape being a story simply of restorative nostalgia. For one, Cemal's memories are couched in humor, rejecting the seriousness of restorative nostalgia. In addition, Cemal's memories are not just of a glorified past. Along with the pleasurable memories of his childhood, Cemal must confront the trauma of his sister's death. It is only by *reflecting* on the related events that Cemal can face his present. We suggest that even as the film presents a reflective nostalgia, it also generates a glimpse at reflective eco-nostalgia that moves away from sentimental pastoralism into the possibilities of complex pastoralism.

Such complexity comes late in the film, post-dam, and arguably confronts the idealism of Cemal's pre-dam eco-nostalgia. It is most apparent in a scene that culminates a subplot woven into the film. Throughout the film, we have been presented with a bit of comedic side action, a young woman laughingly running away from a young man with a cleaver in his hand. The couple is shown periodically traversing the town's locales as other action is foregrounded. Towards the end of the film as we move from scenes of the town recovering from Şehra's death we reencounter the couple.

The two take off through the golden, stonewalled fields – the man yelling he will kill the girl when he catches her because she keeps running away from him, the girl laughing as she runs away. The camera cuts to the barber in the town plaza excitedly announcing the coup d'état that is being enacted across the nation. When the camera cuts again, in long shot, we see the young woman and man running towards us, and along a path by a stream, in the cool shade of dense trees. As she nears us, she rounds a corner, and he manages to grab at her clothes, ripping them, as he falls. When they both rise and straighten, the soundtrack, which is now of a radio broadcast announcement of the coup, fills the airwaves.

In the following shot-reverse-shot sequence, the woman backs against a tree, smiling up at the man. He pauses, then yells out "aaa" and raises his cleaver (see Figure 3.3). She closes her eyes in a moment of fear as the cleaver lands in the tree trunk next to her head. Opening her eyes, she smiles. The camera tracks back, as now, both hands free, the man grasps at her hand, pulling it towards him. When she lets him, the torn clothes she holds up fall away, revealing her breasts. He pulls her to him and they embrace, falling to the leaf-littered dirt ground. Here the camera, in medium shot, rests on her, revealing in her face and gestures the pleasure she feels.

The scene takes place in the outdoors, where the natural environment figures prominently and our two humans find themselves in the joy of a basic animal act. The ecological resonances of the encounter are even more striking when considered in light of the pantheistic Greek legend of Daphne and Apollo that this story references. The historical legends of Antakya, also known as Antioch from Hellenistic times, incorporate the story of love-struck Apollo (by cheeky Eros's arrow) as he chases the water nymph, Daphne. In the legend, when Apollo finally catches her, Daphne, who wants nothing to do with Apollo, begs her father, a river god, for help. Heeding her call, her father transforms her into a laurel tree. Her tears are believed to flow through the waterfalls in Antakya. *Şellale's* adaptation of the story in the constant chase and final encounter between the young woman and

Figure 3.3 Still from *Şellale*: The young woman and her cleaver-wielding man.
Source: Courtesy of Ezel Akay and Yalçın Kılıç, Producers, IFR.

her cleaver-wielding man alerts us to this legend, as well as its narrative of blurred boundaries between human and nonhuman nature.

We get a fleeting glimpse of the complex pastoral in the way the legend's reference in *Şellale* prompts viewers to face the contradictions of such blurring. Specifically, in merging violence with pleasure, it prevents viewers from becoming engrossed in an "idealized escapism" and instead prods them to consider how to face less-than-ideal situations. Apollo, seeking his ideal love, is confronted with her demise as lithe, womanly water nymph. In confronting his loss, he venerates the laurel tree, raising its status in Grecian culture as a symbol of honor. In *Şellale*, violence simmers in the couple's encounter – inherent in the material presence of the man's cleaver, which connotes a fearful affective resonance, and the broadcast's staccato announcements, which for many in Turkey, represent the beginning of intense eco-social disruption. Even though the scene is a heavy-handed way of symbolizing the end of an era of "collective childhood innocence," its reference to the Apollo–Daphne legend complicates simplistic eco-nostalgia "before/after" interpretations and prompts viewers to consider how one might, like Apollo, still engage the natural world, even love and venerate it, despite its compromised fall from the ideal. One might even argue that the woman's pleasure in her man's advances, in contrast to Daphne's loathing, speaks to this possibility of building compromises within a world of shifting nature–human relationships.

Astute viewers might take the complex pastoral resonance of these scenes into the final waterfall scenes that follow and close the film, reflecting on the gap between Cemal's eco-nostalgic longings and the reality of the dammed waterfall. In this case, reflective nostalgia, which recognizes nature as home yet is able to face the realities of shifted nature–human relationships, might productively serve to help rebuild a sustainable, perhaps even nonhierarchical, relationship between these two entities. *Şellale* fleetingly exposes such possibilities through its ecocritical engagements.

Conclusion: *Şellale* as an invitation into ecocinema studies

We began this chapter by suggesting that *Şellale* has ecocritical valences. In describing how, we have explored a number of important concerns in ecocinema studies. First, through the concept of eco-nostalgia we are able to connect Turkish film scholarship on nostalgia with ecocinema studies' interests in ecology. In doing so, we expand the view of both areas of research – demonstrating how ecological concerns weave themselves into narratives that have been theorized in other contexts by Turkish film scholars. Thus, while Suner and others recognize the pastoral narrative as common to popular Turkish cinema, further attention to such narratives complicates a simple, sometimes dismissive understanding of the pastoral as purely sentimental. Likewise, bringing Turkish cinema to the attention of eco-film critics opens ecocinema studies to a national cinema that has been underrepresented in the field. In extending our attention to other popular Turkish films, we might engage a second concern of ecocinema studies' interest – national and transnational cinema.

We have already briefly touched upon this second ecocinematic concern in our exploration of *Şellale's* commentary, but we can further consider whether the prevalence of nostalgic pastoral themes in Turkish cinema is indicative of Turkey's collective ecological anxieties and hopes. While the pastoral narrative is prevalent today, rural themes harken back to an earlier Turkish cinematic period, **Yeşilçam**, that began in the 1950s and lasted until the 1970s. Most Yeşilçam films (which were also classic melodramas) centered Istanbul as the site for drama, portraying it as a metropolis that reflected the hopes, anxieties, and desires associated with Turkey's modernization (Abisel et al. 2005, 77). Within this tradition, films known as *immigration films* portrayed Istanbul as the uncanny and cruel center of the struggle for life.

It is not until the wave of New Turkish Cinema in the mid-1990s that the rural landscape becomes a popular setting for stories. This shift in focus might be attributed to Turkey's own engagement with Western environmentalism post-1980s. As free-market economics and consumerism shaped more affluent, Westernized urbanites, the idea of escaping from the "unnatural" city into the open spaces of the countryside entered popular discourse. In the "back to rural" stories of New Turkish Cinema, the countryside is the place where the ecological aspirations of the urbanite unfold. This is quite different from a common Yeşilçam narrative, in which rural protagonists confronted the ecological dilemmas of urban life, and suggests a changing landscape of environmental preoccupations that permeate Turkish discourse.

Third, and also related, the pastoral narrative might be popular in Turkish cinema, but what might it mean to engage the urban narratives of contemporary Turkish film? Twenty-first-century Turkish environmentalism is part and parcel of the urban landscape. This is perhaps best recognized in the recent and intense Gezi Park demonstrations of 2013. Beginning as a protest against development projects that would overrun this urban green space, the Gezi Park demonstrations resulted in one of the largest social movements in Turkish history. The images of young people hugging trees in protest is engraved in collective memory; reflections of these anxieties can be further explored by ecocritically engaging Turkish cinema's urban narratives.

Fourth, while our focus has been the pastoral narrative in popular Turkish cinema of comedic melodrama, our exploration makes room for ecocinema studies' various genre interests. For example, Suner and other Turkish film scholars also point to New Turkish Cinema's art film industry. As independent film many of these art films might be recognized as slow cinema, with narrative and cinematic conventions that yield their own ecocritical nuances and that are worth exploring further.

Box 3.3   A selected Turkish filmography

Yeşilçam Immigration Films: *Birds of Exile* (Halit Refiğ 1964); *The Return* (Türkan Şoray 1972); Lütfü Akad's trilogy *The Bride* (1973), *The Wedding* (1974), and *Blood Money* (1974).

Independent New Turkish Art Films: *The Small Town* (Nuri Bilge Ceylan 1997); *Clouds of May* (Nuri Bilge Ceylan 1999); *Times and Winds* (Reha Erdem 2006); *Egg* (Semih Kaplanoğlu 2007); *Milk* (Semih Kaplanoğlu 2008); *Autumn* (Özcan Alper 2008); *Summer Book* (Seyfi Teoman 2008); *Kosmos* (Reha Erdem 2010); *Honey* (Semih Kaplanoğlu 2010) and *Winter Sleep* (Nuri Bilge Ceylan 2014).

New Turkish Films with Urban Settings: *Block C* (Zeki Demirkubuz 1994); *Somersault in a Coffin* (Derviş Zaim 1996); *Innocence* (Zeki Demirkubuz 1997); *Laleli'de Bir Azize* (Kudret Sabancı 1999); *A Run for Money* (Reha Erdem 1999); *Elephants and Grass* (Derviş Zaim 2000); *Distant* (Nuri Bilge Ceylan 2002); *Istanbul Tales* (Ümit Ünal, Ömür Atay, Selim Demirdelen, Kudret Sabancı, Yücel Yolcu 2005); *Magic Carpet Ride* (Yılmaz Erdoğan 2005); *Pandora's Box* (Yeşim Ustaoğlu 2008).

New Popular Turkish Rural Films: *Offside* (Serdar Akar 2000); *Vizontele* (Yılmaz Erdoğan 2001); *Vizontele Tuuba* (Yılmaz Erdoğan 2004); *My Father and My Son* (Çağan Irmak 2005); *Ice Cream I Scream* (Yüksel Aksu 2006) and *The International* (Sırrı Süreyya Önder and Muharrem Gülmez 2006), *Ecotopia* (Yüksel Aksu 2011).

Further Reading: Akser, Murat, and Deniz Bayrakdar, eds. 2014. *New Cinema, New Media: Reinventing Turkish Cinema*. Newcastle upon Tyne: Cambridge Scholars Publishing; Dönmez-Colin, Gönül. 2003. "New Turkish Cinema – Individual Tales of Common Concerns." *Asian Cinema* 14.1: 138–145; Dönmez-Colin, Gönül. 2008. *Turkish Cinema: Identity, Distance and Belonging*. London: Reaktion Books; Kaim, Agnieszka Ayşen. 2011. "New Turkish Cinema – Some Remarks on the Homesickness of the Turkish Soul." *Cinej Cinema Journal* Special Issue 1: 99–106.

Fifth, our analysis has focused primarily on emotion, a perceptual dimension that the filmic text works to evoke, and through this we have touched on material and social contexts. However, our analysis leaves room for ecocinema studies' interests in approaches that begin from material or social contexts. We might engage the material ecologies of Turkish filmmaking or the social ecologies of race, gender, class, and other aspects that govern the who, what, and how of ecocinematic representations. Similarly, one might think of other ways of considering the perceptual dimension of filmic ecologies. For example, ecocinema audience reception studies can consider the reactions of Turkish audiences as they engage with these films.

Our analysis of eco-nostalgia in one popular Turkish film, Şellale, is just one example of the myriad productive ways eco-film critics are grounding cinema studies in ecological considerations. It is an attempt to push the boundaries of ecocinema studies' outwards and, in doing so, invites you into the ongoing conversations of this recent, but rapidly burgeoning, field of ecocritical media inquiry.

Acknowledgments: The authors would like to thank Carter Soles and Matt Beehr for their invaluable assistance on the content and copy editing of this chapter.

Keywords

Affect *versus* emotion

Antipastoral

Ecocinema

Ecocinema studies

Eco-nostalgia

Encode *versus* decode

Immigration films

New Turkish Cinema

Nostalgia (restorative, reflective)

Pastoral (sentimental, complex)

Rural/Homeland movies

Yeşilçam

Discussion questions

1   Explore the cinematic language (light, sound, camera angles, color, etc.) of a film that you believe takes an eco-nostalgic approach, and discuss how this cinematography contributes to the ecological and nostalgic narrative of the film. Can you categorize the film as restorative or reflective in its eco-nostalgia?

2   Think of a movie that you believe has a strong emotional hook. Do you think the emotion has an ecological valence? Research ecocritical scholarship and analyze the film to support your response.

3   Şellale references the Greek legend of Daphne and Apollo to connote an ecological resonance. Can you think of another filmic example that similarly references a story that comes from much older traditions than filmmaking? Explain how the story lends symbolic significance to the film and if this significance has ecological dimensions.

4   Engage in an ecocritical exploration of a cinema of a country other than the United States. (Major studios like Hollywood are more transnational than national in their production and distribution.) Would you describe the examples you encounter as rural or homeland movies? Do the films have an urban feel? What might these representations suggest about a nation's culture, sociopolitical circumstances, and environmental concerns?

Further reading

Akser, Murat, and Deniz Bayrakdar, eds. 2014. *New Cinema, New Media: Reinventing Turkish Cinema.* Newcastle upon Tyne: Cambridge Scholars Publishing.

Arslan, Savaş. 2010. *Cinema in Turkey: A New Critical History.* Oxford: Oxford University Press.

Cook, Pam. 2005. *Screening the Past: Memory and Nostalgia in Cinema*. Abingdon: Routledge.

Garrard, Greg. 2004. *Ecocriticism*. New York: Routledge.

Hochman, Jhan. 1998. *Green Cultural Studies: Nature in Film, Novel, and Theory*. Moscow, ID: University of Idaho Press.

Jameson, Fredric. 1997. "The Nostalgia Mode and Nostalgia for the Present." In *Postmodern After-Images, A Reader in Film, Television and Media*, edited by Peter Brooker and Will Brooker, 22–35. New York and London: Arnold.

Marx, Leo. 1964. *The Machine in the Garden: Technology and the Pastoral Ideal in America*. Oxford: Oxford University Press.

Murray, Robin L., and Joseph K. Heumann. 2009. *Ecology and Popular Film*. Albany, NY: State University of New York Press.

Works cited

Abisel, Nilgün, Umut Tümay Arslan, Pembe Behçetoğulları, Ali Karadoğan, Semire Ruken Öztürk, and Nejat Ulusay, eds. 2005. *Çok Tuhaf Çok Tanıdık*. Istanbul: Metis Yayınları.

Boym, Svetlana. 2001. *The Future of Nostalgia*. New York: Basic Books.

———. 2011. "Nostalgia." Atlas of Transformation. Accessed August 20, 2014. http://monumenttotransformation.org/atlas-of-transformation/html/n/nostalgia/nostalgia-svetlana-boym.html

Bozak, Nadia. 2012. *The Cinematic Footprint: Lights, Camera and Natural Resources*. New Brunswick, NJ: Rutgers University Press.

Brereton, Pat. 2006. *Hollywood Utopia: Ecology in Contemporary American Cinema*. Portland, OR: Intellect.

Buell, Laurence. 1995. *The Environmental Imagination: Thoreau, Nature Writing, and the Formation of American Culture*. Cambridge, MA: Harvard University Press.

Carmichael, Deborah. 2006. *The Landscape of Hollywood Westerns: Ecocriticism in the American Film Genre*. Salt Lake City, UT: University of Utah Press.

Cubitt, Sean. 2005. *EcoMedia*. New York: Rodopi.

Davidson, Tonya K., Ondine Park, and Rob Shields, eds. 2011. *Ecologies of Affect: Placing Nostalgia, Desire and Hope*. Waterloo, ON: Wilfrid Laurier University Press.

Erciyes, Cem. 2011. "Türk Sinemasında Taşraya Dönüş." *Radikal Gazetesi*, December 03. Accessed August 08, 2014. http://www.radikal.com.tr/yazarlar/cem_erciyes/turk_sinemasinda_tasraya_donus-1071352

Ingram, David. 2013. "The Aesthetics and Ethics of Eco-Film Criticism." In *Ecocinema Theory and Practice*, edited by Stephen Rust, Salma Monani, and Sean Cubitt, 43–62. New York: Routledge Press.

Garrard, Greg. 2004. *Ecocriticism*. New York: Routledge.

Gifford, Terry. 2014. "Pastoral, Anti-Pastoral, and Post-Pastoral." In *The Cambridge Companion to Literature and the Environment*, edited by Louise Westling, 17–30. Cambridge University Press.

Hageman, Andrew. 2013. "Ecocinema and Ideology: Do Ecocritics Dream of a Clockwork Green?" In *Ecocinema Theory and Practice*, edited by Stephen Rust, Salma Monani, and Sean Cubitt, 63–86. New York: Routledge Press.

Hepper, Erica, Timothy Ritchie, Constantine Sedikides, and Tim Wildschut. 2012. "Odyssey's End: Lay Conceptions of Nostalgia Reflect its Original Homeric Meaning." *Emotion* 12: 102–119.

Howarth, William. 1996. "Some Principles of Ecocriticism." In *The Ecocriticism Reader: Landmarks in Literary Ecology*, edited by Cheryll Glotfelty and Harold Fromm, 69–91. Athens, GA: University of Georgia Press.

Ivakhiv, Adrian. 2013. *Ecologies of the Moving Image: Cinema, Affect and Nature*. Waterloo, ON: Wilfrid Laurier University Press.

—— "Green Ecocriticism and Its Futures." 2008. *Interdisciplinary Studies in Literature and Environment* 15.2: 1–28.

Kääpä, Pietari. 2013. "Ecocinema Audiences." Special issue of *Interactions: Studies in Communications and Culture* 3.4: 107–112.

Kääpä, Pietari, and Tommy Gustafsson, eds. 2013. *Transnational Ecocinemas: Film Culture in an Era of Ecological Transformation*. Bristol: Intellect.

Keyder, Çağlar. 1999. *İstanbul Küresel ile Yerel Arasında*. Istanbul: Metis Yayınları.

Leiserowitz, Anthony A. 2004. "Before and After the Day After Tomorrow: A U.S. Study of Climate Risk Perception." *Environment* 46.9: 23–37.

Lu, Sheldon H., and Jiayan Mi, eds. 2009. *Chinese Ecocinema in the Age of Environmental Challenge*. Hong Kong: Hong Kong University Press.

MacDonald, Scott. 2004. "Towards an Ecocinema." *Interdisciplinary Studies in Literature and Environment* 11.2: 107–132.

Maxwell, Richard, and Toby Miller. 2012. *Greening the Media*. New York: Oxford University Press.

Monani, Salma, Belinda Chiu, and Carlo Arreglo, eds. 2011. "At the Intersections of Ecosee and Just Sustainability: New Directions in Communication Theory and Practice." Special Issue *of Environmental Communication: A Journal of Nature and Culture* 5.1: 141–145.

Murray, Robin L., and Joseph K. Heumann. 2009. *Ecology and Popular Film*. Albany, NY: State University of New York Press.

Murray, Robin, and Joseph Heumann. 2012. *Gunfight at Eco-Corral: Western Cinema and Environment*. Norman, OK: University of Oklahoma Press.

Pick, Anat, and Guinevere Narraway, eds. 2013. *Screening Nature: Cinema Beyond the Human*. New York: Berghahn Books.

Rust, Stephen, Salma Monani, and Sean Cubitt, eds. 2013. *Ecocinema, Theory and Practice*. New York: Routledge.

Seymour, Nicole. 2013. *Strange Natures: Futures, Empathy, and Queer Ecological Imagination*. Urbana-Champaign, IL: University of Illinois Press.

Suner, Asuman. 2010. *New Turkish Cinema: Belonging, Identity and Memory*. New York: I.B. Tauris.

Taylor, Bron, ed. 2013. *Avatar and Nature Spirituality*. Waterloo, ON: Wilfrid Laurier University Press.

Tong, Chris. 2013. "Ecocinema for All: Reassembling the Audience." *Interactions: Studies in Communication & Culture* 4.2: 113–128.

Weik von Mossner, Alexa, ed. 2014. *Moving Environments: Affect, Emotion, Ecology, and Film*. Waterloo, ON: Wilfrid Laurier University Press.

Williams, Raymond. 1973. *The Country and the City*. New York: Oxford University Press.

Willoquet-Marcondi, Paula, ed. 2010. *Framing the World: Explorations in Ecocriticism and Film*. Charlottesville, VA: Virginia University Press.

Yeung, Liu Wai. 2004. "The Politics of Nostalgia: Explorations of Home, Homeland and Identities in the Context of an Accented Cinema." Master Thesis. The University of Hong Kong.

4 The aesthetics of environmental equity in American newspaper strips

Veronica Vold

Introduction

The young discipline of comic studies promises fresh lines of environmental inquiry for new students and experienced scholars alike. Comic genres from funny animal cartoons to comic books sponsored by the nuclear industry to creator-owned environmental justice (EJ) zines are ready to test and reorient enterprising readers. The ecocritical facility of these graphic texts resonates with the ethos and aims of the *environmental humanities*, a collection of disciplines that includes literature and media studies, history, philosophy, the arts, and the social sciences. Together the environmental humanities examine how human beings imagine and ethically respond to the natural world. Scholars in the environmental humanities deploy theory to investigate and critique environmental justice problems in the public sphere. *Comic studies* is congruent to the environmental humanities in that it too convenes a wide range of disciplines to investigate the form, history, and cultural significance of comic art forms. Comic art forms include the single-panel cartoon, the newspaper strip, the comic book, the graphic narrative, the zine, and the webcomic, among others. Iconicity, line art, panel design, color, and page layout demand that readers read in new ways. Readers must activate connections between images and text to make sense of the whole. When approached from an ecocritical perspective, comics compel unique environmental readings because their forms and production histories give us new access to critical environmental engagements.

Comic art forms are sites of formal innovation and cultural production. Though once considered pure junk by the academy, comics are intricate cultural registers of human expression. Comics often converge with ecocritical themes and interests; therefore, it is surprising that little scholarship presently exists about this intersection. This chapter seeks to activate such scholarship by linking the environmental humanities to comic studies, specifically by reframing comic studies through *environmental justice (EJ) ecocriticism*. EJ ecocriticism is integral to the environmental humanities. EJ ecocriticism asks how "issues like toxic waste, incinerators, lead poisoning, uranium mining and tailings, and other environmental equity issues [can] be brought forth more fully in literature and criticism" (Reed 2010, 149), drawing our attention to the intersectionality of gender, race, indigeneity, disability, and sexuality to the environment at a given moment in time. From this perspective, I seek to answer the following questions: What new questions do comic studies generate for the environmental humanities? And how does EJ ecocriticism produce our reading of comic art forms?

In order to respond to these questions, this chapter will review key concepts introduced in existing environmental scholarship about comics. Central to these concepts is a comic's ***environmental imagination,*** or its ethical orientation to the natural world. In a comic, an environmental imagination is developed through the representation of familiar ecological icons, as well as through the representation of environmental problems and movements. To respond to the second question of this chapter, how EJ ecocriticism improves our analysis of comic art forms, we will examine the problem of ***environmental racism*** – the systemic and historical burdening of communities of color with disproportionate rates of environmental risk and lack of environmental protection – in two twentieth-century comics, one mainstream and one alternative American newspaper strip.

After analyzing representations of environmental racism in the dominant post–*Silent Spring* environmentalism in Charles Schulz's *Peanuts* (1950–2000), I offer a close reading of the formal architecture of environmental racism in Jackie Ormes's romance strip, *Torchy in Heartbeats* (1950–1954). Ultimately, I argue that while the environmental imagination of mainstream comics like *Peanuts* often fails to take up the moral claims of environmental justice, Ormes's alternative strip uses a retroactive riskscape to develop an ***aesthetics of equity.*** Aesthetics of equity can be understood as nature as a space of possibility for all people rather than as a zone of impoverished blight or elite leisure. In comics, such aesthetics comprise a range of verbal–visual moves that denote awareness of and resistance to environmental disparity. In *Torchy*, shifting perceptions of risk chronicle the difficulty of proving and stopping environmental racism.

Box 4.1   Talk about it: aesthetics of equity

In *Root Shock* (2004), Mindy Thompson Fullilove, a psychiatrist who studies how the environment affects mental health, defines an aesthetics of equity as design principles that uphold the environmental rights of marginalized communities in architecture, urban planning, and development. These aesthetics include public access for those with disabilities, as well as spaces for recreation and free public exchange. Literary scholar Katie Hogan (2012) adapts Fullilove's aesthetic concept of "planting equity" by analyzing dialogue and characterization in Tony Kushner's *Angels in America* (1991). According to Hogan, the play develops an aesthetics of equity by illuminating "the racial, class, and sexual dimensions undergirding aesthetic perceptions of urban environments" and queering the discourse of environmental justice (6). Based on Fullilove's and Hogan's scholarship, we can conclude that a media (any cultural representation, be it spatial, sonic, or tactile) generates an aesthetics of equity when it incorporates underrepresented dimensions of environmental injustice into its design and content. What media have you encountered that generates an aesthetics of equity? What evidence supports your claim?

Why comics studies matters to ecocriticsm

Environmental scholarship about comics is still quite new. No published anthology or monograph of ecocriticism about comics yet exists. While there is promising ecocriticism about marginalized literary genres often associated with comics, for example, children's literature (Dobrin and Kidd 2004) and animated cartoons (Murray and Heumann 2011; Pike 2012), the distinct medium of comics has not yet been addressed. We can speculate that the absence of scholarship may be the result of cultural confusion about the relevance and availability of comics to ecocritical analysis. As this volume demonstrates, scholars of ecomedia are productively revising academic assumptions about what counts as a text and what makes a text worthy of ecocritical study. As Douglas Wolk attests, "Comics are not prose. Comics are not movies. They are not a text-driven medium with added pictures; they're not the visual equivalent of a prose narrative or a static version of a film. They are their own thing: a medium with its own devices, its own innovators, its own clichés, its own genres and traps and liberties" (2008, 14). Comics have a lot to offer ecocritical scholarship when approached as "their own thing," rather than being misunderstood or dismissed as an uneasy hybrid of existing media forms.

Currently, ecocritical scholars who analyze comics do so using questions and methods familiar to their respective academic fields, and they rarely take up the study of comics as art forms. For example, Kevin de Laplant (2005) approvingly reviews Paul Chadwick's 1989 comic book *Concrete*, yet his assessment relies heavily on the comic book's narrative content rather than its unique verbal–visual construction. De Laplant demonstrates that the comic book invites students to critique anthropocentrism, deep ecology, and environmental sexism. Though de Laplant notes that *Concrete* engages student attention like no other course text, he doesn't speculate about how or why; his analysis treats the comic art form as incidental rather than central to *Concrete*'s potential as an environmental text. His approach is commendable because it shows what environmental philosophy gains when it takes up comics as philosophical literature. However, his approach ignores what environmental philosophy loses when it doesn't take up comics *as comics*; that is, a distinctive medium with its own devices and designs. Comic studies, in contrast, does account for **comic form**, as well as the politics of production and distribution. As Charles Hatfield argues in "An Art of Tensions" (2009), reading comic form means responding to the tensions of the page, including sequence, panel composition, layout, and color. Analyzing the politics of production requires understanding the various formal constraints of serial publication, which include the risk and benefit of securing a third-party contract to syndicate and distribute a comic. Attending to these dimensions situates the work a comic does both on the page and in the world. Yet comic studies has yet to apply its methods toward meaningful environmental critique.

Similar to eco-philosopher de Laplant, some ecomedia scholars have sought to integrate comics into environmental cultural analysis, yet these scholars often don't approach comics as comics. Finis Dunaway undertakes an analysis of Walt Kelly's comic strip *Pogo* as part of the discourse of the first Earth Day (2008, 67). However, his promising endeavor is preoccupied with the implications of a motto attributed to Pogo the Possum in an Earth Day poster ("We have met the enemy and he is us"). Dunaway's approach to *Pogo* concerns this slogan alone. By ignoring the rest of the newspaper strip, its sequencing, iconicity, and design, Dunaway slips away from engaging comics as a unique form of cultural register.

Perhaps the most developed vein of environmental scholarship about comics emerges in a study by American Studies scholars Dale Goble, Paul Hirt, and Susan Kilgore (2005). In "On Environmental Cartoons," the authors focus on single-panel political cartoons, exploring changing environmental imaginations represented by animal icons in nineteenth- and twentieth-century American newspapers. In his corresponding project on the cultural anxieties of the post–*Silent Spring* era, Mark Barrow Jr. (2012) chronicles the social reception of Rachel Carson's watershed book in eleven editorial cartoons and a single newspaper strip, Charles Schulz's *Peanuts*. After examining the use of caricature, irony, and symbolism in these comics, Barrow concludes that "this body of cartoons reveals a shared set of understandings about how modern technology presented potential dangers to both humans and the natural world" (2012, 164). In other words, these comics chronicle the anxieties of the postwar industrial era through unique visual–verbal argumentation. The following analysis continues such environmental analysis by taking up sequential comic arts, of which little is yet written.

Sequential art introduces new dimensions for imagining environments. The standard grammatical unit of comics, **the panel**, spatializes time by dividing and organizing action in a sequence. Reading across the white space between panels, **the gutter**, is a lot like reading the white space of a poem; the conspicuous absence of ink constitutes its own critical presence on the page. Yet the gutter is thoroughly specific to the work that a comic demands of readers. Readers connect the action *between* panels to complete the logic of a given sequence. This is what Scott McCloud (1994) calls "closure" (what Bart Beaty [1999] calls "suturing," borrowing from the analogous but distinct phenomenon in film). The act of closure implicates readers in uniting the frames and making sense of plot. When comics take up environmental themes and questions, the act of closure further involves readers in the relationship between characters, settings, and conflicts. Reading color, line art, and iconicity contributes to a comic's environmental imagination. By setting these tensions in sequence, newspaper strips offer unexplored entry points into environmental discourse.

Box 4.2   Close reading a comic

Choose any webcomic or newspaper strip that might facilitate EJ inquiry. You might begin with Stephanie McMillian's award-winning editorial cartoon *Code Green* (2009–2012), Rebecca Bratspies and Charlie LaGreca's comic book *Mayah's Lot* (2012), or Kate Beaton's webcomic series *Ducks* (2014), all of which are available online. Once you've chosen your comic, sit and look at it for a long time. Consider the tensions of the page, including page layout, panel size, panel-to-panel transitions, effects of word balloon size and shape, lettering techniques, and color palette. Consider how the gutter functions both to separate and unite beats of the narrative. Ask yourself: How much time passes? How would the comic work differently if it ended in a different spot? How would it read if a character weren't there? Does the comic signal an awareness of environmental justice or mainstream environmentalism? How? Take notes on what you discover. Then, looking back over your notes, make a claim about the environmental imagination of the comic itself.

Newspaper strips and the environmental imagination of *Mark Trail* (1946–present)

Anyone who has glanced at the funny pages can imagine their form: a short row of panels with a familiar cast of characters that pull off a quick gag. Newspaper strips usually turn up in the same spot in the paper on a daily or weekly basis. A significant difference between contemporary and mid-century strips is the size of the panels themselves. While contemporary strips are squished into a few square inches, newspaper supplements in the mid-century period allowed for more generous sizing and meticulous artwork.

Reading a newspaper strip's ethical orientation toward the natural world entails a study of its form and content, as well as its production and reception history. Generally, a strip's environmental imagination emerges in one of two modes: a strip may consciously endorse a particular environmental discourse, as in the case of political cartoons and comic poster art, or a strip may disclose a latent investment in environmental concerns. The American newspaper strip *Mark Trail* (1946–present) is a prime example of the former mode. *Mark Trail* is often cited as the representative environmental comic of the postwar American period. For more than 60 years, this adventure strip has enjoyed wide syndication while campaigning for wilderness conservation. *Mark Trail* pursues the adventures of its eponymous leading man, a White, heterosexual, able-bodied photojournalist with a shock of black hair. Mark Trail protects the fictional national park of Lost Forest with "a crushing right cross" (Fruhlinger 2007, np). In addition to fighting off poachers and rural drug dealers, our square-jawed wildlife reporter advocates for many conservationist issues, "including preservation of Alaskan wilderness lands, urging boat speed limits to protect the manatee in Florida, and countering the maligned reputations of coyotes, wolves, mountain lions, and alligators" (Hill 2003, np). The strip's artwork further encodes its hero's storied investment in conserving wilderness. For example, in a typical three-panel daily strip, the first and final panels focus on humans, but the center panel regularly foregrounds extreme close-ups of various animals in mid-flight or mid-leap. In this center panel, tiny human figures meander in the background or vanish to nothing but their speech balloons, perfectly unconcerned with the frame's sudden focus on, for example, an extreme close-up of a dancing trout or startled deer. This dynamic focalization serves to disorient the reader; it can sometimes be difficult to tell if the animals themselves are speaking or if an off-panel human character is talking. The sudden size of the featured animal is further disorienting: diminutive forest creatures can appear astonishingly colossal in the focus on the strip. In the formal tension between animal icons and humans as well as narrative content, *Mark Trail*'s panel sequence imagines a conservationist paradigm that insists on human reverence for and submission to the active interests of the more-than-human world. Its lyrical tribute to wildlife interrupts any anthropocentric narrative flow. Thus, the form of the strip supports its decidedly ecocentric vantage point.

Yet iconicity in *Mark Trail* reiterates several key problems in mainstream American conservationism. The strip effectively erases minority perspectives and relationships to the natural world. The absence of any minority characters defines wilderness in *Mark Trail* as a sanctuary for White people alone. Compounding the erasure of a multiethnic cast, the strip limits female roles to Mark's White girlfriend Cherry, and Cherry's rival, Kelly Welly. These characters concentrate chiefly on Mark Trail's hardlined physique and his readiness to box his wilderness-abusing opponents. In keeping with adventure strip convention, female characters in the strip function as romantic distractions rather than complex people. Thus, women in *Mark Trail* don't challenge the heteronormative conservationism Mark advocates. As ecocritic Mei Mei Evans argues, dominant narratives of the American wilderness are marked by latent racism and heterosexism, which

problematically define nature as "the province of white heterosexual masculinity" (Evans 2010, 183). While the strip constructs dynamic ecocentric
ideals about the relationship between animals and humans, it also privileges
one specific frame of reference, a White heterosexual man, as the authority
of this imagination. This unquestioned authority shores up troubling ideals
of mainstream environmentalism. *Mark Trail* proves that while a comic can
consciously endorse an environmental politics like conservationism, it also
risks reiterating the conceptual limits associated with this politics.

In contrast to the overtly political project of *Mark Trail*, comics can
develop environmental imaginations that aren't conspicuously environmental. For example, the post–*Silent Spring* environmentalism of Charles
Schulz's *Peanuts* (1950–present) and the mid-century EJ ethos of Jackie
Ormes's *Torchy in Heartbeats* (1950–1954) generate environmental imaginations that are more incidental than central to each strip. Yet as prominent
ecocritical scholars from Lawrence Buell to Ursula Heise agree, "ecocriticism becomes most interesting and useful . . . when it aims to recover the
environmental character or orientation of works whose conscious or foregrounded interests lie elsewhere" (Kern 2000, 11). Texts that don't declare
their environmental character, or, alternatively, develop an environmental
imagination not customarily analyzed as such, compel vital and radically
innovative environmental inquiry. *Peanuts* and *Torchy in Heartbeats*, two
mid-century newspaper strips that aren't widely analyzed for the structure of their environmental imaginations, engage my close reading in this
chapter.

Mainstream environmentalism in *Peanuts* (1950–2000)

Even when comics don't endorse an environmental orientation on purpose, they nonetheless inscribe into their form and content the environmental character of their era. For example, in the decade following *Silent
Spring* (Carson 1962), *Peanuts*, along with many other mainstream comics,
responded to the concerns of the **New Environmental Paradigm** (NEP).
As environmental sociologist Dorceta Taylor argues, this paradigm sought
to mobilize legal instruments to mitigate postwar chemical exposures. The
NEP "articulated a bold new vision that critiqued the development of large,
complex, and energy-intensive issues such as nuclear power, population
control, pollution prevention, risk reduction, energy, recycling, and environmental cleanups" (Taylor 2002, 10). It sought to develop technologies that
would address national environmental issues. Yet this era didn't recognize
how environmental issues differ along race and class; although it responded
to experiences of shared risk, it didn't take up the reality of unequal risk. By
failing to consider more comprehensive responses to unequal environmental risk, this era denies the **comprehensive environmental community**. The
comprehensive environmental community includes "poor people, women,
communities of color, Indigenous peoples, and minorities, and citizens of

developing nations" (Dotson and White 2013, 55). The concerns of this group frequently don't find traction in mainstream comics.

Yet comics often help us analyze missed coalition between mainstream environmentalism and environmental justice. For instance, the recent Charles M. Schulz Museum exhibition "Peanuts . . . Naturally" (2013) provides a retrospective look at icons of nature in Schulz's famous strip. *Peanuts* imagines a lively environment of bouncy flowers, thick blankets of falling snow, and kite-eating trees, all drawn in Schulz's sophisticated economy of line and syncopated sense of design. The exhibit also celebrates Schulz's playful incorporation of mainstream environmental figures and institutions, including the strip's homage to Rachel Carson and its farcical depiction of the Environmental Protection Agency antagonizing Charlie Brown. Yet while *Peanuts* introduced Franklin, its first African American character, with grace in 1968, the strip was slow to take up the concerns of environmental racism that might have preoccupied Franklin's family. As an African American outsider to Charlie Brown's neighborhood, Franklin could realistically expect to breathe, drink, and play in poisons that his White friends never had to worry about. As Robert Bullard argues, Black Americans bear disproportionate environmental burdens based not only on class but on race (2000, 5). Like many post–*Silent Spring* newspaper strips, *Peanuts* doesn't take on Franklin's particular knowledge and experience as shaped by his environmental vantage point.

Instead, its environmental concerns remain mainstream. For example, in the wake of *Silent Spring*, *Peanuts* references Rachel Carson by name in several daily strips (Barrow 2012). These strips configure the quiet and controversial ecologist as an incongruous hero for Lucy, the strip's boisterous and often graceless know-it-all. Mark Barrow Jr. argues that Carson, "an articulate, educated female who was not afraid to speak her mind in public," probably served as a role model for Lucy (Barrow 2012, 163). Yet although Lucy might celebrate her hero by carrying a baseball bat emblazoned with Carson's name (Schulz 1962), Lucy has little patience for studying "stupid butterflies" for a school project in a memorable Sunday strip (Schulz 1963). Lucy exhausts herself by shouting in bolded lettering and wildly chasing the hovering specimens with her net. She moves from foreground to background across the thin hatching of the grass, surrounded by the dotted spiral of the butterflies' flight in the air, as though she herself were entangled in the net of their dizzying movement. Her brother Linus stands silently by, his striped shirt and timid air reminiscent of A. A. Milne's Piglet, watching from the periphery of the action. At the peak of the frenzy, as the butterflies have steadily increased from one to two to three in a cloud of trailing dots, Lucy admits to Linus that she needs the stupid butterflies for school. Hereafter, the action in the strip clears and quiets. In the first two panels of the final row of the strip, Linus is suddenly alone with the butterflies. He quietly tilts his open palm up and out, first right, and then left, as though consciously summoning the flying insects. Like clockwork, they float easily to his palm.

When Linus hands them like a still-life bouquet to the wild-eyed Lucy, his tender words of protection ("Promise you'll let them go after you've studied them, will you?") are a marked departure from Lucy's frenetic commands that the butterflies "**HOLD STILL, I SAY!**"

This Sunday strip shows two different mainstream orientations to the natural world between brother and sister: that of romanticized participation and that of abject domination. When Lucy throws her net over Linus' head in frustration, he implies that his perception of the natural world is more like Rachel Carson's than Lucy's: "I can't believe that Rachel Carson would ever let herself get so upset!" Linus here loosens the narrative of perceived human dominance into a reciprocal and respectful participation with the natural world. However, Linus' status as a White, heterosexual male who knows nature better than his belligerent sister reprises the role of Mark Trail in the Lost Forest. The environmental imagination of this *Peanuts* strip is lyrically pastoral, but problematic in its fortification of nature as a space of White, heterosexual male finesse. However, unlike *Mark Trail*, whose earnest tone compromises its capacity to sustain irony, the humor in *Peanuts* disorients a straight-faced reading. Linus *and* Lucy are the butt of the joke here; Linus for his butterfly-catching pretentiousness, and Lucy for her impatience and short-temper. Neither emerges as a clear winner in this contest, complicating the efficacy of the strip's mainstream environmental attitudes.

Animal icons in *Peanuts* cross-pollinate with government-sponsored environmental literature, securing the strip's role in the mainstream environmental movement. After the first Earth Day in 1970 and the surge of new American environmental regulation, including the creation of the Environmental Protection Agency (EPA), the character icons of Snoopy and Woodstock feature prominently in government-sponsored "Johnny Horizon" promotional materials. This campaign includes poster art and pamphlets designed to encourage school children to adopt mainstream environmentalist behaviors (Pilgrim 2014). The U.S. Department of the Interior "recruited" the *Peanuts* animal icons for the campaign and local Bureau of Land Management (BLM) offices distributed promotional materials ("Snoopy Joins Battle Against Pollution" 1972). America's iconic beagle and his faithful bird-friend thus took to Day Glo–colored placards to encourage young civilians to "Bend a Little, Pick Up a Lot" and to "Pounce on Pollution!"

Schulz's striking page design is critical to the mainstream argument these promotional posters pose. Each poster features Schulz's beloved animal icons rendered in his trembling, buoyant black line art. Each icon is paper-white against the neon wash of the background. This punch of color conveys the urgency of the mainstream environmental movement. By addressing young audiences through placards and speech balloons, each poster essentially functions as a large, single-panel cartoon. The national poster campaign connects the icons of *Peanuts* with an ethos of public service and consumer-citizen initiative. As government-sponsored mascots, Snoopy and

Woodstock continue a legacy of cartoon animals pressed into national service for lofty conservationist aims ("Only you can prevent forest fires!" as Smoky Bear reminds us). Educational poster arts exhort youth to identify themselves with an ethic of personal accountability as espoused by a beloved cartoon icon and sanctioned by the Mark Trail lookalike Johnny Horizon.

The "Johnny Horizon" *Peanuts* posters represent the growing anti-toxics discourse in the decade following *Silent Spring*. *Peanuts* recognizes that environmental health is a critical factor in the evolving anti-toxics movement of the postwar nation. Concurrent to the poster campaign, Schulz referenced the newly created Environmental Protection Agency (EPA) in several daily strips. Of course, Charlie Brown is not a very good environmentalist; he is only really good at getting things wrong. Thus, in a March 1977 story arc, when Charlie Brown takes a big bite out of the kite-eating tree in revenge for yet another destroyed kite, he receives a threatening letter from the EPA. The EPA interrupts the tranquil domestic scene of the Brown household: Charlie Brown is neatly seated on a tiny stool in front of the TV when Sally hands him the letter. The arrival of this letter riffs on the poor kid's predictably bad luck. But this sequence also sustains a critique of the EPA's preoccupation with individual rather than systemic environmental change: the EPA wastes its resources by discouraging solitary citizens from biting trees. As Michael Maniates argues, such individualization "diverts attention from political arenas that matter" (Maniates 2001, 44). An intense focus on saving a single tree or picking up a handful of litter displaces a collective focus on the elite powers and corporations that generate environmental harm in the first place.

The individualization that Schulz lampoons is symptomatic of a mainstream environmentalism that fails to counter environmental racism. Despite having roots in the Civil Rights Movement, mainstream environmentalisms tend to elide social disparities that produce different environmental realities. EJ ecocriticism emerges from the critical need for discussions of race in environmental regulation and legal practice. EJ ecocriticsm asks how a text represents access to environmental goods as well as access to legal instruments of environmental regulation; it asks who benefits from a text's framing of nature and whose environmental rights are ignored, forgotten, or outright denied by this framing; and it asks if a text constructs nature as a romantic and/or utilitarian object for human use or as the complex place where people live, work, and play. In short, an EJ ecocritical reading of a text is alive to the legacies of classism, racism, colonialism, sexism, and homophobia that encode a text's environmental imagination.

It's important to note that EJ ecocritical discourse does more than merely acknowledge how environmental experience varies according to human difference; it argues that environmental hazards are the result of multiple kinds of historical abjection and authorized indifference (Dotson and White 2013, 74). Environmental injustice flows from converging institutional structures of racism, homophobia, and sexism. It cannot be resolved without addressing the historical abjection of minority communities. While *Peanuts* remains oblique in its attention to systemic concerns and noticeably omits such concerns in racial and ethnic terms, Jackie Ormes's *Torchy in the Heartbeats* is more forthright in engaging a comprehensive aesthetics of environmental equity.

Environmental racism and the form of the newspaper strip in *Torchy in Heartbeats* (1950–1954)

The EPA and its host of environmental regulations did not exist when Jackie Ormes inked *Torchy in Heartbeats* to paper from 1950–1954. While *Torchy* is often summarized as comic strip ahead of its time, Ormes's project is vital for the very fact that Ormes *does* respond to her time. As Nancy Goldstein (2013) argues, Ormes would have been aware of struggles against garbage incinerators and landfills happening in the 1950s in her own Chicago community: "Many parts of the South Side were low-income neighborhoods whose residents were mostly people of color, and these neighborhoods were well known as dumping grounds for the waste from more affluent communities and industry" (Goldstein 2013, 40). Goldstein reasons that Ormes was most likely inspired by one community action in particular: "In 1953, citizens in South Side Chicago where [Ormes] lived united to protest a defective landfill that released untreated runoff into swamps and lakes" (Goldstein 2013, 40). *Torchy* is thus significant not only because it remains relevant to our contemporary environmental justice era, but because it responds so profoundly to its own, especially at a time when the most prominent environmental imagination in comics was limited to the White, heteronormative conservationism of *Mark Trail* and *Peanuts*. Given the national circulation of the *Pittsburgh Courier*, readers from every major city from Houston to Memphis to New Orleans to Detroit might see their local struggles against environmental racism reflected in Ormes's fictional Southville. Ormes taps into a collective experience of environmental oppression in mid-century African American life by innovating the form of romance, a marginalized comic genre, within the marginalized medium of comics.

While historians nod to the progressive themes that distinguish *Torchy in Heartbeats* (1950–1954) as noteworthy newspaper strip (Jackson 1985, Jones 1985, Reib and Feil 1996, and Robbins 2001), no scholars have examined its formal achievements from an ecocritical perspective. *Torchy* originally appeared in the comic section of the African American weekly newspaper, the *Pittsburgh Courier*. Access to the strip is extremely limited as only a few libraries in the United States hold archives of the supplement in which it appeared, and even these holdings are incomplete (Goldstein 2013, 27). Nancy Goldstein (2008) is the only scholar to examine the environmental justice story arc (1953–1954) at any length. Goldstein summarizes the major events of the EJ sequence and resourcefully contextualizes the year's work of weekly strips against mid-century EJ struggles.

Yet Goldstein's important work does not analyze the sequence's formal construction or the different *risk horizons* that encode environmental racism in the strip. In her analysis of prose novels, Ursula Heise explains that risk horizons reveal character struggles "to gain awareness of . . . riskscapes and find ways of living and dying within them" (Heise 2002, 773). The term refers to a character's perception of toxic risk *as* risk. *Torchy* produces varying risk horizons as an aesthetic of equity, generating an environmental imagination that pulls environmental disparity into the light.

Each of Ormes's cartoon heroines is complex, self-assured, and resourceful, but Torchy Brown is exceptionally well-defined. Ormes reflects that "Torchy was no moonstruck crybaby, and that she wouldn't perish between heartbeats. I never liked dreamy little women who can't hold their own" (Jackson 1985, 25). In the final story arc of *Torchy in Heartbeats*, Torchy applies her talents to fighting the environmental racism of Colonel Fuller, owner of the "huge Fuller Chemical Plant," which "is slowly poisoning the entire community" of the predominantly Black town of Southville (4 July 1953). Ormes uses the form of serial publication to activate a retroactive riskscape, signaling the ethical imperative of responding to the comprehensive environmental community.

Torchy at first doesn't see Southville as an environmental riskscape that will require her to negotiate life and death. Having completed nurse's training in the city for the purpose of assisting her boyfriend Dr. Paul Hammond in his new rural medical practice, Torchy spends the day of her arrival slowly walking through Southville's dusty streets, reuniting with Paul in his shockingly run-down clinic, and walking with him in the dark, cool woods on a house call. After her exploration of the town and woods, Torchy learns that the Fuller Chemical Company is poisoning the community. The June 1953 strips that contain the very moment of revelation are missing from the available archive, but by July, Torchy and Paul have returned from their walk to his ramshackle clinic. Gesturing to a shelf of glass jars bright red with blood samples, Paul explains his plan to isolate the toxin flowing from the nearby chemical plant into the bloodstreams of his Black patients (4 July 1953). With this revelation, all previous strips in the storyline, including Torchy's walk along the town's dusty road and Paul and Torchy's strolls in "the stillness of the cool woodland," are cast in toxic suspicion (Reib and Feil 1996, 31). The environment of Southville is reframed as a riskscape as through the blood of its people.

The early strips featuring Torchy's encounter with a passing farm-cart driver are thus accentuated with latent danger. These strips include at least one panel background saturated with bright red ink. Blood-red backgrounds glow with the same urgency as the blood samples in Paul's clinic. This motif represents the material trace of otherwise invisible harm. Framed by the blood of the community, Torchy is shocked by the rudeness of the White farmer who calls her "girlie" and refuses to help her find Paul's new clinic. She clutches her throat and stares after him as he rides away, her smart

purple dress and astonished expression a sharp contrast to the dehumanizing implications of his insults (18 Apr. 1953). Torchy continues on the road
with dignity and energy, but is visibly disturbed by the malevolence generated in this encounter. Grimly, against the saturated red of the background,
she tells herself, "I guess I'll find out what [the farmer] meant in time!"

Weeks later, the strip again centers on the blood of the community in
Torchy's confrontation with chemical plant owner Colonel Fuller. Torchy
stands in for Paul and relies on her own authority to present his medical
proof. In the strip featuring her confrontation with Fuller, the dance of their
bodies across the page and between panel borders conveys contrasting perceptions of environmental risk (12 Sept. 1953). The presence and absence of
Torchy's body in the sequence communicates defensive and offensive positions. In the opening panel, Torchy wears a smart black-and-white clamshell
hat and a sequined black dress as she waits in the reception area of Fuller's
office. Her dignified ensemble is more elegant than the plain white nurse's
uniform she wears at the clinic; Torchy assumes an unmistakably dignified
air in the reception area. Even so, Fuller's secretary refuses to allow her in to
the private office: "Colonel Fuller will be *out* to see you!" Torchy holds her
temper and ignores the implications of the rejection, vowing, "I've got to
make him see! *I've got to!*" Even as Torchy makes her vow, Colonel Fuller's
fleshy hand appears in the corner of the panel, pushing his private office
door open. Colonel Fuller occupies the entire following panel; Torchy is not
visible. Fuller's chin is slightly raised, his jowls shaven and full. The straight
lines of his suit sharply contrast with the fuzzy, tapioca-colored painting
behind him. In the following row, Torchy and Colonel Fuller finally share
the panel. The sudden blood-red background eliminates the details of the
office. Torchy's face appears in a slim profile along the right edge; Fuller
occupies the panel center, his hands forming fists at his belt, his balding
forehead wrinkled in confusion at Torchy's presence. Action lines radiate
from the folder of blood tests beneath Torchy's chin, suggesting that the
woman is trembling. This impression is supported by the abrupt breaks
in her speech as she stammers out her purpose for visiting: "I – I've come
for Doctor Hammond at the clinic. I've brought his findings – here in this
folder." Color and punctuation suggest that the blood of the Black community is under threat and Torchy is the only one who can shift Fuller's risk
horizon.

Torchy, not Fuller, assumes the center of the page in a medium close-up in
the subsequent panel space. The focus of the panel emphasizes her shoulders
and strong neck; her body is not bound by a clear panel border but by the
borders of the panels that surround her space, encircling her with a generous
measure of white. This design emphasizes her proud posture as she asserts
that Fuller is poisoning the community: "Doctor Hammond has suspected
for some time that the waste products of your plant are poisoning the entire
community through absorption in the water, the very land itself. These
analysis [sic] of blood samples from the clinic patients prove he is right!"

Her steady, strong gaze looking out from the page is piercing. Despite the indignity of meeting Fuller in his reception area, and despite his intimidating body language, Torchy assembles a picture of strength and authority.

Yet Torchy's resolve doesn't prevail over the structure of power on the page. The closing caption entirely hides her body. Only her neat white hat and the back of her head are visible. The caption itself details the action as Torchy looks on:

> The man said nothing for a long moment while his hard eyes continued to probe hers. Torchy was beginning to wonder if he'd heard what she had said when suddenly his body relaxed. Throwing back his head he began to laugh – a laughter that grew till it filled the room!

Despite her forceful presentation of the poisoning of Fuller's Black employees and their families, Fuller rejects Torchy's authority to make any ethical claim on him. The page layout charts the rise and fall of Torchy's argument that Black life must matter to Fuller. While Torchy judiciously pushes back against the Colonel Fuller's apathy for the Black community through her elegant clothing, her assertive posture, and her earnest language, Fuller refuses to value Black life. His risk horizon remains unmoved.

The emotional arc of the epidemic that follows Colonel Fuller's denial is terrifying. The community is wrecked by the physical suffering of children and families. Paul works late into the night to develop a possible treatment, and Torchy communicates with worried patients in his stead. Her role as a medical communicator is pivotal to the rising action of the strip: she proves herself to be a clear-eyed rallying figure. Paul's serum is ready just in time for the worst of the epidemic. Yet it's not until Colonel Fuller's young nephew Jamie becomes severely ill with the same chemical poisoning that Fuller's risk horizons begin to shift. When Jamie's bloodwork leads Fuller's expensive White doctors to confirm Paul's original findings, Fuller realizes he needs the serum Paul's developed to save Jamie. Illness in the Black community becomes real to Fuller only after a White body suffers environmental harm. Paul is keenly aware of the power of Fuller's attachment to Jamie and treats the child in hope of awakening Fuller's own humanity. It seems to work: as Jamie improves, Fuller vows to change for the better.

Yet Torchy is not convinced. By sneering at Colonel Fuller for the remainder of the environmental justice arc, even after Fuller appoints Paul as head physician of the updated medical clinic and installs new holding facilities for the chemical waste, Torchy indicates that Fuller's crimes are not forgotten even when his risk horizon expands to include the Black community. In the absence of any new legal protections, Torchy doubts that Fuller's internal transformation will hold. Torchy's suspicious looks at Fuller suggest that she hasn't found satisfaction in the quiet reckoning of the strip. The story arc's resolution conventionally unfolds as our heroine's boyfriend triumphs over confusion and injustice, but Torchy's silent scorn for Fuller signals her and Ormes's realistic assessment of mobile risk horizons in the strip. Torchy's glaring looks constitute a continuing aesthetic of equity in the strip. She indicts Fuller for his failure to honor the Black community and the lack of any binding legal protections in wake of the epidemic.

Figure 4.1 Torchy in Heartbeats, October 17, 1953, by Jackie Ormes. *Pittsburgh Courier* [Color Comics Supplement], Smith-Mann Syndicate.

Source: Image courtesy of Nancy Goldstein.

Conclusion

Comic forms that register environmental problems deploy a range of verbal–visual tools to communicate the stakes of these problems. *Mark Trail, Peanuts,* and *Torchy in Heartbeats* generate distinct environmental imaginations in their color, page layout, and iconicity. *Mark Trail* relies on disorienting animal icons and speech balloons that disrupt the strip's anthropocentric sequence. Whereas *Peanuts* relies on mainstream environmental concerns like universal risk and conservationism, *Torchy* mobilizes diverse risk horizons in response to environmental racism. *Peanuts* doesn't consciously imagine how race determines experiences of environmental risks, while *Torchy* meditates on the best means of building coalitions and transforming systemic oppression.

This chapter has sought to map out the vitality of EJ ecocriticism in comic studies and vice versa. Scholarship could productively respond to new forms of American nature writing in environmental graphic memoir, or map how webcomics generate digital comics ecologies through online platforms, links, and commenting forums. The environmental humanities renews attention to the formal influence of environmental problems and queries present in comic forms. Comic studies opens the environmental humanities to a range of verbal–visual moves that can deepen interdisciplinary inquiry and offer new methods of analysis.

Keywords

Aesthetics of equity
Audience reception
Comic form
Comic studies
Comprehensive environmental
  community

Environmental humanities
Environmental imagination
Environmental justice ecocriticsm
Environmental racism
New Environmental Paradigm
Risk horizons

Discussion questions

1   What does environmental scholarship about comics lose when it fails to "take up comics *as comics,* that is, as a distinctive medium with its own vocabulary, devices, and designs"?
2   Reread the key concept for "comic studies." Why does this chapter argue that comic studies is congruent with the environmental humanities? What is the benefit of reading for an aesthetics of equity in comics?
3   Examine the October 17, 1953, *Torchy in Heartbeats* strip (Figure 4.1) in which Torchy confronts Colonel Fuller. How much time passes in the story between the panels? How does the layout of the panels on the page and the presence or absence of panel borders affect the pace of your reading? What work does color achieve on the page? Note that

Torchy knows the stream is polluted at this point, yet she meets Jamie there anyway. Why would she do this? What does her presence in the natural environment tell you about the strip's aesthetics of equity? Why is Jamie's presence in the woods significant in a story arc that meditates on environmental racism?

4   This chapter argues that "even when comics don't endorse an environmental orientation on purpose, they nonetheless inscribe into their form and content the environmental character of their era." Do you agree? Is it possible for a comic to *lack* an ethical orientation to nature or somehow remain environmentally neutral? Why or why not?

5   Find a comic you enjoy. How would you perform an ecocritical reading of it? Does the comic encode (through complacency or critique) the environmental imaginations that this chapter suggests are often elided?

Further reading

Adamson, Joni, Mei Mei Evans, and Rachel Stein, eds. 2010. *Environmental Justice Reader: Politics, Poetics, & Pedagogy*. Tucson: University of Arizona Press.

Aldama, Frederick Luis, ed. 2010. *Multicultural Comics: From Zap to Blue Beetle*. Austin: University of Texas Press.

Chute, Hillary. 2010. *Graphic Women*. New York: Columbia University Press.

Cole, Luke, and Sheila Foster. 2001. *From the Ground Up: Environmental Racism and the Rise of the Environmental Justice Movement*. New York: New York University Press.

Eisner, Will. 1985. *Sequential Art*. Melbourne, Australia: Poorhouse Press.

McCloud, Scott. 1994. *Understanding Comics*. New York: HarperCollins Books.

Wolk, Douglas. 2008. *Reading Comics: How Graphic Novels Work and What They Mean*. Cambridge, MA: Da Capo Press.

Works cited

Barrow, Mark V. Jr. 2012. "Carson in Cartoon: A New Window into the Noisy Reception to *Silent Spring*." *Endeavor* 36.4: 156–164.

Beaty, Bart. 1999. "The Search for Comics Exceptionalism." *Comics Journal* 211: 67–72.

Bullard, Robert. 2000. *Dumping in Dixie*. 3rd ed. Boulder, CO: Westview Press.

Carson, Rachel. 1962. *Silent Spring*. Greenwich, CT: Fawcett.

Charles M. Schulz Museum. 2013. "Peanuts . . . Naturally." Traveling Exhibition. Accessed February 6, 2015. http://schulzmuseum.org/explore/traveling-exhibitions/rent-a-traveling-exhibit/peanuts-naturally/

De Laplant, Kevin. 2005. "Making the Abstract Concrete: How a Comic Can Bring to Life the Central Problems of Environmental Philosophy." In *Comics As Philosophy*, edited by Jeff McLaughlin, 153–163. Jackson, MI: University Press of Mississippi.

Dobrin, Sidney I., and Kenneth B. Kidd, eds. 2004. *Wild Things: Children's Culture and Ecocriticism*. Detroit: Wayne State University Press.

Dotson, Kristie, and Kyle White. 2013. "Environmental Justice, Unknowability, and Unqualified Affectability." *Ethics and the Environment* 18.2: 55–79.

Dunaway, Finis. 2008. "Gas Masks, Pogo, and the Ecological Indian: Earth Day and the Visual Politics of American Environmentalism." *American Quarterly* 60.1: 67–99.

Evans, Mei Mei. 2010. "Nature and Environmental Justice." In *Environmental Justice Reader: Politics, Poetics, & Pedagogy*, edited by Joni Adamson, Mei Mei Evans, and Rachel Stein, 181–193. Tucson: University of Arizona Press.

Fruhlinger, Josh. 2007. "Fists of Fury and/or Justice." *Comics Curmudgeon*, April 19. http://joshreads.com/?p=1039

Goble, Dale, Paul Hirt, and Susan Kilgore, 2005. "On Environmental Cartoons." Environmental History 10.4: 776–792.

Goldstein, Nancy. 2008. *Jackie Ormes: The First African American Woman Cartoonist*. Ann Arbor: University of Michigan Press.

———. 2013. "The Trouble with Romance in Jackie Ormes' Comics." In *Black Comics: Politics of Race and Representation*, edited by Sheena C. Howard and Ronald L. Jackson. London: Bloomsbury.

Hatfield, Charles. 2009. "An Art of Tensions." In *A Comics Studies Reader*, edited by Jeet Heer and Kent Worcester, 132–148. Jackson, MI: University Press of Mississippi.

Heise, Ursula K. 2002. "Toxins, Drugs, and Global Systems: Risk and Narrative in the Contemporary Novel." *American Literature* 74.4: 747–778.

Hill, Jack. 2003. "Talk before the Pleasant Oaks Gem and Mineral Club of Dallas." *Preservation Society for Spring Creek Forest*, June 5. Accessed May 30, 2015. http://www.springcreekforest.org/mark_trail.htm

Hogan, Katie. 2012. "Green *Angels in America*: Aesthetics of Equity." *Journal of American Culture* 35.1: 4–14.

Jackson, David. 1985. "The Amazing Adventures of Jackie Ormes." *Chicago Reader*, 14–23.

Jones, Stephen Loring. 1985. "From 'Under Cork' to Overcoming: Black Images in the Comics." In *Ethnic Images in the Comics*, edited by C. Hardy and G. F. Stern: 21–30. Philadelphia: Balch Institute for Ethnic Studies.

Kern, Robert. 2000. "Ecocriticism: What Is It Good For?" *Interdisciplinary Studies in Literature and Environment* 7.1: 9–32.

Maniates, Michael. 2001. "Individualization: Plant a Tree, Buy a Bike, Save the World?" *Global Environmental Politics* 1.3: 31–52.

McCloud, Scott. 1994. *Understanding Comics*. New York: HarperCollins Books.

Murray, Robin, and Joseph Heumann. 2011. *That's All Folks: Ecocritical Readings of American Animated Features*. Lincoln, NE: University of Nebraska Press.

Ormes, Jackie. 1950–54. *Torchy in Heartbeats*. Pittsburgh Courier [Color Comics Supplement], Smith-Mann Syndicate. Image courtesy of Nancy Goldstein.

———. 1953. *Torchy in Heartbeats*, April 18. *Pittsburgh Courier* [Color Comics Supplement], Smith-Mann Syndicate. Image courtesy of Nancy Goldstein.

———. 1953. *Torchy in Heartbeats*, July 4. *Pittsburgh Courier* [Color Comics Supplement], Smith-Mann Syndicate. Image courtesy of Nancy Goldstein.

———. 1953. *Torchy in Heartbeats*, September 12. *Pittsburgh Courier* [Color Comics Supplement], Smith-Mann Syndicate. Image courtesy of Nancy Goldstein.

Pike, Deidre. 2012. *Enviro-toons: Green Themes in Animated Cinema and Television*. Jefferson, NC: McFarland & Company.

Pilgrim, Caren. 2014. "Johnny Horizon." *Collect Peanuts*. Accessed February 6, 2015. http://www.collectpeanuts.com/wp/promotional-materials-giveaways/johnny-horizon/

Reed, TV. 2010. "Toward an Environmental Justice Ecocriticsm." In *Environmental Justice Reader: Politics, Poetics, & Pedagogy*, edited by Joni Adamson, Mei Mei Evans, and Rachel Stein, 145–162. Tucson: University of Arizona Press.

Reib, Susan, and Stuart Feil. 1996. "Torchy Brown Faces Life." *American Legacy* 2.2: 25–32.

Robbins, Trina. 2001. *Great Women Cartoonists*. New York: Watson-Guptill, Print.

Schulz, Charles. 1962. *Peanuts,* November 12. *Go Comics*. Accessed February 6, 2015. http://www.gocomics.com/peanuts/1962/11/12#.U3ZxfoUjzRc

———. 1963. *Peanuts,* May 12. *Go Comics*. Accessed February 6, 2015. http://www.gocomics.com/peanuts/1963/05/12#.U3ZyLoUjzRc

———. 1977. *Peanuts,* March 1. *Go Comics*. Accessed February 6, 2015. http://www.gocomics.com/peanuts/1963/05/12#.U3ZyLoUjzRc

"Snoopy Joins Battle Against Pollution." 1972. *Eugene Register Guard*, Jan. 6. 30. Accessed February 6, 2015. http://news.google.com/newspapers?nid=1310&dat=19720106&id=tdhVAAAAIBAJ&sjid=QeEDAAAAIBAJ&pg=5186,1442857

Taylor, Dorceta. 2002. "Race, Class, Gender, and American Environmentalism." *Forest Service General Technical Report PNW-GTR-534*. United States Dept. of Agriculture. Chicago State University, April 2002. PDF.

Wolk, Douglas. 2008. *Reading Comics: How Graphic Novels Work and What They Mean*. Cambridge, MA: Da Capo Press.

Part II
Flow

5 Overview

Flow – an ecocritical perspective on broadcast media

Stephen Rust

Introduction

As students and scholars of such *broadcast media* as radio and television, we can further develop the critical skills and research methods necessary to address the challenge of analyzing media *and/as* ecology by merging the academic discourse of *ecomedia studies* with that of *media ecology*.

Over the past twenty years, ecomedia studies has developed in response to actual environmental changes occurring on a global scale, including climate change, biodiversity loss, deforestation, and air and water pollution. It generally operates by approaching media texts and contexts through the disciplinary and methodological lenses of environmental philosophy (for example, Gaard 1993; Morton 2009), rhetoric (for example, Dobrin and Morey 2009; Ross 1994), visual anthropology (for example, Vivanco 2002; 2004), history (for example, Bousé 2000), and cultural studies, which combines these disciplinary angles (for example, Chris 2006; Sturgeon 2008). As such, ecomedia studies can be understood as a historically situated, ideologically motivated, and ethically informed approach to the intersections of media, society, *and* the environment.

Despite having a similar name, media ecology has developed as a very different field of study. Building on the work of communication theorists such as Marshall McLuhan, Walter Ong, and Neal Postman, the Media Ecology Association was established in 1998 by scholars interested in studying media *as* environments. In this field, ecological terms are used primarily as metaphors for studying the relationships between various forms of media. Notice, for example, how television scholar Jonathan Gray employs metaphoric language when he asserts in his 2010 book *Show Sold Separately* that video games, merchandise, advertisements, and other media texts have become "as organic and naturally occurring a part of our mediated environment as are movies and television" (23). Gray's description resonates with many readers because it uses familiar language to make an important point about the ubiquity of media in our everyday lives. Yet his point does not directly comment on the interaction between media and the actual material environment of the planet. In effect, the two fields of ecomedia studies and media ecology have developed in recent decades with different goals and methodologies.

The chapters in this section of *Ecomedia: Key Issues*, however, offer us a new way of looking at media by taking important steps toward the convergence of ecomedia studies and media ecology through considerations of both the cultural and material aspects of broadcast media and/as ecology. This overview chapter contributes to the convergence by offering an ecocritical perspective on one of the most important metaphors used in the field of media studies – *flow*. A central concept in media studies, flow has not often been applied in ecocritical analyses of media. It is imperative to reflect on established concepts like flow so that ecomedia scholars can interrogate the discourse of media studies itself and contribute to the field from its center, rather than its periphery. As discussed below, reevaluating the idea of flow can serve both fields well, as it draws attention to the fluid boundaries between media as an abstract, cultural concept and its material, environmental groundings. Thus, in the first part of this chapter, we will explore the theoretical aspects of the convergence of ecomedia studies and media ecology using the concept of flow. In the latter part of this chapter, we will ground this theoretical discussion in textual analysis by examining a single television documentary, the 2010 Emmy-nominated Public Broadcasting exposé *Ghana: Digital Dumping Ground*, to consider the practical applications of theorizing flow ecocritically.

Media flow

In media and communication studies, the keyword *flow* commonly refers to the stream of content (advertisements, entertainment, news, etc.) distributed by broadcasters through radio waves, airwaves, satellite transmissions, and cable wires and consumed by radio listeners and television viewers. Flow can refer to the entire stream of content that is being broadcast at any one time on radio and television (imagine all the songs and shows you could access right now at this very moment) or a particular portion of content, such as the 24-hour cycle of programming (Barnard 2000, 197–199; Butler 2010, 6–11). While the word "flow" has been used in the English language for more than a thousand years to refer to the movement of water and air (or other liquids and gasses), cultural historian Raymond Williams in his seminal 1974 book *Television: Technology and Cultural Form* introduced flow into media studies. Williams was interested in the layering of discourses and meaning produced by viewers' collective experience of television programming. As Will Brooker (2005) puts it:

> Williams was describing the disruptive, dreamlike experience of watching American television, with its constant flash-forwards of promised shows to come and flashback reminders of stories born? before; its snatches of teaser-trailers for current affairs sliced into the middle of drama series, and its lack of obvious distinction between commercials and programs.

As television viewers (and radio listeners), we have the capability of producing multiple levels of meaning by simultaneously considering the meanings produced from individual segments of flow, the relationships between segments of flow, and the relationships between these segments and the entire flow of content available (Williams [1974] 2003, 87–90). As you read Sarina Pearson's essay on New Zealand television in this section, for example, you might consider how meanings can be produced from individual episodes of shows like *Hunting Aotearoa*, the relationship between the episodes and the commercials that might have played while those episodes aired, and the relationship between an individual episode of the show and every other show available to viewers at the same moment on other channels.

Williams himself was most interested in how flow refers to the overall experience of television programming and viewing rather than to the individual units of content we might be watching at any one point in time. This was because he was concerned with the control that broadcasters exert over this televisual flow. He points out that while viewers ultimately produce meaning from television flow, patterns of flow are carefully planned by broadcasters to influence viewers, for example by pairing particular advertisements with particular programs to reach certain segments of television audiences ([1974] 2003, 86). Media scholars often refer to this process as targeted marketing or agenda setting by attempting to exert control over the potential meanings that viewers can produce from advertisements. As Mike Budd, Steve Craig, and Clay Steinman assert in their 1999 book *Consuming Environments*, it is in the best interests of broadcasters to maintain the attention of viewers and listeners so that advertisers can reach the widest possible audience and thus sell more products to those viewers (150–151). While Williams had not experienced the stream of flow produced by the hundreds of cable television and satellite radio stations available to us today, his analysis of media flow provided scholars a starting point to delve more deeply into the study of radio and television as serious academic pursuits.

Box 5.1   Broadcasting as ecological metaphor

Ecological metaphors generate comparisons between two seemingly unrelated objects or ideas through the use of objects or ideas associated with the natural world. The keyword *broadcasting* is an ecological metaphor that takes its meaning from the relationship between human agricultural and industrial practices. In agriculture, the term broadcasting was first used in the mid-1700s to describe the traditional practice of spreading seeds by hand across a broad area of land. During the nineteenth century, this agricultural practice was replaced by the use of seed drills and other farm tools and the term broadcasting was used instead to describe the process of spreading political ideas across society (Hamilton 2007, 290). In the 1920s, the term was first used to describe the broadcasting of wireless radio signals. As radio and television emerged as industrial technologies during the second half of the twentieth century, they benefited from the fact that the term broadcasting, borrowed from agriculture, evokes pastoral images of farmers living in harmony with nature. Yet the history of radio and television broadcasting has its roots in the increasing disruption of the natural world through industrialization, not in the pastoral past as the term suggests.

Further reading

James Hamilton. 2007. "Unearthing Broadcasting in the Anglophone World." In *Residual Media*, edited by Charles R. Acland, 283–301. Minneapolis: University of Minnesota Press.
Sue Thomas. 2013. *Technobiophilia: Nature and Cyberspace*. New York: Bloomsbury Press.

Over the past four decades, scholarship on flow has expanded to refer to more than just the transmission of content by broadcasters and the reception of that content by viewers and listeners. Sociologist Manuel Castells has theorized more broadly that contemporary global society is "constructed around flows," including "flows of capital, flows of information, flows of technology, flows of organizational interactions, flows of images, sounds, and symbols" (2000, 442). Building on Castell's work, Daya Kishan Thussu uses flow to describe the increasingly globalized process of media production, consumption, and circulation. In the twenty-first century, broadcast media content and infrastructure primarily flow outward from highly urbanized cultural hubs like New York and London to the peripheries of society, thus contributing to the concentration of information and wealth in these centers of power (2007, 15–22). As Joseph Straubhaar points out, media flows are intertwined not only with technology but with economic and political structures, as well as historical factors such as colonization, immigration, and education (2007, 14–15, 42–51). In his chapter in this section, Sean Cubitt does not directly discuss flow, but his argument reflects these ideas. He considers not only how radio listeners in the 1960s and 1970s initially produced meaning from FM radio programs that played environmentally themed songs by musicians like Captain Beefheart, but also how those transmissions were part of a broader shift in radio broadcasting during the era. Given these expanding definitions of flow, it is no surprise that the term is among the most broad and varied concepts used by media scholars to describe the complex processes at play when we surf through television channels or the radio dial.

Considering flow ecocritically

As the examples from Cubitt's and Pearson's chapters in this section indicate, ecocritics are making important contributions to our understanding of media flow and its impact on societies around the globe. Now, let us investigate why ecocritics are interested not only in media content but also what we might call media's *material flows*. Scholars such as Richard Maxwell and Toby Miller, Nadia Bozak, Charles Corbett and Richard Turco, Nicole Starosielski, and Lisa Parks (another contributor to this section) are beginning to consider the complex ecological processes involved in the global flows of media content – from the extraction of natural resources used to manufacture screens and media hardware through the lifecycle of media equipment to its disposal in landfills or reprocessing as *electronic waste* (Maxwell and Miller 2012; Bozak 2012; Corbett and Turco 2006; Starosielski 2011b; Parks 2005).

These scholars have begun to redirect media studies attention to the ways in which media texts and systems are produced from and embedded in material conditions and cultural histories. In their groundbreaking study, *Greening the Media* (2012), for example, Richard Maxwell and Toby Miller document "the myriad ways that media technology consumes, despoils, and wastes natural resources" (1). Acknowledging that students and professors of media "rarely address where texts and technologies physically come from or end up," Maxwell and Miller consider such questions as why consumers treat technology as disposable, how labor practices and bureaucratic regulations contribute to the throw-away culture of media consumption, and how toxic chemicals are part and parcel of the manufacturing and recycling of media hardware (10). It is precisely this ability to foreground our understanding of figurative concepts like flow in what Maxwell and Miller call the "*materialist ecology*" of media that distinguishes ecocriticism from traditional approaches to media studies (9).

Nicole Starosielski brings an ecocritical perspective directly to bear on the concept of flow in work such as her article "Underwater Flow" (2011b) for the highly regarded online media journal *Flow*. Starosielski usefully reminds us that the flow of information and images on the Internet cannot be detached from material conditions. Building on Parks's (2005) examination of the material conditions necessary for satellite technology to distribute television signals around the globe, Starosielski explains that although "we tend to think of the Internet as less and less wired," in actuality "almost all of the texts, images, and videos on the Internet are transformed into light and transported by fiber-optic cables" (2011b). By "tracking media flows as they extend underwater" across oceans and between continents, she argues, our attention is drawn "to the ways that seemingly nebulous digital circulations are always anchored in material coordinates" (2011b). By grounding her analysis of media flow in a consideration of media's material impacts on the environment, Starosielski contributes to our understanding of media from an ecocritical perspective.

Like Starosielski, Lisa Parks is also concerned that we pay attention to the material coordinates of media flow. In her 2007 essay "Falling Apart: Electronics Salvaging and the Global Media Economy," she challenges us to rethink our use of the term *residuals*, a term that most scholars use in reference to the financial royalties earned by actors and producers when their shows are rebroadcast or syndicated. Parks, however, defines residuals as "the waste products of a media and information society," including "the old radio and television sets, computers, stereos, VCRs, telephones, and printers that have piled up in people's basements and garages, neighborhood repair shops and thrift stores, and electronics recycling and salvage centers" (2007, 33). When we use terms like residuals (or flow) without ecocritical reflection and analysis, we risk "reinforcing the [profit-driven] imperatives of electronics manufacturers and marketers" (33), who benefit financially when we turn a blind eye to the issues of toxicity and social injustice associated with the salvaging, recycling, and disposal of media technology. In her contribution to this section, Parks brings a similar materialist approach to bear on her analysis of broadcast infrastructure in the United States.

Along with examples such as Parks's, Pearson's, and Cubitt's that constitute the following chapters in our flow section, below let's directly apply materialist flow thinking to one specific text, the Emmy-nominated television documentary *Ghana: Digital Dumping Ground*, which first aired on the Public Broadcasting program *Frontline* in 2009.

E-waste: Visualizing media *and/as* ecology

During the past decade, technological advancements, consumer demand, and government regulations led to a worldwide transition from analog to digital television broadcasting. In the United States, for example, this transition was completed in June 2009, when the last mainstream analog broadcasts were shut down and replaced by digital signals. One result of this transition is that tens of millions of analog television sets have become obsolete. According to the U.S. Environmental Protection Agency, between 2006 and 2009, Americans disposed of an estimated 1.4 billion pieces of electronic equipment, including 89 million television sets ("Electronics Waste Management" 2011, 26). While approximately 17% of these televisions were domestically recycled (27), the rest either ended up in landfills or were sent overseas to developing countries for salvaging. Responding to this dramatic rise in *e-waste* (electronic waste), University of British Columbia journalism professor Peter Klein and a team of graduate students undertook an effort to track several shipping containers full of discarded televisions, computers, and mobile devices from North America to their destinations in Ghana and China. What they document in *Ghana: Digital Dumping Ground* demonstrates how understanding the complex global issue of e-waste involves a flow of ecomedia studies' concerns into the realm of media ecology studies (and vice versa).

Box 5.2   Talk about it: tracking the flow of e-waste

What did you do with your television, stereo, computer, or mobile phone the last time you upgraded to a new device? Did you donate it, toss it in the trash, or take it to a local e-waste recycler? How can you be sure that your used electronics have been disposed of safely and locally? Visit your local sanitation center, a local electronics repair business, or your college or university computer center to find out where they send broken or obsolete media technologies for recycling. Are they willing and able to disclose that information, or do they seem unable or unwilling to cooperate with your request? Consider contacting your local and state elected officials and urge them to regulate the e-waste industry more carefully. We all want to be able to upgrade our devices without feeling guilty that we are contributing to environmental injustices such as those documented in *Ghana: Digital Dumping Ground*.

For more information on e-waste, check out the Basel Action Network at http://www.ban.org.

As an individual segment of televisual flow, *Digital Dumping Ground* works by combining words and images intended to produce a powerful intellectual and emotional impact on the viewer. The documentary opens in the Ghanaian city of Agbogbloshie, where millions of tons of e-waste arrive each year on cargo ships from developed countries in the West. These images provide visual confirmation of Klein's description of the area as "a smoldering wasteland, a slum carved into the banks of the Korle Lagoon, one of the most polluted bodies of water on earth." The exposé continues by cutting between establishing shots featuring enormous piles of old television sets and computers that litter the lagoon and surrounding fields and medium and close-up shots of workers breathing in highly toxic fumes as they burn these discarded devices over small open-air fires. Workers burn the devices to extract small amounts of valuable metals such as copper and iron, which they can sell to e-waste brokers in order to buy food and clothing for their families. The apparent lack of concern for the workers' health and safety on the part of the government and those profiting from the workers' efforts can leave the average viewer with a profound sense of environmental injustice. According to Klein's narration, while Ghanaians initially thought they would be receiving donations of usable electronics when shipments began arriving in the early 2000s, Western exporters quickly began to exploit the system as a cheap way of sending junk electronics oversees. By shipping our e-waste overseas, those of us living in developed countries are diverted from thinking about the problem. Out of sight, out of mind, as the saying goes. Yet as Ghanaian environmental journalist Mike Anane tells Klein and his team, the health implications for the workers involved are deeply troubling and the pristine wetland where Anane played soccer as a child is gone forever.

The documentary then shifts to the United States, where Klein's graduate students visit an undisclosed electronics recycling center on the West Coast. A worker interviewed on camera tells the team that the computers they have brought in will be recycled locally. Using a hidden camera, however, the filmmakers note the numeric codes on the shipping containers leaving the facility and use public records to trace the flow of the containers to the port of Hong Kong. Their reporting then takes them to the southern Chinese city of Guiyu, which "has been completely built around the e-waste trade. Miles and miles of nothing but old electronics." As Klein explains, "In China, e-waste has become big business." E-waste businesses in Guiyu employ tens of thousands of workers, primarily women, to literally "cook" computer motherboards to melt the circuitry so that trace amounts of gold and other precious minerals can be salvaged.

Historically, environmental injustices have gone underreported in China due to tight control over media by the country's central government (de Burgh and Rong 2011, 4; Yang, this collection). Although the situation is changing due to such forces as globalization and liberalization in China, the health impacts of the e-waste trade in Guiyu were first widely disclosed by Western journalists working with the Basel Action Network (Yeung 2008). Jim Puckett (the first journalist to document the situation in Guiyu) tells the filmmakers, "I was there first in 2001 and it was shocking enough then. . . . And what is happening there [now] is rather apocalyptic." Using hidden cameras, which adds an additional layer of drama to the show, the filmmakers interview a Chinese e-waste broker in one of the documentary's final scenes. The broker explains that since millions of shipping containers are sent to the West each year filled with consumer electronics and other products that are cheaper to produce in China, it is more cost effective for Western countries to return those containers filled with e-waste rather than recycle that waste locally. "If you want to do it environmentally," he says, "you have to pay. They have to invest in labor, machinery, everything. It isn't worth it to pay so much money."

As a single segment of televisual flow, this documentary is clearly quite powerful. Yet its meaning takes on an even greater relevance when one considers it in relationship to the hundreds of other shows competing for viewers' attention at the moment the program first aired in 2009. Public Broadcasting programs air without commercial interruption, but consider, for example, the number of commercials for computers, smart phones, televisions, and other electronic devices that ran on every other channel available to viewers during the program's original broadcast. One can also consider the relationship between the documentary and other films produced by Klein and his students, one on illegal logging (www.internationalreporting.org/cut), one on Brazilian forests (www.internationalreporting.org/landbrazil), and one on China's environmental movement (www.internationalreporting.org/greenchina).

Beyond the multiple layers of flow relevant to the meanings produced by viewers of *Ghana: Digital Dumping Ground* one must also consider the environmental footprint of the show's production itself. It is worth noting that even the producers of *Digital Dumping Ground* neglected to fully consider the ecological impacts of their own production, which is ironic considering the topic of the documentary. That said, in an email correspondence in 2014, Professor Klein explained to us, "I have been thinking about the environmental impact of our own work – and have been exploring how to at least mitigate the carbon footprint of our work. We are looking into this quite seriously."

One of the key lessons we can take away from close readings of documentaries like *Ghana: Digital Dumping Ground* is that the flow of media content does not exist in some abstract ether. In fact our experience of media content is inextricably linked to the economic, social, *and* ecological factors involved in media's material flows. Although this statement should in no way seem to be a revelation of some new truth, it is surprising how little attention has been paid to this issue in media studies until quite recently. In addition to the carbon footprint generated by electronics manufacturing and the shipping of containers filled with residuals around the globe, the environmental and health issues facing workers in countries like Ghana and China as a result of e-waste salvaging can be directly linked to our collective consumption of media technology and content.

As we have examined in this chapter, the media content we enjoy on our radios, televisions, and computers is not immaterial. Thinking through the various ways that media scholars have used the ecological metaphor flow to describe aspects of the production, consumption, and circulation of media content reminds us that we can also engage in ecocritical analysis of broadcast media flow from a variety of angles, from textual analysis to investigations of media infrastructure. As you read the chapters in this section by Sean Cubitt, Sarina Pearson, and Lisa Parks, keep in mind the various ways that each author considers the fluid interaction between broadcast media and/as environment.

Keywords

Broadcast media	Material flows
Ecological metaphor	Materialist ecology
Ecomedia studies	Media ecology
E-waste	Residuals
Flow	

Discussion questions

1   How do radio and television programs differ in their ability to engage listeners and viewers in environmental thinking and action? List and

discuss some of the formal characteristics that are unique to each of these different forms of media and how these characteristics help shape the responses of listeners and viewers.

2 Track the flow of one broadcast media text – including both its place in the flow of radio or television programming and its material flow from production to distribution. What, if any, environmental content does it have at the textual level? How is this content affected by its relationship to other texts? What, if anything, can you determine about the environmental impacts of its production?

3 List several examples of ecological metaphors that are used to describe aspects of media – for example, the term "web" as a synonym for the Internet. How do these ecological metaphors shape the way we think about media? Do you think these metaphors are helpful? Harmful?

4 Do media production courses at your university, community college, or high school teach methods of sustainable production? If not, why do you think this issue is so commonly overlooked? If so, list some specific methods of sustainable production methods taught at your school and discuss why they are taught.

Further reading and viewing

"Following the Trail of Toxic E-Waste." November 9, 2008. *60 Minutes*. Produced by Solly Granatstein. CBS News. Television Broadcast.

Greenlit. 2010. Produced and directed by Miranda Bailey. Los Angeles, Ambush Entertainment. DVD.

Postman, Neil. 2000. "The Humanism of Media Ecology." *Proceedings of the Media Ecology Association* 1: 10–16. Keynote Address Delivered at the Inaugural Media Ecology Association Convention Fordham University, New York, June 16–17, 2000.

Ross, Andrew. 1994. "The Ecology of Images." In *The Chicago Gangster Theory of Life: Nature's Debt to Society*, 159–201. New York: Verso.

Thomas, Sue. *Technobiophilia: Nature and Cyberspace*. 2013. New York: Bloomsbury Press.

Yeager, Patricia. 2008. "Editor's Column: The Death of Nature and the Apotheosis of Trash, or Rubbish Ecology." *PMLA* 123.2: 321–339.

Works cited

Barnard, Stephen. 2000. *Studying Radio*. London: Arnold.

Bousé, Derek. 2000. *Wildlife Films*. Philadelphia: University of Pennsylvania Press.

Bozak, Nadia. 2012. *The Cinematic Footprint: Lights, Camera, Natural Resources*. New Brunswick, NJ: Rutgers University Press.

Brooker, Will. 2005. "Everything Will Flow." *Flow* 1.12. Accessed June 4, 2014. http://flowtv.org/2005/03/everything-will-flow/

Budd, Mike, Steve Craig, and Clay Steinman. 1999. *Consuming Environments: Television and Commercial Culture*. New Brunswick, NJ: Rutgers University Press.

Butler, Jeremy G. 2010. *Television: Critical Methods and Applications*, 3rd ed. New York: Routledge.

Castells, Manuel. 2000. *The Rise of Network Society: The Information Age: Economy Society and Culture*, Vol. 1, 2nd ed. Oxford: Blackwell.

Chris, Cynthia. 2006. *Watching Wildlife*. Minneapolis: University of Minnesota Press.

Corbett, Charles J., and Richard J. Turco. 2006. *Sustainability in the Motion Picture Industry*. Los Angeles: University of California Los Angeles Institute of the Environment and California Integrated Waste Management Board.

De Burgh, Hugo, and Zeng Rong. 2011. *China's Environment and China's Environment Journalists*. Bristol, UK: Intellect.

Dobrin, Sidney I., and Sean Morey, eds. 2009. *Ecosee: Image, Rhetoric, Nature*. Albany: State University of New York Press.

"Electronics Waste Management in the United States through 2009." 2011. U.S. Environmental Protection Agency Office of Resource Conservation and Recovery. Washington, DC. Accessed June 6, 2014. http://www.epa.gov/epawaste/conserve/materials/ecycling/docs/fullbaselinereport2011.pdf

Gaard, Greta, ed. 1993. Ecofeminism: Women, Animals, Nature. Philadelphia: Temple University Press.

Ghana: Digital Dumping Ground. June 23, 2009. *Frontline World*. Reported by Peter Klein. Public Broadcasting. Television Broadcast.

Gray, Jonathan. 2010. *Show Sold Separately: Promos, Spoilers, and Other Media Paratexts*. New York: New York University Press.

Hamilton, James. 2007. "Unearthing Broadcasting in the Anglophone World." In *Residual Media*, edited by Charles R. Acland, 283–301. Minneapolis: University of Minnesota Press.

Klein, Peter. 2014. "Re: One more question Re: 'Digital Dumping Ground'." Email to the Author. October 13.

Maxwell, Richard, and Toby Miller. 2012. *Greening the Media*. London: Oxford University Press.

Morton, Timothy. 2009. *Ecology Without Nature*. Cambridge, MA: Harvard University Press.

Parks, Lisa. 2005. *Cultures in Orbit: Satellites and the Televisual*. Durham, NC: Duke University Press.

———. 2007. "Falling Apart: Electronics Salvaging and the Global Media Economy." *Residual Media*, edited by Charles R. Acland, 32–47. Minneapolis: University of Minnesota Press.

Ross, Andrew. 1994. "The Ecology of Images." *The Chicago Gangster Theory of Life: Nature's Debt to Society*. New York: Verso: 159–201.

Starosielski, Nicole. 2011a. "Beaches, Fields, and other Network Environments." *Octopus: A Visual Studies Journal* 5: 1–7.

———. 2011b. "Underwater Flow." *Flow* 15.1. Accessed June 4, 2014. http://flowtv.org/2011/10/underwaterflow/

Straubhaar, Joseph D. 2007. *World Television: From Global to Local*. Los Angeles: Sage.

Sturgeon, Noel. 2008. *Environmentalism in Popular Culture: Gender, Race, Sexuality, and the Politics of the Natural*. Tucson, AZ: University of Arizona Press.

Thussu, Daya Kishan. 2007. "Mapping Global Media Flow and Contra-Flow." In *Media on the Move: Global Flow and Contra-Flow*, edited by Daya Kishan Thussu, pp. 10–29. Abingdon, UK: Routledge.

Vivanco, Luis. 2002. "Seeing Green: Knowing and Saving the Environment on Film." *American Anthropologist* 104.4:1195–1204.

———. 2004. The Work of Environmentalism in an Age of Televisual Adventures."
   Cultural Dynamics 16.1: 5–28.
Williams, Raymond. 2003 (Orig. 1974). *Television: Technology and Cultural Form.*
   London: Routledge.
Yeung, Miranda. April 21, 2008. "There's a Dark Side to the Digital Age." *South China
   Morning Post.* Accessed December 15, 2015. http://www.scmp.com/article/64615/
   theres-dark-side-digital-age

6 "I took off my pants and felt free"

Environmentalism in countercultural radio

Sean Cubitt

Introduction

This chapter looks at a distant moment of media history in order to draw out lessons for contemporary ecomedia studies. It takes a case study of early FM, pirate and free radio, and looks in particular at the musical legacy of Captain Beefheart, a pioneer of environmentally oriented rock. Tracing the interconnections between ideas of freedom and ecology with the ideology of underground radio as an environment for freedom, it looks into the changing meanings of individuality in environmental politics as formed in the counterculture of the 1960s and 1970s. Cultural studies use the term *subject* to describe the human individual, emphasizing two features: that individuality is formed socially and historically and is therefore a dynamic system rather than a fixed ego; and that this subject is constructed both as subject of and subject to larger social and environmental systems. This concept of subject, the chapter argues, took a specific form in *countercultural ecopolitics*, but one still grounded in a third feature of the theory of the subject: that subjects are always construed in opposition to objects, the object in this case being the alienated and objectified environment. The inference of the chapter, drawn out in the conclusion, is that contemporary ecomedia, especially networked and mobile media, have yet to unravel and address the contradictions first worked through nearly fifty years ago at the birth of the modern Green movement through the broadcast medium of radio.

Box 6.1 Turn off that racket

In the era before personal stereos and MP3 players, radio was the preferred medium for listening to music outside the home and remains so for many marginalized communities today. The already polluting din of cars was only increased by teenagers playing radio music as they cruised favorite shopping areas in their vehicles, while the transistor radio, a major fashion item as well as a listening device in the 1960s, was a constant source of complaint because of its use in parks and on beaches. Noise pollution is blamed for many indicators of stress in humans and animals, notably changing the singing habits of birds, making them sing louder or at different frequencies (the "Lombard reflex") or to sing at night when noise levels tend to be lower (Birkhead 2012, 59). The typically poor bass response of radio speakers did minimize effects on ground-dwelling animals, but the increased power of bass woofers is suspected of causing hearing-sensitive animals to attempt to move habitat, an often dangerous or impossible task in or near urban environments.

Legends surround the album *Trout Mask Replica* (1969) by Captain Beefheart and the Magic Band. By the accounts of Magic Band member Bill Harkleroad (1998) and John French (2010), the recording was an ego-driven experience of deprivation – of food notably – and a kind of cult-like manipulation, even to the point of violence. At the same time, the Captain (singer-songwriter Don Van Vliet) was rumored to have sent for tree surgeons to ensure the surrounding woods were not being adversely affected by the volume of their rehearsals.

Album opener "Frownland" is all attack: swift-bubbling bass, two guitars scattering shards in opposite directions, broken and elliptic drums and Beefheart's torn baritone roaring in off the beat. It is followed by "The Dust Blows Forward and the Dust Blows Back," an unaccompanied, improvised field recording on a Bush tape deck, of observations from a fishing expedition in the desert where the recordings were being made. Quiet percussions indicate the points where the tape has been started and stopped. After nightfall, the lyrics turn from the visual record (even wilderness is infected by "a lipstick Kleenex") to the sounds of nocturnal mammals. Like many Beefheart tracks, the song has enough verbal play to stand free of any claim to straightforward reference to reality. Nonetheless, obvious environmentalist themes reappear throughout this album and the band's two follow ups, *Lick My Decals Off Baby* (1970) and *The Spotlight Kid* (1972), where songs like "Wild Life," "Petrified Forest," and "When It Blows It Stacks" make clear Beefheart's ecological commitment. In an interview first published in *The Georgia Straight* in 1973, Beefheart says:

> You can help animals – people are very hard to help. When The Beatles were singing "I Want To Hold Your Hand" I was singing to watch out for Strontium 90, let's put it that way. And you see how big they made it, compared to me. But I'm still going. All of *Trout Mask Replica* was about ecology.
>
> (McGrath 1973)

Like the album's producer Frank Zappa, a friend since Van Vliet's teenage years, Beefheart cannot be considered a joiner of movements. Yet the combination of environmental themes, countercultural rock tropes, removal from corporate recording studios (in favor of a remote cabin and the desert setting of recording) and the lyrics and recording technique of tracks like "The Dust Blows Forward and the Dust Blows Back" link the album to the back-to-the-land communes of California and the southwestern US states during this time. The line from the song quoted in the title of this chapter certainly sums neatly the configuration of nature and natural living as it appeared in countercultural classics like *The Whole Earth Catalog* (see Chris Russill's chapter in this volume).

Released on Zappa's independent label Straight Records and distributed without major label marketing muscle, *Trout Mask* was too spiky, too tightly compressed a rereading of African American music – of the sparsest forms of Delta blues with the further reaches of free jazz improvisation – and too formally and ideologically weird to have anything but the remotest chance of radio airplay. No doubt the sheer obscurity, in all senses, of the record helped make it a cult classic of the era. When it did find airtime, it would be on two new forms of radio emerging on either side of the Atlantic, FM **underground** or **free form** stations in the United States, and **pirate** stations in Europe. This chapter traces the congruence between Beefheart's album and a critical moment in radio history to ask how changing concepts and discourses of "freedom" overlaid both the environmentalist themes of late 1960s and early 1970s rock music and the briefly flourishing alternative media scene in a period, between Rachel Carson's *Silent Spring* (1962) and Ernest Callenbach's *Ecotopia* (1975), when the idea of a new media ecology was just beginning. Artists like Neil Young ("After the Goldrush"), Joni Mitchell ("Big Yellow Taxi,") and Country Joe McDonald ("Save the Whales") voiced a generational concern with environmental issues, while Alan "Blind Owl" Wilson of Canned Heat devoted much of his short life to the ecological movement (Davis 2013). The relation between this early green surge in rock and pop and its audiences is in many respects the story of radio.

Countercultural radio

Although the tale is probably oversimplified and certainly hagiographic (Frost 2010), the story of how the AM (Amplitude Modulation) radio cartel blocked the development of FM (Frequency Modulation) technology is an impressive instance of the powers of capital to block invention. Edwin H. Armstrong received patents for frequency modulation in 1933. The following year, Armstrong joined communications giant Radio Corporation of America (RCA), one of the three networks that dominated broadcasting in the United States from its introduction in 1920 until the launch of cable in 1948. RCA had no intention of investing in new technologies merely to improve the signal when there was no prospect of increasing advertising revenues on radio, which had a healthy proportion of total national advertising spending. The corporation used its legal and political muscle to deny Armstrong any opportunity of developing the technology commercially on his own. According to media historian Douglas Gomery (2008, 160), "Through the network era, David Sarnoff's RCA controlled the needed AM patents and he did everything he could to prevent FM" from competing. But as [RCA subsidiary] National Broadcast Corporation (NBC) became a television empire, Sarnoff abandoned his opposition to FM. Armstrong was able to start commercial application through manufacturing giant General Electric. Sadly, television was also formative in securing Federal Communications Commission (FCC) rulings in 1945 forcing experimental FM broadcasts out of their allocated area of the radio spectrum. This made the FM receivers Armstrong had sold thus far useless. Broadcast industry insiders saw FM as competition no longer with AM but with television: consumers emerging from the Depression were only going to buy one piece of equipment. Armstrong, however, saw it as a conspiracy to strangle his brainchild. FM was born in a spirit of rebellion against corporate America, albeit a revolution fully financed by smaller radio networks, and by General Electric radio receivers.

In the early 1960s, the FCC moved to maximize commercial exploitation of the FM waveband by forcing AM and FM stations to differentiate their content. This decision opened up the radio sector to new broadcasters for the first time, while the new stations also began to exploit their capacity to transmit in stereo sound (see Frost 2010). Colliding with the emergence of multitrack recording in the popular music industry (a field in which Beefheart's producer Frank Zappa was a pioneer), the combination of technical qualities and cultural forms associated with the counterculture's drugs of choice (Whiteley 1992) created the space for **freeform** radio to emerge. Low-powered, compared to the large AM stations, and more local, FM radio represented a way of escaping the intensely programmed forms of AM top 40 stations, encouraging long-form tracks that had begun to emerge on albums by bands like The Grateful Dead and Cream and providing the kind of aural response already exploited by domestic stereo systems and albums made for them like *Pet Sounds* (1966), *Sergeant Pepper's Lonely Hearts Club Band* (1967) and *Electric Ladyland* (1968).

Steve Post (1993) names New York station WBAI as the forerunner of freeform radio with Bob Fass's show *Radio Unnameable*, first broadcast in 1963. College stations like Upsala College's WFMU-FM in New Jersey used their freedom from commercial imperatives to expand their programming styles, including interviews and discussions on environmental issues, and their alumni soon spilled into commercial city-based stations including WNEW-FM and WPLJ in New York and KMPX and KSAN in San Francisco, followed by stations in Los Angeles, Boston, and Pasadena. The revolution was short-lived, however. Executives were antipathetic to "hippy radio," advertisers stayed away, unsure of the audience, and the FCC attempted to crack down on drug-oriented tracks. Gradually though, the college-educated listenership of FM, especially those who avoided the commercialism of TV, became attractive to advertisers to the point that it was worth reining in the freedom allowed freeform DJs (Douglas 1999, 276–279), and reinstituting the key tool of AM Top 40 radio:

> Top 40 as practiced and preached by consultant Drake Chenault even moved to FM. His modification of WOR-FM New York (which received a hybrid of oldies, album cuts, and touches of the Top 30) included expansion to a Top 40 playlist, less DJ chatter, and more contests. His "Hit Parade" – an adult-appeal pop format – was eventually fully automated . . . Any disc jockey who did not conform might receive a corrective call . . . His formatting of FM would prove the wave of the future.
> (Gomery 2008, 160)

By the end of the 1970s, as the last of the counterculture's energies waned, FM radio in the USA lost its last traces of radicalism. Environmental issues would continue to be aired on PBS public service talk radio, but its moment in the vanguard of popular culture was ebbing away.

In the UK, radio had a very different history. Regarded as a national resource, the radio spectrum was initially requisitioned for military and maritime use, only reluctantly freed for government-sponsored technical experiments (Briggs 1961). In the wake of World War One, internal memoranda of the Post Office, then in charge of broadcasting, noted the risk of radio hams (amateurs) creating anarchy on the airwaves, and the ominous threat that Russia, now in the first throes of post-revolutionary consolidation, might commence broadcasts into the void left by the absence of radio entertainment (Briggs 1961). The compromise was to establish a government licensed radio broadcaster, the British Broadcasting Corporation: the BBC. The struggle over content was subject to both the terms of the BBC charter – to educate, inform, and entertain – and to the determination of its first governor, Sir John Reith, to ensure this order of priorities. Only during World War Two did the BBC open up to forms of light entertainment (Scannell and Cardiff 1991), and only within very tight constraints, especially on broadcasts of popular music. Only Radio Luxembourg, broadcasting from Europe, attempted to thwart the monopoly granted to the BBC's public service, beaming advert-laden programs to Britain and Ireland, but with a signal that could rarely be heard in daylight hours (medium-wave broadcasts carry farther at night). In 1964, however, shipboard radio stations, known as the **pirates**, began broadcasting daytime programming of pop music to the UK. Unlike the FM experience in the US, the pirates' enemy was not heavy-handed commercialism but state monopoly, and in a striking reversal, far from subverting top 40 programming, that was exactly what the pirate radio stations set out to offer.

In the late-night graveyard slot, however, when little advertising revenue could be expected but which was useful in keeping listeners tuned to the stations, more experimentation was feasible. Notable among the late-night DJs was the legendary John Peel, an alumnus of radio stations in Dallas, Oklahoma, and San Bernardino, whose program *The Perfumed Garden* pioneered the kinds of programming that FM stations of the same period were promoting in the US. Peel was, among other things, famed for nurturing and providing a platform for acts like Pink Floyd and other UK psychedelic bands and the West Coast sound of bands like The Doors and Captain Beefheart. As Chapman (1992, 124–125) has said, "The evolution of *The Perfumed Garden*, where nightly the underground communicated with itself, mirrored a corresponding stage in the evolution of a whole subculture." Legislation forced most of the pirates off-air in 1967, but they had proved the demand for pop radio, to which the BBC responded by creating its own youth station, Radio 1, largely staffed by ex-pirate DJs. Moving to the BBC in 1967, for 18 months Peel ran a show called *Night Ride* which emulated the freeform style of the US FM counterculture stations: mixing minority rock bands, world music, electronica, and avant-garde music from jazz to formal, alongside poetry readings, interviews with journalists, musicians, and friends including discussions of topics like drug laws, venereal disease, and environmental issues. The show, like the station that hosted it, was, however, designated by the BBC as a youth-oriented music station. Older listeners of light music had Radio Two; Radio Three was devoted to classical music. Any discussion of environmental issues was henceforth concentrated on Radio Four, the talk station oriented to documentary, drama, and news programming. Thus after the early 1970s, as had happened in the USA, the brief marriage of environmentalism and popular music radio was annulled.

A third source of countercultural radio emerged across Europe in the later 1960s and 1970s in the form of Free Radio. Closely associated with libertarian left movements like Poetere Operaia and the Italian Autonomists who evolved from them, European free radio resisted state monopolies on broadcasting, the conservatism of Christian churches closely associated with government, and the Stalinist Communist Parties that then dominated the European left. Although the most famous of continental European pirates, Radio Alice, only started broadcasting in 1976, it encapsulated the harder-edged, more self-conscious politics of the period between counterculture and punk, as recalled by Franco "Bifo" Berardi in a 2010 interview. The station, he comments, worked with small groups:

> feminists, gays, workers. I emphasize this "little group" character because we did not conceive of the radio as a political organisation that has to "state/decide" who can speak or can't speak. We considered the radio as the point of intersection of different experiences – every experience being different from the other. We did not think about attempting to homogenise these different groups and points of view.
>
> (Berardi 2010)

This group ethos is even more apparent in Felix Guattari's (1996, 75) account of "the assumption of direct speech" in various free radio stations across Europe, in which "the way opened up by the free radio phenomenon seems to go against the whole spirit of specialization. What becomes specific here are the collective arrangements of enunciation that absorb or 'traverse' specialities." Free radio absorbed and traversed genres and professional specialisms with equal ambition. The sense of collectivity, as in Bologna's Radio Alice, extended beyond phone-ins to open doors to the management of the station, open sessions with audience members pitching program ideas, broadcasting cassettes compiled by listeners and using the radio to retransmit phone messages tracking police action during demonstrations. In Ireland, radio became a key medium for feminists seeking a voice against Catholicism and the ban on abortion (D'Arcy 2000), but also a significant arena for contesting the environmental aspects of government policies. Throughout Europe, with the exception of the UK where the BBC was established at arm's length from government, most radio was directly run by government departments, often tied specifically to the governing political party and with monopoly over the use of the radio spectrum (Tracey 1998). Rather than commercial opposition, many French, German, Austrian, and Dutch stations, the latter strongly associated with the Kabouters green movement, promoted radical politics, including the early stirrings of ecology and green parties deriving from the protest movements of 1968.

Modelled on the BBC, Australia ABC national broadcaster included a strong strand of environmental debate. The same cannot be said for state broadcaster Akashvani (All India Radio) in India, whose central function was national unity and which lost much support as a free medium when Indira Gandhi backed up her sterilization program by offering a transistor radio in exchange for the procedure, leaving a long period of recovery spent building alternative networks (Pavarala and Malik 2007). On the other hand, Valerie Alia documents the large number of indigenous radio stations in North and South America, the Pacific and Southern Africa, many documenting struggles for control over the natural environment. Canadian indigenous radio has been vital in debate over the exploitation of natural resources, especially in the North (Alia 2010).

Radio had several qualities that made it a key medium for early green politics. It was relatively cheap and easy to produce professional quality broadcasts (whereas, for example, the available video equipment was well below broadcast standard). It could engage directly with popular audiences through the significant place of music in youth cultures of the time. For all three instances of countercultural radio – US freeform FM, UK late-night pirates, and European radical free radio – the greatest contribution was the radio's ability to create, in Squier's (2003) phrase, "communities of the air." Susan Douglas evokes the American experience: "The feeling isn't some naive, bathetic sense of universal 'brotherly love' (although under certain circumstances . . . such an illusion is possible), but there is a sense of camaraderie and mutuality coming from the sky itself" (Douglas 1999, 40). This would be an apt description of the role of underground programming on UK pirates and later of Peel's programs on the BBC's Radio One. The radical free radio of Europe went much further than the construction of an *imagined community*, to borrow Benedict Anderson's (1983) term. It sought to confirm the existence of communities as "but one central element of a whole range of communication means, from informal encounters in the Piazza Maggiore to the daily newspaper – via billboards, mural paintings, posters, leaflets, meetings, community activities, festivals, etc." (Guattari 1996, 75). This suture of broadcasts and audiences has been emulated in UK and US commercial and public service radio, for example, through stations' live broadcasting from music festivals they sponsor, but never with the goal of producing such communitarian politics.

Instead, like much of the ecopolitics of the English-speaking world in the period, freeform radio oriented itself to listeners presumed to be alone, to be seeking identification with an imaginary community of like-minded folks, but not connected to them in the real life of political struggle, as in the European stations. UK and US radio, even in freeform genres, kept their audiences quite distinct from the *"specialist"* broadcasters that Guattari so assiduously excluded from definitions of free radio.

Beefheart, environmentalism, and freedom

David Ingram is certainly correct to argue that Beefheart's "identification of the self with the rest of the universe is complicated by an appeal to a more individualistic notion of personal autonomy" (Ingram 2010, 133). "The most important figure to emerge from the rock era of the 1960s and 1970s" according to John Peel (1997), Beefheart was not closely identifiable with any scene, ploughing his idiosyncratic musical furrow and environmental commitments without close engagement in any form of social movement. In this extreme cultural isolation, he is in certain respects typical. Beefheart's exceptionalism takes the form of intense individualism, of the kind engendered in the broadcaster-audience model that pervaded the freeform FM and pirate underground radio where his music was championed. As in the case of most of the electronic "revolutions" that followed, the main market for FM radio in the 1950s and early 1960s was a cadre of male electrical and hi-fi buffs (Douglas 1999, 266). Beefheart's music was also very much part of a masculine rock scene, which saw few if any female DJs, and a culture of machismo that continued throughout the history of alternative radio into the 2000s (Goodlad 2003: WNEW-FM's Alison Steele was a rare exception; Annie Nightingale joined BBC Radio One in 1970 as their first female presenter three years after the station's launch: see Michaels and Mitchell 2000). Likewise Beefheart is easily placed in the tradition of countercultural masculinist surrealism that extended from the French avant-garde (Gauthier 1971) to Firesign Theatre's sonic comedies on KPPC-FM Los Angeles and Peel favorite Vivian Stanshall's "English as tuppence" monologues *Sir Henry at Rawlinson End*. Even in the persona he adopted in interviews such as the one published by *Rolling Stone* under the title "I'm not even here: I just stick around for my friends" (Winner 1970), Beefheart adopts the pose of the avant-garde genius-eccentric which, while largely alien to the rock scene, placed him in the discourse of misunderstood artist-loners. In each of these congruences of the music with significant cultural tropes of the day, Beefheart conforms to highly recognizable discursive constellations at the very moment of asserting his uniqueness. At the same time, his musical lexicon, which both attenuates and bloats the rural and electric blues that forms his basic musical material, expresses this uniqueness in the fundamentally familiar form of the radio-friendly three-minute track (rather than the long jam sessions preferred by many bands of the period).

As Theodor Adorno (1997, 202) notes, "The more specific the work, the more truly it fulfills its type": Beefheart's eccentric blues vanguardism is intensely particular, but at the same time concentrates a particular individualist tradition of environmental subjectivity in the counterculture of North America, a tradition traceable to Thoreau, and strongly marked in the writings of John Muir, Aldo Leopold, and Gary Snyder (Heise 2008, 28–49). This rugged individualism contrasts with the contemporaneous development of a more systems-theoretic approach to scientific ecology associated with Buckminster Fuller and Stewart Brand (Turner 2006, 43–45). Brand's *Whole Earth Catalog* provided a Sears Roebuck for the back-to-the-land communes who shared in some degree the allegiance to place, if not the personal self-sufficiency of the older Transcendental tradition, in which Beefheart can be placed. But Brand also owed his allegiance to the connection between everything in a system, a tendency that would lead him to the emerging computer scene in California and away from his ecological roots.

Beefheart's commercial failure can be ascribed to a failure to understand – or to wish to understand – the workings of any system, but especially the media system in which his music was recorded and distributed. Where *systems ecology* looked to mutual dependencies, and in certain respects therefore pointed forward not only to the formation of cyberculture among young Californians on the brink of the move into Silicon Valley, as Fred Turner argues, but the free market extremism of neo-liberalism, at that time in formation in the economics department of the University of Chicago. This notion of a system whose freedom is more important than the freedom of its elements was alien to Beefheart's aesthetic and his environmentalism, even though he might be read in the context of hip entrepreneurs of the kind that launched publications, food stores and record labels in the late 1960s. Much like Edward Abbey (1968) at the same time, in the track "Blabber 'n Smoke" from *The Spotlight Kid*, Beefheart pillories those who talk about environments without action to match. In this respect the song represents his turn away from joining with others, and as much a critique of a lack of affect ("I can't help but think you treat love like ah joke") as of lack of activity.

Here the specific structure of Beefheart's subjectivity demands attention, both for what it tells us about how his work draws to a fine focus the concerns of his epoch and for how an artist exceeds his own times. *Decals* has several references to dinosaurs in "The Smithsonian Institution Blues (Or the Big Dig)" and "Petrified Forest," both identifying the extinct saurians with the oil industry, and in a complex metaphor in the latter song hinging on the phrase "Bow your eyes 'n heads to the duty of the dead." In the history of aesthetic theory, Kant's propositions concerning the *sublime* have had a huge impact on environmentalism. Kant (1952, §23–29) argues that while beauty is a matter of taste, and therefore of community standards, debate and social agreement, the sublime confronts us with the strictly unspeakable: that which exceeds human discourse. The nineteenth-century Transcendentalists held to this Kantian position: nature exceeds (transcends) anything we might say about it. A critique of the sublime, which has also become a key phrase in contemporary art criticism (Krauss 1996), would argue that this distinction between human and natural is itself unnatural, a product precisely of human discourse, because it removes nature from history and therefore either denies humanity's effects on it in the past or that we can mend our relations with it in the future.

But there is another way of understanding the environment as unspeakable Other suggested in the line from "Petrified Forest." If we understand the fire-breathing dinosaurs as standing in for all extinct species, including the many indigenous tribes who fell victim to genocide in the settler colonies, and for the fossil legacy of hydrocarbon fuels, then we confront in nature – in landscapes, in oil, and in our transformations of both – an alien form of subjectivity: the dead. To treat the dead as objects is to deny them their existence. At the same time, to speak on their behalf is to deny their silencing (Mladek and Edmundson 2009). Beefheart's injunction to bow our heads in duty to the dead then suggests that we cannot forget, objectify or ventriloquize the unaccounted dead, human and nonhuman, but instead should subject our subjectivity to theirs, lost as it is. The environmentalist subject cannot abandon, ignore, or even mourn these lost, since mourning is a form of healing. These wounds are unhealable as well as unspeakable. The ecopolitical subject is then forced either to become melancholic, to the point of withdrawal from the world, or to embrace the joy of life denied these Others: hence the joy of Beefheart's cast-off pants. Melancholia leads to fatalism and the kind of green apocalypticism that would happily see the world ended so it can say "I told you so!", and joy to Beefheart's freedom. But this freedom is entirely subjective and individual. Freeform radio was historically a celebration of just this form of freedom, but one that, in reaching out to form a "community of the air," realizes the limitations of individualism even in the pursuit of joy.

Nature, Raymond Williams noted, is "perhaps the most complex word in the language" (1983, 219); the same could be said of *freedom*. Berlin (1969) helpfully distinguished negative freedom (being left alone) from positive freedom (the provision of education, health, and welfare such that people had the opportunity to learn how to be free and experience freedom). An exacting critic of Berlin, Nicholas Rose adds a further distinction, between "freedom as a formula of resistance from freedom as a formula of power. Or rather, to be more circumspect, freedom as it is deployed in contestation and freedom as it is instantiated in government" (Rose 1999, 65). Rose's point is that the term "freedom" is employed in liberal democracies to describe and define a specific operation of government, an agreement on the part of citizens to obey the laws, for example, in order to be able to exercise other freedoms, such as that of trade. At the same time it is employed by protestors and other political and cultural agents to claim freedoms that are not recognized morally or politically, such as freedom of sexual choice.

If we place these two complex terms together, we begin to understand the complexities of ecopolitics implicit in Beefheart's moral imperative to pay respect to the dead, the unspeaking Others of "nature." Beefheart's freedom in "The Dust Blows Forward" implies free access to wilderness, today a zone marked out by National Parks, that is by state fiat, and in many instances founded on land seized from First Nations from which they are now excluded. The freedom of freeform, alternative radio belongs to a similarly permitted, and therefore governed, space. Despite its claims to autonomy, even the European free radio depended on commercially produced radio receivers, especially portable transistor radios which replaced larger domestic receivers (and simultaneously replaced older radio-phonogram cabinets with modern stereo hi-fi's) creating waste of old sets and new demands for materials to build the new ones.

Box 6.2   Talk about it: more material impacts – radio and radiation, boxes and batteries

The vast majority of scientific studies on living near radio masts and antennae suggest that the effects on humans are negligible. Radio waves are usually broadcast parallel to the ground and attenuate rapidly with distance. There is some evidence, however, that smaller animals, such as house sparrows, are affected by EM (Electromagnetic) radiation (Everaert and Bauwens 2007). There is also the question of waste radiation from radio antennae, which radiate in a circle from the mast toward receivers that only pick up a small proportion of the total emission. This waste radiation has little known impact on human activities, although radio astronomers complain of its interference with their instruments. In addition, the energy required to broadcast signals, while small compared to the energy requirements of the Internet, is a significant dispersal of unused energy into the environment as well as a measurable proportion of the planet's total energy budget.

Boxes and batteries

The invention of FM radio, while an engineering triumph, required listeners to buy a new box to receive the new wavebands it opened up. Mass manufacturing these boxes of electronics required significant quantities of metals and plastics, while the old boxes they replaced made their way gradually to landfills. The transistor radio ran on batteries of the "primary" type, such as alkaline and zinc-carbon batteries labelled as "disposable." Rechargeable batteries became available on the mass consumer market only in the 1980s and were not universally adopted. Battery recycling, which is now taken seriously in most industrial countries, was not for the first twenty years or so of the transistor radio and its successor, radio-equipped personal stereos. Much of the debris from this period of waste is still in landfills, and includes substantial amounts of toxic acids.

Listeners to freeform FM and pirate radio were participating in freedom, a freedom that they wanted to extend to the environment. That this freedom was imaginary is not a fundamental problem: historically freedom has often been imagined before it was experienced. The problem rather is the constitution of the auditor as unique individual, rather than as either part of a human community or, and this surely is the point of ecocriticism, as an integrated element in a far vaster confluence of organic activities that constitutes our planet. As Mark Pedelty (2012, 2) has argued with reference to monster stadium tours like U2's 360° Tour, "Pop spectacle is clearly at odds with the environment." The same, he observes, is true of the recording industry, playback equipment, distribution mechanisms (including the Internet) and of course radios. Still we seek, in our privatized soundscapes, what Philip Tagg (2006) describes as a generalized longing among alienated urban dwellers for a sonic environment that is distinctly our own.

Music critic John Street (1997) recalls playing *Trout Mask* for the first time as a teenager:

> I'm not sure that I actually enjoyed the experience, but I know that my friends and enemies at school hated it, and that was enough. I had achieved in that small gesture an element of individuality, albeit one sustained by the thought that out there in the world of rock journalism, in hip circles in London and America, "people like me" were nodding appreciatively to "Ella Guru."

This is just the kind of spectacularly individual listening that Tagg identifies: identification not only with the unique but with an imaginary community of the like-minded, which is the special preserve of underground music and underground radio, and equally of Transcendentalist environmentalism championed by wilderness advocates from Thoreau to Abbey. Yet it is also, to use an oxymoron, the typically paradoxical fate of such sounds to address the sovereign subject, that is someone who is not only subject to rule, but subject of it, who is invited to identify with the uniqueness of the artist, and thereby to deny the individuality of listener and artist alike. This contradictory subject position, recognizable as a relation of Val Plumwood's "ecosocial feminism" (Plumwood 1994), is at the core of Beefheart's ecological freedom, his renunciation of success, his flight to the desert and its still potent appeal; and it is this contradiction which lies at the heart of the contradictory messages of mediated environmentalism under conditions of commercial or state-sanctioned radio.

It is for this reason, in turn, that Beefheart's most joyous expressions of union with the ecology like "Wild Life" from *Trout Mask Replica* ("Find me uh cave 'n talk them bears/In t' takin' me in") are in the end less persuasive than later, darker songs like "Petrified Forest" ("The rug's wearing out that we walk on") or "Grow Fins" ("I'm gonna grow fins 'N go back in the water again"). In such songs, Beefheart seems to confront the sublimity of nature as a product of its exclusion from the human, its objectification, and its construction as irremediably external surroundings, the environing nonhuman, defined by its difference and distance from humanity. Such an understanding echoes the traditional wilderness advocacy stance, which has been roundly criticized over the years (most famously by William Cronon's 1995 essay "The Trouble with Wilderness"). Here the self-contradiction of the sovereign subject meets the results of its sovereignty: that the unthinkably other is unthinkable precisely because humanity has chosen to exclude it from the realm of the thinkable, yet that unthinkable status is a necessary result of human thinking, human discourse made mental and cultural reality.

Freedom and community

Human sovereignty has brought freedom but at the same time and as a direct result has alienated itself from nature. This realization then leaves us with two related questions concerning popular music and radio: the question of freedom and the question of community. On the former, Adorno argues that artworks produced in freedom cannot thrive under an enduring social unfreedom whose marks they bear even when they are daring. Indeed, in the copy of style – one of the primal aesthetic phenomena of the nineteenth century – that specifically bourgeois trait of promising freedom while prohibiting it can be sought (Adorno 1970/1997, 206).

If we substitute for Adorno's phrase "the nineteenth century" the phrases "rock and pop music" and "radio playlists," we can see the same contradiction acted out in more contemporary terms. Beefheart's retreat from the centers of the music industry to make *Trout Mask* (in what Berlin would call negative freedom), and his authoritarian style of managing his group to produce exactly the sounds he wanted (Berlin's positive freedom) do encode both the formal discipline of a music creating its own sonic logic rejecting social authoritarianism, and also an equally formal submission of the work, however crazy it sounds to other ears, to its own, idiosyncratic authoritarianism. Learning from preindustrial music of the ex-slave plantations of the southern United States, electrifying and reconstructing it as an alternative to repressive white urban cultures, Beefheart takes a music of oppression, the blues, and turns it toward angry eco-utopianism. In *Trout Mask* we can hear the refusal of the kind of freedom "instantiated in government" that Rose analysed. Unsurprisingly, despite its cult status, the record was and remains difficult to listen to and resoundingly unpopular, a condition Adorno ascribes to the impossibility of true freedom to thrive under the conditions of social repression that he believed intrinsic to capitalism.

However, in the turn to "the duty of the dead" on *Decals*, which Beefheart produced himself a year later under his birth name Don Van Vliet, both the increasingly formal qualities of the music (without Zappa's interspersed bits of studio knockabout on *Trout Mask*) and the turn to the ethical debt owed to the nonhuman world change the terms of the relationship between environmentalism and freedom. Now responsibility takes precedence over liberty, especially in the increasing references to oil as a link between past and present masters of the planet ("The new dinosaur is walkin' in the old one's shoes" as he sings on "The Smithsonian Institute Blues"). There is a moral gesture here that in one move sacrifices negative, purely personal liberty in order to sabotage the false promise of freedom embedded in capital's self-styled free market and liberal democracy's controlled and controlling freedom to vote. That call of duty denies the freedom of the individual as it does that of the state and the market, one reason why this album feels so much denser and darker than its predecessor. Given Beefheart's notorious imposition of his style at this time at whatever cost to the members of the Magic Band and his extreme individualism, the result of this renunciation is a definitively tragic tone.

Yet tragedy is not a necessary outcome, unless we are to believe that Beefheart was destined by his upbringing (in suburban Glendale, California) to the macho individualism so characteristic of North American eco-warriors of his generation like wilderness advocate Edward Abbey and avant-garde filmmaker Stan Brakhage (Rosenbaum 1983, 47; for a defence of Brakhage see Brenez and Martin 2003). Like Brakhage, Beefheart sought a personal salvation in retreating from the urban world, but his sense of the history immanent in the landscape would not allow any easy resolution of the debt owed by the living to the dead. Destabilizing the subjectivity so deeply founded on the concept of personal liberty in the USA, and even more so in California, was not only a matter of stripping away ascriptions ("Lick My Decals Off, Baby, meaning get rid of the labels": Beefheart in interview in Coley and Carey 1979) and casting off (musical and cultural) influences but of assuming the burden of responsibility to "clean up the air and treat the animals fair" ("Blabber 'n Smoke"). If this results in a tragic art, it is not because of Beefheart's considerable ego, but because of the failure of countercultural environmentalism to transcend the ideologies of freedom that permeated hippy culture and the culture of freeform radio. The loss of freedom and the terrible burden of duty are too much for one person to bear. Simply to become humanly possible, at psychological, ethical, and political levels, they require community.

Community is another complex and divergent word. Etymologically it carries the sense of bringing into one, of communion with God, or with one another in "the communion of the saints" for example, and thus a deeply spiritual axis. It shares its roots with "communication," which media scholarship identifies as the media we use to form groups and societies. Here too it has a utopian aspect in the older and newer aspirations of communism, including the communes of the counterculture, for whom communication is both the means for doing politics and the goal of perfect communion. The initial challenge of environmentalist community is already in place in Beefheart: to commune with the animals and with nature. The second, however, is visible in the British English usage "the community," referring typically to Black, gay, Asian and other communities, implying a strong sense of shared values tying a group together in struggle. Beefheart's rugged macho individualism and the similarly strongly male world of radio DJs points out what John Peel notoriously referred to as "white boys with guitars" (a much-quoted 1988 comment on the listener-voted "Festive Fifty"). Though feminists from Rachel Carson to Vandana Shiva (see for example, 2007) have had a powerful impact on environmentalism, racism has only recently been acknowledged both as integral to environmental history, in which slaves and ex-slaves, the colonized and indigenous peoples have borne the brunt of environmental crises, and as going beyond accounts of victim status toward an environmental justice movement that would include "justice for people of color, justice for women, and justice for nature" (Merchant 2003, 390).

Our definitions of freedom are based on the electoral sovereignty of the state, the free market, and the notion of a rights-bearing individual. They exclude those who have no rights: usually migrants (who under UN Charter are only granted rights if they are recognized as refugees, whence the reluctance of governments to use any term but "asylum-seeker" to categorize them), indigenous peoples and other "second-class citizens." The community that was imagined in radio listening (and to a great degree in racially segregated radio in North America still is imagined) in radio listening rarely includes working-class Blacks, migrants, or Native Americans in anything but stereotypical or consumerist form, and in the heyday of freeform radio also marginalized women or defined them as consumer housewives. It was the dearth of this primary community of humans that was missing in Beefheart and that the European free radios and indigenous and post-colonial radios across the globe attempted to construct. Despite the proliferation of Internet radio, that challenge remains largely unmet, with stations working to cater to subcategories of increasingly differentiated "markets," or at best to support self-identified communities of the like-minded. Popular music, while it retains its capacity to create, especially in live events and clubs, temporary autonomous zones (Bey 1991) of communal celebration, has lost much of the cultural and political centrality it had in the 1960s and 70s. Radio itself, which at one time tried to define itself against television's mass culture, is now a minor feature of a media landscape where activism has moved increasingly to mobile and network media, especially at time of writing, largely voiceless microblogs. The lessons from this study of Captain Beefheart and underground radio remains nonetheless relevant to the challenges faced by ecomedia studies. We still need to understand the limits of freedom in our dealings with the environment and with each other, and to understand the necessity of forming communicative communities capable of assuming communally the burdens of our responsibility to the past and present of the planet.

Keywords

Community	Pirate
Countercultural ecopolitics	Subject
Freedom	Sublime
Freeform	Systems ecology
Imagined community	

Discussion questions

1   Draw up a list of the environmentally inspired songs you know. Do the artists have anything in common? Are there any musical genres and styles that seem not to be interested in environmentalism? What might that tell us about the reach of environmentalism today?
2   The chapter makes a distinction between imagined communities of listeners and real communities of activists. Given our evolving media landscape, does that distinction still work?
3   Today radio is known as "the 2% medium": two per cent of the audience, and two per cent of the advertising revenue. Under these conditions, is radio dead?
4   The biggest audience for radio is in-car, "drive-time" radio. Does that create an opportunity or a barrier for environmental content?
5   Where would you go now to find or create free-form media?

Further reading

Barnes, Mike. 2011. *Captain Beefheart: The Biography*. London: Omnibus.
Chapman, Robert. 1992. *Selling the Sixties: The Pirates and Pop Music Radio*. London: Routledge.
Courrier, Kevin. 2008. *Trout Mask Relica*. London: Bloomsbury.
Guattari, Felix. 1996. "Popular Free Radio." In *Soft Subversions*, edited by Sylvère Lotringer, translated by David L. Sweet and Chet Wiener, 73–78. New York: Semiotext(e).

Ingram, David. 2010. *The Jukebox in the Garden: Ecocriticism and American Popular Music Since 1960*. Amsterdam: Rodopi.

Post, Steve. 1993. "Son of Playlist: The Decline and Fall of Commercial Free-Form Radio." In *Radiotext(e)* (=*Semiotext(e)* #16, VI[1]), edited by Neil Strauss. New York: Semiotext(e).

Works cited

Abbey, Edward. 1968. *Desert Solitaire: A Season in the Wilderness*. New York: McGraw Hill.

Adorno, Theodor W. 1970/1997. *Aesthetic Theory*. Edited by Gretel Adorno and Rolf Tiedemann, translated by Robert Hullot-Kentor. London: Athlone Press.

Alia, Valerie. 2010. *The New Media Nation: Indigenous Peoples and Global Communication*. New York: Berghahn Books.

Anderson, Benedict. 1983. *Imagined Communities: Reflections on the Origin and Spread of Nationalism*. London: Verso.

Berardi, Franco "Bifo." 2010. "Radio Alice." Interview by Carlos Ordonez. Retrieved 24 May 2014. http://www.zgpress.com/?p=36

Berlin, Isaiah. 1969. *Four Essays on Liberty*. Oxford: Oxford University Press.

Bey, Hakim. 1991. *T.A.Z.: The Temporary Autonomous Zone, Ontological Anarchism, Poetic Terrorism*. New York: Autonomedia.

Birkhead, Tim. 2012. *Bird Sense: What It's Like to Be a Bird*. London: A&C Black.

Brenez, Nicole, and Adrian Martin. 2003. "Serious Mothlight: For Stan Brakhage." *Rouge* 1. Retrieved 26 May 2014. http://www.rouge.com.au/1/brakhage.html

Briggs, Asa. 1961. *The History of Broadcasting in the United Kingdom. Volume 1: The Birth of Broadcasting*. Oxford: Oxford University Press.

Callenbach, Ernest. 1975. *Ecotopia: The Notebooks and Reports of William Weston*. New York: Bantam.

Carson, Rachel. 1962. *Silent Spring*. New York: Houghton Mifflin.

Chapman, Robert. 1992. *Selling the Sixties: The Pirates and Pop Music Radio*. London: Routledge.

Coley, Bryon, and Robert Carey. 1979. "Captain Beefheart Pulls a Hat Out of His Rabbit." Originally published in *The New York Rocker*. Beefheart.com. Accessed November 14, 2014. http://www.beefheart.com/captain-beefheart-pulls-a-hat-out-of-his-rabbit-by-byron-coley-and-robert-carey/

Cronon, William. 1995. "The Trouble with Wilderness, or Getting Back to the Wrong Nature." In *Uncommon Ground: Rethinking the Human Place in Nature*, edited by William Cronon, 69–90. New York: W. W. Norton.

D'Arcy, Margaretta. 2000. "Galway's Pirate Women." In *Women and Radio: Airing Differences*, edited by Caroline Mitchell, 167–181. London: Routledge.

Davis, Rebecca. 2013. *Blind Owl Blues: The Mysterious Life and Death of Blues Legend Alan Wilson*. Blind Owl Blues.

Douglas, Susan J. 1999. *Listening In: Radio and the American Imagination*. Minneapolis: Minnesota University Press.

Everaert, Joris, and Dirk Bauwens. 2007. "A Possible Effect of Electromagnetic Radiation from Mobile Phone Base Stations on the Number of Breeding House Sparrows (Passer domesticus)." *Electromagnetic Biology and Medicine* 26: 63–72.

French, John. 2010. *Beefheart: Through the Eyes of Magic*. London: Proper Music Publishing.

Frost, Gary L. 2010. *Early FM Radio: Incremental Technology in Twentieth-Century America*. Baltimore: Johns Hopkins University Press.

Gauthier, Xavière. 1971. *Surréalisme et sexualité*. Paris: Gallimard.

Gomery, Douglas. 2008. *A History of Broadcasting in the United States*. Oxford: Blackwell.

Goodlad, Lauren M. E. 2003. "Packaged Alternatives: The Incorporation and Gendering of 'Alternative' Radio." In *Communities of the Air: Radio Century, Radio Culture*, edited by Susan Merril Squier, 134–163. Durham NC: Duke University Press.

Guattari, Felix. 1996. "Popular Free Radio." In *Soft Subversions*, edited by Sylvère Lotringer, 73–78, translated by David L. Sweet and Chet Wiener. New York: Semiotext(e).

Harkleroad, Bill. 1998. *Lunar Notes: Zoot Horn Rollo's Captain Beefheart Experience*. London: SAF Publishing.

Heise, Ursula K. 2008. *Sense of Place and Sense of Planet: The Environmental Imagination of the Global*. Oxford: Oxford University Press.

Ingram, David. 2010. *The Jukebox in the Garden: Ecocriticism and American Popular Music Since 1960*. Amsterdam: Rodopi.

Kant, Immanuel. 1952. *The Critique of Judgement*. Translated by James Creed Meredith. Oxford: Oxford University Press.

Krauss, Rosalind E. 1996. "'Informe' Without Conclusion." *October* 78 (Autumn): 89–105.

McGrath, Rick. 1973. "Know What I Mean? The Don Van Vliet Interview." March. *The Georgia Straight*. Accessed 25 May, 2013. http://www.rocksbackpages.com/Library/Article/know-what-i-mean-the-don-van-vliet-interview

Merchant, Carolyn. 2003. "Shades of Darkness: Race and Environmental History." *Environmental History* 8.3: 380–394.

Michaels, Kim, and Caroline Mitchell. 2000. "The Last Bastion: How Women Become Music Presenters in UK Radio." In *Women and Radio: Airing Differences*, edited by Caroline Mitchell, 238–249. London: Routledge.

Mladek, Klaus, and George Edmundson. 2009. "A Politics of Melancholia." In *A Leftist Ontology*, edited by Carsten Strathausen, 208–233. Minneapolis: University of Minnesota Press.

Pavarala, Vinod, and Kanchan K. Malik. 2007. *Other Voices: The Struggle for Community Radio in India*. New Delhi: Sage.

Pedelty, Mark. 2012. *Ecomusicology: Rock, Folk, and the Environment*. Philadelphia: Temple University Press.

Peel, John. 1997. *The Artist Formerly Known as Captain Beefheart*. Directed by Elaine Shepherd. BBC. 50 mins. Broadcast.

Plumwood, Val. 1994. "Ecosocial Feminism as a General Theory of Oppression." In *Key Concepts in Critical Theory: Ecology*, edited by Carolyn Merchant, 207–219. Atlantic Highlands NJ: Humanities Press.

Post, Steve. 1993. "Son of Playlist: The Decline and Fall of Commercial Free-Form Radio." In *Radiotext(e)* (=*Semiotext(e)* #16, VI[1]), edited by Neil Strauss. New York: Semiotext(e).

Rose, Nicholas. 1999. *Powers of Freedom: Reframing Political Thought*. Cambridge: Cambridge University Press.

Rosenbaum, Jonathan. 1983. *Film: The Front Line 1983*. Denver: Arden Press.

Scannell, Paddy, and David Cardiff. 1991. *A Social History of British Broadcasting: Volume One 1922–1939 – Serving the Nation*. Oxford: Basil Blackwell.

Shiva, Vandana. 2007. *Democratizing Biology: Reinventing Biology from a Feminist, Ecological and Third World Perspective.* Boulder CO: Paradigm Publishers.

Squier, Susan Merril. 2003. *Communities of the Air: Radio Century, Radio Culture.* Durham NC: Duke University Press.

Street, John. 1997. *Politics and Popular Culture.* Philadelphia: Temple University Press.

Tagg, Philip. 2006. "Subjectivity and Soundscape, Motorbikes and Music." In *The Popular Music Studies Reader*, edited by Andy Bennett, Barry Shank and Jason Toynbee, 44–50. London and New York: Routledge.

Tracey, Michael. 1998. *The Decline and Fall of Public Service Broadcasting.* New York: Oxford University Press.

Turner, Fred. 2006. *From Counterculture to Cyberculture: Stewart Brand, the Whole Earth Network, and the Rise of Digital Utopianism.* Chicago: University of Chicago Press.

Whiteley, Sheila. 1992. *The Space Between the Notes: Rock and the Counter-Culture.* London: Routledge.

Williams, Raymond. 1983. *Keywords: A Vocabulary of Culture and Society.* New York: Fontana.

Winner, Langdon. 1970. "I'm not even here: I just stick around for my friends: The Odyssey of Captain Beefheart." *Rolling Stone*, 14 May. Retrieved 25 May 2013. http://www.beefheart.com/im-not-even-here-i-just-stick-around-for-my-friends-the-odyssey-of-captain-beefheart-by-langdon-winner/

7 New Zealand reality television
Hostile or hospitable?

Sarina Pearson

Introduction

Television and the environment have a long and rich but sometimes vexed association. Since the earliest days of television, the medium has traded in ecological imagery along a spectrum that ranges from the explicit to the implicit. Cultural Studies scholar Andrew Ross describes the most explicit end of this spectrum as "images of ecology for ecology," while the implicit end of the spectrum have "some kind of ecological content incorporated into the daily fabric of public and popular culture: images of ecology that are not necessarily about ecology" (1994, 181). This chapter builds on Ross's early observations to examine how television has represented the environment and to what effect. It then turns specifically to New Zealand television to consider how although some of its popular shows might appear to forward seemingly celebratory messages about the nation's environment, they in fact signify complex historical and social discourses about legitimacy and belonging that require critical interventions.

Explicit ecologies on television

Wildlife and natural history programming on television is arguably the most popular genre of explicit imagery of the natural world, whereas news and current affairs have been where environmentalism (defined here as an appreciation for the earth's finite resources and for its intrinsic worth rather than its exploitive value) has been most consistently expressed. Early wildlife and natural history programming effectively subspeciated into three types: series that featured domesticated wildlife in zoos, shows that took viewers on exotic adventure-filled spectacles in the wild (Mittman 1999; Davies 2000), and educational programs like the sober natural historian's lecture accompanied by expertly guided ethology, field study, and evidentiary recording (Davies 2000). Bousé argues that by the 1980s and 1990s, wildlife films had evolved into their own genre (quite distinct from earlier nature documentaries) by exhibiting a set of conventions that repeatedly focused upon large predators, dramatic narratives, and a notable absence of history, humans, politics, or much science (1998, 134). Perennially compelled to straddle the divide between entertainment and education, earlier forms of wildlife programming at least paid some lip service to conservation values. More recently, however, educational and conservation values appears to be under pressure as wildlife programming adapts to the rapidly changing conditions of what Cottle refers to as its "*production ecology*" (2004, 82). Production ecologies are "the organizational relationships and dynamics that exist within a particular field of media production" (Cottle 2004, 82). In order to survive deregulation, intensifying market competition, and changing audience tastes, wildlife and natural history makers have increasingly blurred the boundaries between wildlife and television genres more commonly associated with entertainment (Chris 2006; Kilborn 2006; Horak 2006; Louw 2006).

On current affairs and news programming, where environmental issues and their dilemmas have historically been most prominent, critics argue that ecological discourses are fundamentally shaped by the dictates of newsworthiness, which select for sensationalism, immediacy, relative simplicity, and singular events as opposed to chronic complex situations (Allan, Adam, and Carter 2000; Shanahan and McComas 1999). News media therefore tend to overemphasize violent radical one-off environmental events such as earthquakes, tsunami, and nuclear accidents at the expense of equally catastrophic slow-moving events such as climate change or bioinvasion (Allan, Adam, and Carter 2000, 6). News media "routinely visualize 'nature' and the environment in terms of deeply felt cultural oppositions that resonate with and help constitute an environmental sensibility . . . where 'nature' and the 'environment' are now widely felt to be under threat" (Cottle 2000, 43). While news and current affairs may play a role in escalating anxieties about the environment, critics accuse most other television genres of depoliticizing, dehistoricizing, and decontextualizing environmental issues (Howard-Williams 2011; Shanahan 1993) in favor of uncritically celebrating nature, reducing it to personality-driven spectacle (Vivanco 2004; Chris 2006, 92–99) or commodifying it (Japp and Japp 2002).

Implicit ecologies on television

Environmental cultivation theorists have researched links between entertainment (non-news) television and attitudes toward environmentalism. They correlate increasingly heavy television viewership with a diminishing sense of concern or agency about environmental issues (Good 2007; Shanahan and McComas 1999; Shanahan 1993). Some scholars attribute this lack of correlation to prime-time television's tendency to elide or "symbolically annihilate" environmental content altogether (Shanahan and McComas 1997). Others suggest that television undermines environmentalist values because it endorses materialist acquisitiveness (Good 2007). More than merely serving as a medium for materialism, television is structurally predicated upon an arrangement whereby networks deliver audiences to advertisers. This arrangement is considered fundamentally incompatible with environmental conservation and sustainability because it sublimates everything to consumption (Howard-Williams 2011; McComas, Shanahan, and Butler 2001; Budd, Craig, and Steinman 1999; Shanahan and McComas 1997). Television entertainment's capacity to use images of the environment and discourses of sustainability to drive rather than critique or curtail materialism and consumption underscores this tendency. For example, *The Good Life* on the popular and globally broadcast HGTV (House and Garden TV) shows its audience how once harried, stressed, and burnedout professionals leave the rat race behind to live simple, better, and more fulfilled lives in "nature" envisioned as pastoral or rural places. To achieve their new "good lives" they purchase rural property and set up small-scale enterprises that produce artisanal consumer goods and/or leisure services. Crucially, they do so with a simple, elegant style that is ". . . necessary to separate the middle-class good life from the inadvertent and unavoidable simplicity of poverty and lower-class existence" (Japp and Japp 2002, 89). Appropriately constrained and stylized (nothing threatening here) nature becomes a commodity, the consumption of which enhances happiness and satisfaction (Japp and Japp 2002, 92).

The Good Life exemplifies how nature images can signify discourses that are unconnected or even antithetical to environmentalism. On *The Good Life*, nature becomes a commodity much like a new car, diamond-studded watch, or luxury Caribbean cruise through which a consumer can signal taste, sophistication, superiority, and happiness. Another instance of how television represents discourses that are not expressly or explicitly about environmental issues is New Zealand *reality television*. Popular series such as *Border Patrol* (2003–2013) and *Piha Rescue* (2001–present), as well as hunting, fishing, and food programming such as *Hunting Aotearoa* (2004–present) and *Topp Country* (2014) invoke images of the natural environment and ecology to produce other discourses, such as difference, legitimacy, authenticity, and belonging.

Reality television in New Zealand offers a particularly fertile space in which identities are constructed and represented. Despite the fact that New Zealand reality television consists largely of formats devised offshore (for example, *New Zealand Idol* [2004–2006] and *Changing Rooms New Zealand* [1998–2002] originated in the U.K., *New Zealand's Next Top Model* [2009–2011] originated in the United States, and *The Block New Zealand* [2012–present] adapts the Australian show), the shows themselves are produced locally and therefore give audiences a robust sense of place (Kavka 2004, 223). Consequently, New Zealand reality television has been described as a site where competing local cultural agendas can play out, where *settler colonialism* reenacts and reinforces anxious and tenuous claims to the landscape (West 2008), and where *indigenous* Māori have appropriated and adapted global idioms to revitalize *te reo* (language) and normalize *tikanga* (culture and custom) (Smith and de Bruin 2011, 306; Smith 2006, 32–33). Contemporary *settler colonialism* and Māori indigeneity are often understood as incommensurable because of incompatible or antagonistic conceptions of how humans and the environment relate. Settlers (referred to as New Zealand European or *Pakeha*) are credited with a largely instrumental approach to alienable resources, whereas indigenous Māori relations to the environment are understood as spiritually based, genealogically linked, and immutable with little or no distinction made between the animate and the inanimate (Roberts et al. 1995). Although many reality series appear to reinforce distinctions between settlers and indigenes, this chapter suggests that some New Zealand reality television interrupts prevalent academic and popular discourses about settler/indigenous antipathies. Instead, these series progressively ally settlers *with* indigenes, thereby effectively reaffirming a collective claim to the landscape against escalating claims made by more recent immigrants.

Suburban pastoral versus primordial wilderness

The popularity of real estate renovation reality programming is often cited as evidence of New Zealand reality television's complicity in consolidating and naturalizing settler claims to the country's landscape and resources. These shows tap into deeply rooted settler attachments for property ownership (Kavka 2004, 232). Their focus upon "making over" and "doing up" residential property can be seen as an allegory for the colonial logics of transforming and improving New Zealand's environment (West 2008). The ubiquity of this televisual genre supports the contention that "the settler nation must continually code, decode and recode social norms and social spaces so as to secure a meaningful (read: proprietary) relationship to the territories and resources at stake" (Smith 2011, 111). Seemingly benign and even banal acts of building, decorating, and landscaping on *Mitre 10 Dream Home* (1999–2013) and *Firth Ground Force* (1999–2003) reinforce the production of locality by repeatedly subjugating and refashioning potentially chaotic and unruly elements, including the untamed and uncultivated natural world often referred to as the "bush" (Appadurai 1996) and the historical and ongoing presence of indigenes (West 2008, 29).

Box 7.1   Appadurai and the production of locality

Appadurai points out that place is not just a geographic location but that it is produced socially (1996). What he means is that our understanding and experience of place is shaped through repeated acts of physical, conceptual, and spiritual labor. He uses the neighbourhood as an example where "the building of houses, the organization of paths and passages, the making of and remaking of fields and gardens, the mapping and negotiation of transhuman spaces and . . . terrains is the incessant, often humdrum preoccupation of many small communities . . ." (Appadurai 1996, 180). Appadurai's thinking about the production of locality applies to New Zealand renovation *reality television* because the carpentry, painting, and gardening featured on these shows is very similar to the kind of labor that transformed parts of New Zealand from natural places into British colonial places in the nineteenth century. The audience's desire to repeatedly watch local home renovation and maintenance is symptomatic of the repetitive nature of maintaining particular kinds of place and the ongoing anxiety descendants of European settlers feel about the legitimacy of their occupation.

Perhaps paradoxically given the popularity of "realty television" and its representation of the busywork involved in producing New Zealand as a settled space, New Zealand's environment is simultaneously conceptualized as primordial, pristine, and untouched by suburbanizing pastoral impulses (Gurevitch 2010, 58–75). Many contemporary New Zealanders seek refuge from the vexed and vexing legacies of imperialism by investing in a national vision predicated upon "nature." Symbolically, this nature remains firmly "outside [of] and antecedent to the colonial project" (Ginn 2008, 335). The utility of a nationalism predicated upon nature is, at least theoretically, that diverse constituencies, *Pakeha*, Māori, and recently arrived migrants from East and South Asia, can unite under it. Emptied of politics, people, and history, nature is imagined by eco-nationalists according to a distant but curiously definitive ecological baseline some time before European settlement. Conservation thus takes on heightened significance and particular urgency because the nature eco-nationalists venerate is perceived to be especially vulnerable to the dramatic acceleration and increasing amplitude of bioinvasive agents. The popular television series *Border Patrol* links increased fears about bioinvasion with anxieties about cultural contamination.

Securitainment's environmental imaginary

Initially scheduled on Monday nights in prime time on state-owned broadcaster TVOne, *biosecurity* and immigration, coastal surveillance, and marine search-and-rescue shows began to proliferate, primarily though syndication but also through format sales to overseas markets such as Australia. Seemingly overnight, shows like *Border Patrol* (which illustrates how passengers, cargo, and mail are surveilled and processed for entry into the country), *Coastwatch* (where audiences accompany maritime police and fisheries officials as they regulate recreational and commercial marine exploitation), and *Piha Rescue* (where audiences can follow volunteer lifeguards who ensure the safety of hapless beachgoers) were available on free-to-air television every night of the week, as well as on demand and even DVD. Whether broadcast for the first time or as repeats, these shows consistently rated in the top five shows each week for more than a decade. In effect, these reality formats supplanted previously popular current affairs and magazine programs for significant parts of the year (Philpott 2013) suggesting that forms of "edutainment" were replacing more conventional forms of broadcast journalism historically associated with producing national imagined communities (Anderson 1983). *Border Patrol* attracted an average national audience of 500,000 and as many as 830,000 at its peak in 2012 (New Zealand Customs Service 2012). This is a significant constituency in a country of 4.4 million inhabitants. Critics observe that these shows' immense appeal lies in their mix of observational documentary, soap opera dramatics, and processual, procedural pedagogies of managing ecological, political, social, and physical risk (Andrejevic 2011; Hughes 2010). Andrejevic refers to this particular constellation of risk response and distribution of responsibility as "*securitainment*" (Andrejevic 2011, 170). Securitainment is perhaps best described as a hybrid genre that provides instruction in strategies for risk management and security training as adjuncts to its entertainment content (Andrejevic 2011, 167). Although undeniably influenced by the spectre of terrorism in the post-9/11 era, the risks that are most commonly manifest on New Zealand screens are ecological rather than associated with politically motivated violence.

The focus upon surveillance, enforcement, and spectacle on *Border Patrol* and *Piha Rescue* produces a powerful repertoire of images and concepts about the environment around which national identity is constructed. On a weekly or nightly basis, they instruct local audiences about what it means to be a "real" New Zealander by repeatedly demonstrating how tourists and "new" New Zealanders (recent immigrants and tourists) express casual disregard or duplicity about biosecurity and naiveté about the hazards of the country's natural environment.

Produced with full cooperation from New Zealand's Ministry of Primary Industries, Immigration, and the Customs Service, each half-hour episode of *Border Patrol* typically follows three stories, each from a different port of entry. By far the most popular trope of the show is the passenger arriving off a long haul international flight and either unwittingly or duplicitously carrying biological contraband. These passengers are shown being searched, lectured, and usually dispatched with a stern verbal and/or written warning rather than the legislated $200 spot fine. Particularly intractable or criminally premeditated cases are threatened with more severe punishment that can include prosecution leading to a prison term and a $100,000 fine, although the show rarely, if ever, pursues these options.

The series adopts a "*firm but fair*" approach toward enforcement supporting critics' contentions that these genres function as instruments of governmentality. The work and ethos of risk management is represented as benign, reasonable, and normal (Hughes 2010). *Border Patrol* and similar shows have also been considered symptomatic of the development of late modern neoliberal risk societies, which privatize and personalize risk (Hughes 2010; Rose 1996; Beck 1992). Viewers at home are encouraged to assume greater personal responsibility as travelers who now know better. They are invited to assume civic responsibility alongside *Border Patrol*'s professional enforcement personnel, who are consistently introduced on a familiar first name basis and who unfailingly address the television audience as compatriots, thus producing a collective "we" who must defend the nation's fragile ecology. Habitual viewers become acutely aware that fresh fruit, vegetables, leaves, and seeds are strictly verboten, as are many types of meat products, honey, freshwater fish, eels, coral, and live fauna of any kind. At the conclusion of each search and seizure, either the official involved or the voice-over narrator reiterates the need for collective vigilance.

Despite its focus upon the workaday world of biosecurity surveillance and enforcement, depicted almost exclusively in nondescript airport arrivals halls, port facilities, or mail centers, the series nevertheless produces a powerful image of New Zealand's environment. Without so much as an image of a tree, mountain, stream, or beach, audiences are in no doubt that the landscape under ubiquitous and constant threat is pristine and natural. Rather than represent New Zealand's natural environment explicitly, *Border Patrol* evokes it through discourses of fragility, vulnerability, and risk. Most of *Border Patrol*'s biosecurity inspections take place at Auckland International Airport in a cavernous windowless, clinical space dominated by stainless steel inspection tables and portable office partitions. Wearing latex gloves, inspectors cautiously and systematically poke, prod, and extract contraband. Bright yellow, plastic-lined quarantine bins are almost always in shot. The case of a heavily accented woman caught concealing fresh slices of ginger root and curry leaves in her luggage exemplifies the strategies through which *Border Patrol* implicitly produces a sense of New Zealand's nature. This sequence opens with Ministry of Agriculture and Forestry (MAF) officer "Kylie" in the midst of conducting a thorough inspection of the suspected smuggler's suitcases. Kylie justifies her suspicions to the camera, showing the audience at home the extraordinary array of foreign foods she has managed to extract from this passenger's case. Kylie proceeds to explain how sliced ginger and curry leaves were concealed between two packages of vegetarian duck and then duplicitously shrouded in plastic. The inspection is intercut with images of the bright yellow signage in the arrivals hall emphatically instructing incoming passengers to "Protect New Zealand's Beautiful Environment." The voice-over narrator comments, "This [the ginger and leaves] might not look like much but the risks of disease and infestation are too high." The sequence concludes with a MAF official of South Asian descent lecturing the passenger about the risk of foreign insects. Finally the audience watches the now-chastened passenger paying a $200 dollar fine in crisp $100 notes. *Border Patrol* encourages its television audience to draw upon their own fantasy of New Zealand's pristine nature and place this successfully averted potential environmental crisis in relation to existing biosecurity catastrophes, such as the 30 million Australian brush tailed possums munching their way through New Zealand's native bird and tree life or the now ubiquitous algae *Didymosphenia geminata* (also known as didymo or rocksnot) that chokes most South Island rivers.

According to *Border Patrol*, foreign tourists and visibly different migrants constitute the most significant threats to New Zealand's biosecurity. While the show does not exclusively target East Asian and Polynesian arrivals, it reinforces a pervasive sense of suspicion about non- or new-New Zealanders by consistently associating ethnic and racial difference with illegal activity such as drug smuggling and illegal immigration. Typically, one story in every episode's three segments refers to a foreign tourist carrying suspicious plant or animal material. The other two stories are likely to be about drugs, contaminated cargo, or passengers with incorrect papers, unreported criminal convictions, and/or highly suspicious itineraries. The show therefore produces an isomorphic relationship between visible difference and criminality or pestilence.

The relationship between contamination and ethnic difference is not a recent phenomenon in New Zealand. Contemporary perceptions of East and South Asians have been fundamentally shaped by social attitudes toward Chinese immigration beginning in the mid-nineteenth century. Shortly after arriving in the goldfields of Otago in New Zealand's South Island in 1866, Chinese were represented in the popular print media as unclean, disease ridden, addicted to opiates, immoral, and fundamentally duplicitous (Ip and Murphy 2005). These discriminatory representations were ideologically reinforced by Victorian-era sanitary reforms that linked foreign contagion with foreign bodies, effectively producing discourses that linked whiteness with purity and nonindigenous or nonnative nonwhiteness with contamination. Although there have been significant economic and social changes in the interim, the notion that non-British, non-Māori immigrants are polluting has remained consistent. According to urban anthropologist Eveline Dürr:

> The binary of 'tidy Kiwi/dirty Asian' does very specific work in New Zealand by generating and reinforcing ideals about New Zealand's identity and representation. Narratives of migration entail fear of waste and environmental concerns serve as rhetorical warnings that New Zealand's national self-image is exposed to dramatic changes – and under threat of being polluted.
>
> (Dürr 2010, 32)

Border Patrol reinforces existing anxieties about Asian immigration by associating immigrants with cavalier tourists and conniving criminals. For example, series 6 episode 8 (November 5, 2012) contains four stories, including the extended interrogation of a Romanian couple who arouse suspicion upon arrival in Auckland. They seem to know little about each other and have no set itinerary, only vague travel plans, and an inappropriately large amount of luggage. Furthermore, they fit the profile of a cluster of similarly suspicious arrivals in previous weeks. This story frames three other stories in the episode, one that finds evidence of drug smuggling at the mail center, another that shows a Chinese tourist failing to declare meat in her luggage, and the last which focuses on an immigrant family arriving off a flight from Malaysia with boxes of food. In this last story, we meet the family and MAF Inspector Sue as she is taping up one box of food that appears to have just passed inspection. As Sue works, she conducts a friendly conversation with an articulate middle-class gentleman, who is clearly the head of the family. His wife (wearing hijab) and their two children can be seen in the background. Unlike many passengers undergoing this type of examination, the gentleman is relaxed and confident. Sue asks him if the food is halal. He answers "yes" and then volunteers that the boxes contain delicacies that are difficult to source in New Zealand. As she opens the second box, she asks him about its contents. He replies with a smile, "chips, lots and lots of chips." The box contains bags of onion chips, banana chips, anchovy chips, dried galama fish, and a special delicacy called chicken floss. Sue explains that galama fish is permitted because it is a saltwater species, but the chicken floss is not permitted and will have to be confiscated. She does not elaborate as to specifically why, although habitual viewers of the show will know that items are usually confiscated because they might harbor pests or diseases. Sue does, however, explain that floss is comparable to sandwich fillings. The language Sue uses to describe the comparison reveals how *Border Patrol* typically reinforces anxieties about unassimilable alterity. She says to the camera "so, we have marmite or jam or marmalade or peanut butter and they have floss on their sammies, yummy." Despite the fact that *Border Patrol* has a multiethnic cast of inspectors, the "we" Sue refers to is a television audience imagined as people like her, "real" New Zealanders of European descent and "them" as new immigrants with threatening exotic tastes. Although the Malaysians are law-abiding New Zealand citizens, the show does little to visually or narratively distinguish them from duplicitous travellers who potentially imperil the nation, such as the South Asian woman who conceals sliced ginger and curry leaves, the Chinese tourist who smuggles meat, or the Romanians who are deported upon suspicion of being part of an international credit card–skimming gang. The Malaysians become sources of contamination as much if not more by association than by importing hazardous food items.

Box 7.2   Talk about it: what's on television?

New Zealand isn't the only country where border security is popular on television. Either look at your own television schedule or look online to see what other countries have similar shows. Canada, Australia, and the U.K. all have similar types of series. To what degree do these shows express similar anxieties to those outlined in relation to New Zealand? Consider how these shows imagine their country's environment, what they say about how they imagine society, and why.

Further readings

Andrejevic, Mark. 2011. "'Securitainment' in the Post-9/11 Era." *Continuum: Journal of Media and Cultural Studies* 25.2: 165–175.
Caluya, Gilbert. 2014. "Fragments for a Postcolonial Critique of the Anthropocene." *Rethinking Invasion Ecologies from the Environmental Humanities* 13: 31–44.
Hughes, Peter. 2010. "Governmentality, Blurred Boundaries, and Pleasure in the Docusoap Border Security." *Continuum: Journal of Media and Cultural Studies* 24.3: 165–175. Accessed June 1, 2014. 10.1080/10304311003703116.
Price, Emma, and Amy Nethery. 2012. "Truth-Telling at the Border: An Audience Appraisal of Border Security." *Media International Australia* 142: 148–156.

Defending New Zealand's nature against foreign contamination is contingent upon denying the extent to which it has been anthropogenically modified. Clark reminds us that the imperial project was "as much a biological process as it was an economic, cultural or political one" (2003, 163). Colonists have been described as transporting everything required to recreate European life in the temperate regions of the colonial periphery. In 1832, Darwin observed that at the Waimate mission station in the far north of New Zealand:

> there were large gardens, with every fruit and vegetable which England produces . . . around the farmyard a blacksmith's forge . . . in the middle was that happy mixture of pigs and poultry, lying comfortably together, as in every English farmyard. . . . At the mill, a New Zealander was seen powdered white with flour, like his brother miller in England.
>
> (Darwin in Lamb 1999)

If the process of European settlement in the nineteenth and twentieth centuries so dramatically altered New Zealand's ecosystem, how might one account for current anxieties about biological contamination?

In part, the answer lies in Turner's observation that settlement is a contradictory process characterized chiefly by forgetting (Turner 1999, 20):

> The new country is the site of contradictory demands: the need, ultimately to forget the old country, and the need to ignore the people who already inhabit the new country. . . . Yet the idea of a new country is strictly impossible, as it is founded in the initial contradiction, or disjunction, of competing demands. There is no such thing as an absolutely new country. Quite apart from the indigenous presence, the idea of a new country is built on the displacement or overflow of old-country

passions. . . . it is a site of loss, a place where the self is made void, where cultural identity must be reconstructed. What marks the distinctiveness of the new country is this very self-distancing, a cultural identity that has been split off from the old country.

(Turner 1999, 21)

Amnesia enables contemporary New Zealanders to ignore contradictions posed by the weedy legacies of their forebears. The temperate peripheries (Australasia, South America, and South Africa) were often far more hospitable to European flora and fauna than their habitats of origin. Whether brought by design as in the case of livestock or by default as in the case of Eurasian weeds, the extraordinary vigor with which introduced species took hold and proliferated in places like New Zealand have often been forgotten, as has the fact that not all of these invasions were catastrophic (Clark 2002). Forgetting, conveniently or otherwise, permits the consolidation of naturalized settler identities against which contamination by contemporary human and nonhuman agents must be vigilantly defended. On television these identities are often expressed as ways of being in and relating to the environment.

Not just another day at the beach

Although *Border Patrol* and *Piha Rescue* produce similar discourses about belonging and legitimacy, they envision New Zealand's environment quite differently. Whereas *Border Patrol* imagines the environment as vulnerable to inbound contagion, *Piha Rescue* depicts New Zealand's environment as deceptively benign to those who lack the requisite competencies to safely negotiate it. *Piha Rescue* uses competency in and around the ocean to distinguish between authentic New Zealanders and unassimilable others. Filmed on location at several popular recreational beaches, including Piha near Auckland, Raglan near Hamilton, and Hotwater Beach on the Coromandel Peninsula, *Piha Rescue* follows volunteer surf lifesavers on patrol. Using handheld and helmet-mounted cameras, the makers of the show offer audiences at home a highly kinetic, intimate, and often first-person point of view of maritime crises and dramatic ocean rescues. Drowning is both a significant cause of accidental death and a potent recurrent symbol in New Zealand popular culture. *Piha Rescue* depicts a range of victims, but a disproportionate number of the swimmers swept out by riptides, boogie boarders thrashed by rogue swells, and fatalities are South and East Asian. Most of the hour-long episodes make at least one and most make multiple visual or narrative references to the fact that the people most likely to underestimate the ocean are visible minorities. In many cases, these particular stories constitute a significant proportion of the show's broadcast hour. Two dramatic but representative examples from Season 10 are worth recounting here. A substantial part of episode 7, which initially aired December 9,

2013, takes place at the popular surfing beach, Raglan. The story begins as lifesavers are alerted to a swimmer in distress. They launch their inflatable rescue boat (IRB) and head out. They find the barely-conscious swimmer with a surfer who has managed to get the swimmer onto his surfboard. The television audience can discern that the victim in the IRB is Chinese. His condition deteriorates dramatically on the way back to the shore. Once on the beach, the lifeguards begin to suspect he might also have a spinal injury. The narrator observes that medical personnel on the scene cannot determine the extent of his injuries because of his poor English. He is finally transferred by ambulance to Waikato hospital with a grim prognosis. In the epilogue that follows, the audience learns that the swimmer makes a full recovery. However salutary this news is, the audience is nevertheless left with a distinct impression of who or what kind of New Zealander is most at risk at the beach, an impression confirmed by another story from the same season that traces the emerging tragedy of a double drowning at Piha. In this episode, several off-duty lifeguards are called to the beach where a man lies seriously injured at dusk. Although his face is blurred in the television footage, he appears to be of South Asian descent. The audience learns that he went into the water with two friends but they have failed to return. In the fading light the situation becomes progressively more desperate until the lifeguards acknowledge that the likelihood of the men's survival is virtually nonexistent. The injured man is transported to hospital while the police begin recovery (rather than rescue) patrols along the high tide line. The next morning, just before dawn, the victims' bodies are located on the shore just meters from where they entered the water. The audience is never told their identity nor shown any distinguishing characteristics; nevertheless, the television audience gains a powerful impression that the victims were of South Asian descent, partly because of what they can see of the injured man and because previous episodes of the show have habituated audiences to expect that victims of maritime misadventure will be East or South Asian. This impression is indeed borne out. The victims are Bhawandeep Gill and Yagnik-Kumar Patel from Papatoetoe, who entered the water at dusk fully clothed (Koubaridis 2013).

Belich and Wevers ask, "If pristine scenic vistas constitute the landscape of our imagined community, then who belongs in it?" (Belich and Wevers 2008, 8). On *Piha Rescue*, belonging is represented by competency and confidence in and around the ocean. The lifesavers themselves are the most obvious example. With the exception of one or two American exchange lifesavers (who are clearly identified by lower third titles and by the show's omnipresent narrator), the lifeguards on *Piha Rescue* are nearly all *Pakeha*. Most, but not all, are men. Regardless of gender, however, all of them exhibit composure and pragmatism under pressure, physical aptitude on land and in the water, and expertise driving all-terrain vehicles and inflatable rafts in challenging circumstances. The series also reinforces the sense that *Pakeha* belong, through vignettes such as the one that opens the episode that ends with the critically injured young Chinese man. This vignette shows a class of primary school children undergoing instruction about beach safety and the perils of riptides. Wide shots of the class assembled in the clubhouse and on the foreshore reveal that they are mostly of European descent. One child is selected to demonstrate how easy it is to be caught in a rip and how best to extricate oneself. The child chosen to demonstrate is Gabriel, a fit, blonde ten-year-old girl who reveals that she is part of a junior lifesaving squad. The audience then sees Gabriel both in the whitewater and from the shore as she swims parallel down the shoreline to find a suitable channel back to the beach. Ten minutes later she runs up the beach. Viewers of the show might reasonably assume that most victims of recreational drowning at beaches are Asian. Statistics show, however, that New Zealand Europeans account for 39% of victims, while Māori make up 23% and Asians just 13%. The series therefore reinforces the impression that Asians are perennial interlopers consigned to misapprehend and misconstrue an essentially hostile environment with predictably tragic consequences.

Neither *Border Patrol* nor *Piha Rescue* explicitly differentiate Māori from *Pakeha* within the collective that defends New Zealand's fragile ecosystem against foreign bioinvasion or rescues hapless migrants from the hostile seas. Consequently, it is possible to interpret these programs as yet more anxious settlercentric acts of forgetting, denying, or active erasure. Turner's characterization of the beach as a space where the trauma of first encounters with Māori has been sublimated or forgotten by its reincarnation as a site for settler leisure would certainly seem to support this interpretation (1999, 31). Despite ongoing and fundamental sociopolitical tension between *Pakeha* and Māori however, these genres of New Zealand *reality television* depicts them as more similar than dissimilar. The sensitivity to and appreciation for nature and competency in the landscape in *Border Patrol* and *Piha Rescue* effectively signal an ecological habitus that differentiates "real" New Zealanders from more recent migrants. *Ecological habitus* can be thought of "the embodiment of a durable yet changeable system of ecologically relevant dispositions, practices, perceptions, and material conditions" (Kasper 2009, 319). On New Zealand television, "who belongs in the landscape" is perhaps most powerfully manifest in shows about hunting and food.

Box 7.3   Habitus

Drawing upon Marx's notion of capital, which can be accrued and expended to one's advantage or the lack of such advantage, Pierre Bourdieu argued that life experiences, tastes, skills, knowledge, material possessions, and qualifications can also be thought of as a type of capital – *cultural capital*. How cultural capital is embodied and/ or performed (consciously and unconsciously) is referred to as *habitus*. Habitus is often so ingrained that it is considered innate rather than acquired. For example, the refined tastes of the dynastically wealthy are considered "natural" rather than the sum of generations of collecting and appreciating fine art, quaffing expensive wine, and wearing haute couture fashion. What constitutes cultural capital is entirely context specific. The context can be thought of as a "field." For example, knowing how to swim, sail a dinghy, and shoot a rifle might be advantageous in New Zealand and seem "naturally suited" to the landscape; however, these skills and experiences might not be particularly advantageous or seem especially natural in Beijing or Paris. Swimming, sailing, and shooting become propensities through the interaction between individuals and their social field.

Bourdieu, however, has argued that in general social classes have been able to reinforce their relative privilege and class standing by accruing and passing on particular forms of social knowledge and ways of being (cultural capital), which can translate into material capital (Bourdieu 1986, 241–258). In the ecocritical literature, ecological habitus is used in different ways. Haluza-DeLay (2008) defines *ecological habitus* as a way of being environmentally sensitive and acting sustainably. He argues that one of the reasons ecological habitus is so difficult to achieve on a large scale, despite mounting evidence that environmental degradation is a direct consequence of human activity, is that the social field within which we live is not ecologically oriented. Our current habitus is to act unsustainably (even if we are sympathetic to environmental causes). The key to changing existing conditions would be to harness habituation and routinize sustainable behavior, which if collectively enacted would ultimately transform our social field. In this chapter, I use ecological habitus more in line with Bourdieu and less so like Haluza-Delay, to suggest that New Zealanders (both Māori and *Pakeha*) have ways of being and interacting with nature that have evolved over a long period of settlement, which reinforce their social power and legitimacy. This habitus includes knowing what can and cannot be imported, successfully being in and around the ocean, and hunting.

Māori and *Pakeha* – hunting, fishing, and putting *Kai* (food) on the table

Hunting Aotearoa is a popular long-running prime time hunting series on New Zealand's indigenous broadcaster Māori Television. Currently in its tenth season, the series has more than 200 episodes, most of which, except for occasional offshore trips to other islands in the Pacific, take place in New Zealand. It is perennially among Māori Television's top-rated shows, with a dedicated Māori and non-Māori audience (Turner 2011, 45). Initially presented by Howard Morrison Jr. (seasons 1 to 7) and thereafter by former professional rugby player Matua Parkinson (seasons 8 to 10), each episode typically focuses upon a particular type of prey in a specific location, for example, feral pigs in the Far North, deer and goats in the Marlborough Sounds, or Himalayan thar on Aoraki Mt Cook. Although the show's hunters pursue an impressive array of animals, pigs are by far the most common prey. The fact that New Zealand has no endemic land mammals save for two species of bat means that hunting axiomatically coincides, albeit imperfectly, with eco-nationalist conservation values. Stalking and subsequently killing animals is simultaneously described as pest management and a natural New Zealand activity. The feral ecology is thus seen as both imperial legacy and authenticated as profoundly natural (Clark 2002, 114).

Hunting Aotearoa's episodes are relatively formulaic, beginning with the introduction of local hunters in each location, followed by dramatic and beautiful images of the landscape intercut with the pursuit of prey. Cooking and conversation punctuate the narrative structure of the hunt. The show also has expert-sponsored inserts provided in earlier seasons by a spokesperson from the retailer Hunting and Fishing New Zealand and in later seasons by butcher James Brown, who offers tips that include how to singe an adult boar over an open fire and detach the hind quarters of a deer. In addition to spectacular scenery, violent animal deaths, and butchery, the show features an impressive array of boats, all-terrain and utility vehicles, and the occasional helicopter. Viewers are repeatedly shown physical competence, confidence, and ease in New Zealand's nature. There is a certain irony in characterizing *Pakeha* as "at ease" in New Zealand's rural environment, given the significant literature that describes settlers' relation with the landscape as one of "unease,"particularly in cinema (Neill et al. 1995). The shows discussed here, however, do not appear to reiterate similar feelings, suggesting perhaps that domestic television performs quite different types of ideological work.

A significant proportion of *Hunting Aotearoa* takes place in the Māori language, either through Howard Morrison Jr.'s sync dialogue or by a voice-over narrator in the later episodes hosted by Parkinson. English subtitles are provided for non- or novice Māori speakers. Parkinson periodically introduces or reinforces Māori vocabulary. Both Māori and *Pakeha* hunters are profiled. The series is often cited as a prime example of Māori Television's capability of producing high-quality local content that reinforces Māori language and culture while appealing to a national audience (Smithies 2014). Richard Curtis, the show's producer, attributes its popularity to the way in which *Hunting Aotearoa* reflects the rural heritage that Māori and *Pakeha* share. In a behind-the-scenes interview shot for the series' 200th episode, Curtis says, "Everyone in New Zealand, both Māori and *Pakeha*, grew up on hunting – their grandfathers [and] their grandfathers before them taught them how to hunt, how to live off the land and that's the very New Zealand natural thing to do, live off the land" (Curtis 2014). Although the show occasionally includes stories about trophy hunting, most of its participants stress hunting's role in providing sustenance for their families.

Hunting Aotearoa taps in to a rich legacy of celebrating rural life on New Zealand national television. The most iconic of this type of programming is *Country Calendar* (1966–present), which has represented farmers and New Zealand's pastoral landscape continuously for more than 46 years. A number of other shows that feature television personalities traveling up and down the country profiling local people, places, and events have aired periodically, including *North* (2011) and *South* (2009) in the last decade and the very popular program *Heartland* in the 1990s. Presented by poet and raconteur Gary McCormick, *Heartland* (1991–1996) was designed to show a national audience "the real" New Zealand (McCormick 1994, 7). From week to week, he would visit places that loom large in the iconography of the nation, interviewing the locals and celebrating country life. *Heartland* was not a specialized hunting show, nonetheless the series and its attendant coffee table book both included many images of hunting and dead animals. Longhurst and Wilson suggest "these images emphasize the importance of the kill to the frontier man and how masculine bloodied bodies are naturally positioned and identified in the rural landscape" (Longhurst and Wilson 1999, 53). While images of hunting are clearly implicated in the production of hegemonic masculinity in New Zealand, they also appear to function more broadly as foundational symbols of cultural authenticity and legitimacy.

The symbolic centrality of hunting and killing in envisioning a "real" New Zealand where Māori and *Pakeha* are socially aligned rather than fundamentally differentiated persists well into the present. *Topp Country*, starring the iconic twin lesbian, yodeling, country and western–singing Topp Twins, aired in primetime on Sunday evenings in the autumn of 2014 to an audience of almost 500,000 viewers ("Topp Country" 2014). Essentially a food tourism series, the show features Lynda and Jools Topp as they travel the country interviewing rural food producers, urban food purveyors, and long-established families who share their signature homemade dishes. Episode 9, titled "Heritage," reinforces New Zealand television's tendency to imagine who belongs in New Zealand's landscape as *Pakeha* and Māori united under a history of hunting and producing food from the land. "Heritage," the penultimate episode out of ten, consists of three story segments, beginning with veterinarians Jeff Niblett and Bridgette Karatai who breed and release pheasants and other fowl for hunting in the Hawke's Bay on the East Coast of New Zealand's North Island. Montages in this sequence show beautiful images of pastoral landscape populated by photogenic children fishing in the river and walking down country roads with their gun dogs. The message is clear, pastoral rural life is morally and physically wholesome. Lynda Topp hunts with Jeff for pheasant while Bridget and Jools Topp bake pheasant pie (see Figure 7.1). As Jeff congratulates Lynda on successfully shooting a pheasant, they both admire the bird and speculate about

Figure 7.1 Lynda Topp holding pheasants in *Topp Country*.
Source: Image courtesy of Diva Productions.

what good eating it will make. Their skill in hunting and matter-of-factness about the pheasant as food legitimize their presence in the landscape. The pheasant likewise appears natural in the landscape, despite the fact that it too is a "weedy" European import.

The final segment of episode 9 is curiously neither about a food producer, as most segments are, nor a purveyor, but instead visits the Bowman family at home in suburban Christchurch. Ostensibly about a famous family recipe for tart apple shortcakes, the segment tells the story of the Bowman's recently deceased matriarch referred to as "Grandma." Grandma, it turns out, descended from Kamariera Wharepapa, a Māori Ngapuhi chief who travelled to England as part of a delegation sponsored by Wesleyan Missionary William Jenkins in 1863 and a young British girl named Elizabeth Reid. The Topps bake with Grandma Bowman's grandson and talk about her history with her son. During this conversation, special note is made of a journal entry or letter in which Elizabeth comments on the beauty of Kamariera Wharepapa's facial tattoos, attesting to her attraction and respect for the Ngapuhi chief rather than the contempt and derision colonists often expressed toward Māori. The segment concludes with the Bowmans and Topps eating Grandma's apple short cake and singing in Māori.

"Heritage," in *Topp Country*, refers to hunting, deriving sustenance from the land, and a history of European and Māori interrelations. Concluding this episode with the Bowmans could be viewed as yet another calculated and cynical attempt to naturalize settler presence by appropriating or unjustifiably amplifying settler connections with indigeneity. In the context of a steady xenophobic anti-Asian hum in public discourse, however, *Topp Country*, *Border Patrol*, and *Piha Rescue* might instead be seen as producing national identity borne out of settler *and* indigenous encounters with New Zealand's landscape. Against what has been described as excessive immigration from East and South Asia (Coddington 2006) and, more recently, anxiety about high-profile dairy farm purchases by Chinese consortia (Adams 2012), the delineation of who legitimately belongs in New Zealand and who does not seems to be popularly imagined through physical confidence and competency in the natural environment and an ability to derive sustenance from it. In the end, it seems hardly coincidental that those who least belong in New Zealand seem especially insistent on importing food from some other "home"land.

Conclusion

New Zealand's environment is popularly imagined as pristine and primordial and is advertised domestically and internationally as "100% Pure." At least theoretically, this image of the environment circumvents some of the longstanding debates about European settler entitlement and "at homeness" that characterize postcolonial identity politics in New Zealand (Huggan and Tiffin 2010, 82–83). Conveniently emptied of *Pakeha* settler conflict and history, the utility of such imagery lies in its apparent inclusiveness. However, this ecocritical exploration of some of New Zealand's most popular television programs suggests that New Zealand's pristine environment can be used to divide rather than unite its populace. New Zealand's nature is mediated in ways that continue to marginalize visible ethnic difference. In the meantime, *Pakeha* reinforce claims to the pastoral landscape and the wilderness by invoking the rural heritage they share with Māori. This maneuver appears to be a continuation of the earlier tactics in which European settlement asserts and secures belonging by aligning itself with indigenous communities. What is perhaps new is how allegiances between *Pakeha* and Māori are invoked at the same time that anxieties about violent colonial possession are deflected by displacing them onto East and South Asian tourists and immigrants. Furthering postcolonial ecocriticism, this chapter offers a critique to the underacknowledged and underrepresented relations between the environment and colonialism and suggests that television is a potentially productive medium to examine increasingly complex social formations in postcolonial settler sites.

Keywords

Biosecurity
Ecological habitus
Indigenous
Production ecology

Reality television
Securitainment
Settler colonialism

Discussion questions

1   Look at the prime time television schedule (6–10 pm) across various channels (free-to-air and cable, if possible) for a few evenings. Which shows deal explicitly with environmentalism? How many of them are there? Are there any shows that visualize the natural environment but are not about sustainability and ecological values? What types of shows are they?

2   Select a television genre (ideally one that has aired over the years and undergone change, such as daytime soap opera, cooking show, game show). What is its production ecology? You might want to think about how the genre is financed, where it airs, and who watches it and how. Research the history of the genre. Has the genre acted like an organism responding to changing conditions in its habitat? Explain.

3   Using *Border Patrol* as an example, consider how watching threats to the environment on television might lessen rather than heighten environmental concern. Explore other shows that might alleviate anxieties about environmental concerns rather than intensify them, and discuss how.

4   What sorts of nationalist and postcolonial anxieties are reinforced by the shows discussed here? Can you think of other shows that represent similar anxieties? Why is it important for environmental scholars to take such anxieties into account?

5   Box 7.3 defines the idea of habitus. Is there a tension in the two types of ecological habitus described? Make an argument for Haluza-Delay's notion of ecological habitus as demonstrated by the shows, then critique it.

Further reading

Anderson, Benedict R. O. 1983. *Imagined Communities: Reflections on the Origins and Spread of Nationalism*. London: Verso.

Caluya, Gilbert. 2014. "Fragments for a Postcolonial Critique of the Anthropocene." *Rethinking Invasion Ecologies from the Environmental Humanities* 13: 31–44.

Clark, Nigel. 2000. "Botanizing on the Asphalt? The Complex Life of Cosmopolitan Bodies." *Body and Society* 5.3–4: 12–33.

Clark, Nigel. 2013. "Mobile Life: Biosecurity Practices and Insect Globalization." *Science as Culture*, 22.1: 16–37.

Cubitt, Sean. 2005. *EcoMedia*. New York: Rodopi.

Darwin, Charles. 1902. *Journal of Researches During the Voyage of the Beagle*. London: John Murray.

Hinchcliffe, Steve, and Nick Bingham. 2007. "Securing Life: The Emerging Practices of Biosecurity." *Environment and Planning* 40: 1534–1551.

Huggan, Graham. 2004. "'Greening' Postcolonialism: Ecocritical Perspectives." *MFS Modern Fiction Studies* 50.3: 701–733.

Huggan, Graham, and Helen Tiffin. 2010. *Postcolonial Ecocriticism: Literature, Animals, Environment*. New York: Routledge.

Meister, Mark, and Phyllis M. Japp. 2001. *Enviropop: Studies in Environmental Rhetoric and Popular Culture*. Westport, CT: Praeger.

Price, Emma, and Amy Nethery. 2012. "Truth-Telling at the Border: An Audience Appraisal of Border Security." *Media International Australia* 142: 148–156.

Works cited

Adams, Christopher. 2012. "Crafar Dairy Farms Deal Finally Settled." *New Zealand Herald*, 1 December. Accessed November 5 2014. http://www.nzherald.co.nz/business/news/article.cfm?c_id=3&objectid=10851202

Allan, Stuart, Barbara Adam, and Cynthia Carter. 2000. "Introduction: The Media Politics of Environmental Risk." In *Environmental Risks and the Media*, edited by Stuart Allan, Barbara Adam, and Cynthia Carter, 1–26. London: Routledge.

Anderson, Benedict R. O. 1983. *Imagined Communities: Reflections on the Origins and Spread of Nationalism*. London: Verso.

Andrejevic, Mark. 2011. "'Securitainment' in the Post-9/11 Era." *Continuum: Journal of Media and Cultural Studies* 25.2: 165–175.

Appadurai, Arjun. 1996. *Modernity at Large: Cultural Dimensions of Globalization*. Minneapolis: University of Minnesota Press.

Beck, Ulrich. 1992. *Risk Society: Towards a New Modernity*. London: Sage.

Belich, James, and Lydia Wevers. 2008. "Understanding New Zealand Cultural Identities." Discussion paper prepared by the Stout Research Centre for New Zealand Studies, Victoria University of Wellington, for the Ministry of Culture and Heritage.

Bourdieu, Pierre. 1986. "The Forms of Capital." In *Handbook of Theory and Research for the Sociology of Education*, edited by John G. Richardson, 241–258. New York: Greenwood Press.

Bousé, Derek. 1998. "Are Wildlife Films Really "Nature Documentaries?" *Critical Studies in Mass Communications* 15.2: 116–140.

Budd, Mike, Steve Craig, and Clay Steinman. 1999. *Consuming Environments: Television and Commercial Culture*. New Brunswick, NJ: Rutgers University Press.

Chris, Cynthia. 2006. *Watching Wildlife*. Minneapolis: University of Minnesota Press.

Clark, Nigel. 2002. "The Demon-Seed Bioinvasion as the Unsettling of Environmental Cosmopolitanism." *Theory, Culture & Society* 19.1&2: 101–125.

Clark, Nigel. 2003. "Feral Ecologies: Performing Life on the Colonial Periphery." *The Sociological Review* 51.2: 163–182.

Coddington, Deborah. 2006. "Asian Angst: Is It Time to Send Some Back?" *North and South* 249: 38–47.

Cottle, Simon. 2000. "TV News, Lay Voices and the Visualisation of Environmental Risks." In *Environmental Risks and the Media*, edited by Stuart Allan, Barbara Adam, and Cynthia Carter, 29–44. London: Routledge.

Cottle, Simon. 2004. "Producing Nature(s): On the Changing Production Ecology of Natural History TV." *Media, Culture & Society* 26.1: 81–101.

Curtis, Richard, Producer. *Hunting Aotearoa*. July 17, 2014. http://www.maoritelevision.com/tv/shows/hunting-aotearoa/S10E011/hunting-aotearoa-series-10-episode-11

Davies, Gail. 2000. "Science, Observation and Entertainment: Competing Visions of Post-war British Natural History Television 1946–1967." *Cultural Geographies* 7.4: 432–459.

Dürr, Eveline. 2010. "Tidy Kiwis, Dirty Asians: Cultural Pollution and Migration in Auckland, New Zealand." *Urban Pollution: Cultural Meanings, Social Practices*, edited by Eveline Dürr and Rivke Jaffe, 30–56. Oxford: Berghahn Books.

Ginn, Franklin. 2008. "Extension, Subversion, Containment: Eco-Nationalism and (Post) Colonial Nature in Aotearoa New Zealand." *Transactions of the Institute of British Geographers* 33.3: 335–353.

Good, Jennifer. 2007. "Shop 'Til We Drop? Television, Materialism and Attitudes About the Natural Environment." *Mass Communication and Society* 10.3: 365–383.

Gurevitch, Leon. 2010. "100% Pure Imperial Ecology: Marketing the Environment in Antipodean Film and Advertising." *New Zealand Journal of Media Studies* 10.1: 58–78.

Haluza-DeLay, Randolph. 2008. "A Theory of Practice for Social Movements: Environmentalism and Ecological Habitus." *Mobilization: The International Quarterly* 13.2: 205–218.

Horak, Jan-Christopher. 2006. "Wildlife Documentaries: From Classical Forms to Reality TV." *Film History* 18: 459–475.

Howard-Williams, Rowan. 2011. "Consumers, Crazies and Killer Whales: The Environment on New Zealand Television." *International Communication Gazette* 73.1–2: 27–43.

Huggan, Graham, and Helen Tiffin. 2010. *Postcolonial Ecocriticism: Literature, Animals, Environment*. New York: Routledge.

Hughes, Peter. 2010. "Governmentality, Blurred Boundaries, and Pleasure in the Docusoap Border Security." *Continuum: Journal of Media and Cultural Studies*, 24.3: 165–175. Accessed June 1, 2014. 10.1080/10304311003703116.

Ip, Manying, and Nigel Murphy. 2005. *Aliens at My Table: Asians as New Zealanders See Them*. Auckland: Penguin Books.

Japp, Phyllis M., and Debra K. Japp. 2002. "Purification Through Simplification: Nature, The Good Life, and Consumer Culture." In *Enviropop: Studies in Environmental Rhetoric and Popular Culture*, edited by Mark Meister and Phyllis M. Japp, 81–94. Westport, CT: Praeger.

Kasper, Debbie. 2009. "Ecological Habitus: Toward a Better Understanding of Socioecological Relations." *Organization and Environment*. 22.3: 311–326.

Kavka, Misha. 2004. "Reality Estate: Locating New Zealand Reality Television." In *Television in New Zealand: Programming the Nation*, edited by Roger Horrocks and Nick Perry, 222–239. Auckland: Oxford University Press.

Kilborn, Richard. 2006. "A Walk on the Wild Side: The Changing Face of TV Wildlife Documentary." *Jump Cut: A Review of Contemporary Media* 48. Accessed October 12, 2014. http://www.ejumpcut.org/archive/jc48.2006/AnimalTV/text.html

Koubaridis, Andrew. 2013. "Piha Rip Claims Another Two Lives." *New Zealand Herald*, 25 February. Accessed April 15, 2014. http://www.nzherald.co.nz/nz/news/article.cfm?c_id=1&objectid=10867512.

Lamb, Jonathan. 1999. "The Idea of Utopia in the European Settlement of New Zealand." In *Quicksands. Foundational Histories in Australia and Aotearoa New Zealand*, edited by Klaus Neumann, Nicholas Thomas, and Hilary Ericksen, 79–97. Sydney: University of New South Wales Press.

Longhurst, Robyn, and Carla Wilson. 1999. "*Heartland* Wainuimata: Rurality to Suburbs, Black Singlets to Naughty Lingerie." In *Masculinities in Aotearoa/New Zealand*, edited by Robin Law, Hugh Campbell, and John Dolan, 50–61. Palmerson North: Dunmore Press.

Louw, Pat. 2006. "Nature Documentaries: Eco-tainment? The Case of MM&M (Mad Mike and Mark)." *Current Writing: Text and Reception in Southern Africa* 18.1: 146–162.

McComas, Katherine A., James Shanahan, and Jessica S. Butler. 2001. "Environmental Content in Prime-Time Network TV's Non-News Entertainment and Fictional Programs." *Society & Natural Resources* 14.6: 533–542.

McCormick, Gary. 1994. *Heartland*. Auckland: Moa Beckett.

Mittman, Greg. 1999. *Reel Nature: America's Romance with Wildlife on Film*. Cambridge, MA: Harvard University Press.

Neill, Sam, Judy Rymer, Grant Campbell, and Paula Jalfon. 1995. *New Zealand Cinema: Cinema of Unease*. Wellington, NZ: New Zealand Film Commission. DVD.

New Zealand Customs Service. "Border Patrol Returns to TV Tonight." Last modified September 17, 2012. Accessed June 20, 2014. http://www.customs.govt.nz/news/stories/Pages/Border-Patrol-returns-to-TV-tonight.aspx

Philpott, Chris. 2013 "Baffling Ratings at 7pm." *On the Box* January 29. Accessed June 25, 2014. http://www.stuff.co.nz/entertainment/blogs/on-the-box/8233366/Baffling-ratings-at-7pm

Roberts, Mere, Norman Waerete, Nganeko Minhinnick, Del Wihongi, and Carmen Kirkwood. 1995. "Kaitiakitanga Maori Perspectives on Conservation." *Pacific Conservation Biology* 2.1: 7–20.

Rose, Nikolas S. 1996. "Governing 'Advanced' Liberal Democracies." In *Foucault and Political Reason: Liberalism, Neo-liberalism, and Rationalities of Government*, edited by Andrew Barry, Thomas Osborne, and Nikolas S. Rose, 37–64. Chicago: University of Chicago Press.

Ross, Andrew. 1994. *The Chicago Gangster Theory of Life: Nature's Debt to Society*. New York: Verso.

Shanahan, James. 1993. "Television and the Cultivation of Environmental Concern: 1988–92." In *The Mass Media and Environmental Issues*, edited by Anders Hansen, 181–197. Leicester: Leicester University Press.

Shanahan, James, and Katherine McComas. 1997. "Television's Portrayal of the Environment: 1991–1995." *Journalism & Mass Communication Quarterly* 74.1: 147–159.

———. 1999. *Nature Stories, Depictions of the Environment and Their Effects.* Cresskill, MA: Hampton Press.

Smith, Jo T. 2006. "Parallel Quotidian Flows: Māori Television On Air." *New Zealand Journal of Media Studies* 9.2: 27–35.

———. 2011. "Aotearoa/New Zealand: An Unsettled State in a Sea of Islands." *Settler Colonial Studies* 1: 111–131.

Smith, Jo T., and Joost De Bruin. 2011. "Survivor-styled Indigeneity in Two Reality Television Programmes from Aotearoa/New Zealand." *Australasian Journal of Popular Culture* 1.3: 297–311.

Smithies, Grant. 2014. "The Little Station That Could." *Sunday Star Times* 23 March. Accessed August 1, 2014. http://www.stuff.co.nz/entertainment/tv-radio/9854340/The-little-station-that-could

"Topp Country." 2014. *New Zealand on Air.* Website. Accessed July 22, 2015. http://www.nzonair.govt.nz/television/showcase/topp-country/

Turner, Richard James. 2011. "Non-Māori Viewing of Māori Television: An Empirical Analysis of the New Zealand Broadcast System." MA Thesis, Media Studies, Massey University.

Turner, Stephen. 1999. "Settlement as Forgetting." In *Quicksands: Foundational Histories in Australia and Aotearoa/New Zealand*, edited by Klaus Neumann, Nicholas Thomas, and Hilary Ericksen, 20–38. Sydney: University of New South Wales Press.

Vivanco, Luis A. 2004. "The Work of Environmentalism in an Age of Televisual Adventures." *Cultural Dynamics* 16.1: 5–27.

West, Amy. 2008. "Dream Home (Land): Anxious Fantasies of Settlement in Home Improvement Television." *New Zealand Journal of Media Studies* 11.2: 27–37.

8 Earth observation and signal territories

U.S. broadcast infrastructure, historical network maps, Google Earth, and fieldwork

Lisa Parks

Introduction

The Earth-observing computer platform Google Earth now has the ability to show a map of the United States with an application layer called FCCInfo activated. This Google Earth–FCCInfo interface reveals the country to be one giant *signal territory* – a landscape not only defined by its sovereign boundaries but also blanketed with color-coded icons and lines representing an array of broadcast facilities, including stations, towers, antennas, and microwave links. Such facilities are vital to the operation of broadcast systems and the production of media cultures. These facilities did not emerge overnight, however. They surfaced gradually over the past century as urban and rural communities developed radio and television stations both independently and in conjunction with national broadcast corporations. Each of the technological objects represented by color-coded balloons is embedded within a set of material conditions and local histories, within what Maxwell and Miller call a *"materialist ecology"* of media (2012, 9). In this sense, the Google Earth–FCCInfo interface serves as a discursive space for inquiry as it isolates and directs attention to a multitude of sites and objects that invite historical, critical, and phenomenological investigation.

Historically, such cartographic overviews of broadcast systems have been preserved for industry experts, whether corporate players, regulators, network administrators, or electrical engineers. The presentation of this information within publicly accessible digital platforms is a relatively recent practice that presents opportunities to research broadcast technologies in different ways. While most media scholars and consumers are familiar with radio and television receivers, computers, and mobile phones, fewer are familiar with the network infrastructures and localized sites that transmit signals to such devices. What would it mean to shift critical focus away from the fetishized objects of consumer electronics and toward the broadcast infrastructure sites that turn vast swaths of the Earth's surface into signal territories?

Building on work by communication scholars and cultural critics, I approach the practice of broadcasting as a technologized practice and material phenomenon that cannot be reduced to sites of the screen, the studio, or the home, but rather exists as an enduring potential in vertical space. Broadcasting is spectral, atmospheric, environmental, and ideological (Batchen 1997; Milutis 2006; Peters 1999). As broadcast signals move through the air, it is often hard to grasp them through our human senses. Their movements and trajectories must be put into perceivable forms or discourses, whether maps, visualizations, sounds, descriptions, or creative mediations. The process of transmission can only be perceived indirectly, inferred or intuited through discourse, and yet it is happening around us perpetually as we inhabit and move through various signal territories.

By engaging with different types of Earth-observing practices – historical network maps, Google Earth interfaces, and fieldwork – we can expand the repertoire of materials, sites, objects, and processes that media researchers tend to focus upon and, following Leigh Star, call for further exploration of the "boring" stuff of infrastructure (Star 1999; also see Marvin and Graham 2001, and Bowker et al. 2010). Since much information about U.S. broadcast infrastructure has historically been off limits or assumed to be of little interest to most people (particularly to women), I also want to assess the different kinds of *infrastructural intelligibilities* (Parks, 2015) that Earth-observing practices can help to generate. In charting the signal territory in this way, I hope to shift our critical practice beyond textual and screen-based media studies alone, which tend to privilege processes of production and consumption, or encoding and decoding, and work toward an analysis of technologies of distribution as well as toward more environmental and resource-based understandings of media (Bozak 2011; Cubitt 2005; Maxwell and Miller 2012). I also hope to build upon Nick Couldry's (2003) critique of the *mediated center* by concentrating upon facilities that are located on the outskirts or fringes of what media studies usually focuses its attention (or centers) on, but which are essential to media industries and the distribution of local, national, and global media cultures.

The chapter begins with a discussion of nineteenth- and early-twentieth-century maps of telegraphy, railroad, and radio networks to explore historical precursors to the Google Earth–FCCInfo interface and identify cartographic conventions for representing modern infrastructures of transportation and telecommunication. The second section situates Google Earth's capacity for infrastructure mapping within this longer history and explains how the Earth-observing platform is used to communicate information about U.S. broadcast infrastructure. The final section uses the Google Earth–FCCInfo interface as a springboard for a more phenomenological investigation and offers *new materialism's* "creative mediation" (Kember and Zylinska 2012) of a broadcast infrastructure site, approaching the technology in a more proximate and embodied manner. By moving to and around our case study site, the Google Earth–FCCInfo interface, investigating the resources and materials it is made of, and identifying the signals that it receives and transmits, we can approach the site as part of a broader *"media ecology"* (Fuller 2007) and set out to investigate its complex materialities (Coole and Frost 2010).

Historical network cartographies

During the past several decades, communication scholars have conducted key studies of broadcast systems, transoceanic cables, satellite constellations, and digital networks. Collectively, this path-breaking scholarship has examined the political and economic strategies that undergird national and international communication networks, the cultural impacts of their emergence, and the imperializing dimensions of their use. This work has articulated the rise of communication networks with the administrative maneuvers of nation-states and multinational corporations; processes of modernization, urbanization, and globalization; and various stages and forms of capitalism (Carey 1989; Castells 1996; Innis 1951; Mattelart 2000; Price 2002; Schiller 1969). Crucially, this scholarship has also delineated the relations between communication networks, geopolitics, and regulation.

What is often missing from this work, however, is a detailed investigation of the multiple ways that these infrastructures have historically become intelligible to citizen-consumers and intersect with cultures of everyday life, as well as a sense of the contrasts across industrialized and developing regions, rich and poor areas, urban and rural settings, and literate and oral cultures. I want to begin, then, by examining several U.S. *network maps* from the late nineteenth and early twentieth centuries. These maps approximated the vectors of transportation, commerce, and communication and developed a symbolic language that transformed massive, physically decentralized technological systems into icons that could fit within a visual frame. They not only provide a platform for thinking about the ways infrastructures have historically been rendered through cartographic practice, but also serve as telling precursors to Google Earth's FCCInfo layer as they foreground the scattered locations of infrastructures as well as issues of ownership, regulation, and technological literacy. Although there are many historical studies of infrastructures such as electrical grids (Hughes 1993), railroad tracks (Schivelbusch 1987), telephony (Fischer 1994), radio networks (Hilmes 2011), and global telecommunication systems (Headrick, 1981, 1988, 1991; Hugill 1999; Winseck and Pike 2007), there are fewer studies of the historical mapping of such systems (Challis and Rush 2009; Dodge and Kitchen 2004; Edney 1999).

Early network maps of the late nineteenth and early twentieth centuries, whether of telegraphy, railroad, and radio maps, were often hand-drawn and/or painted on paper. Mapmakers inscribed the locations of interlinked nodes (whether train, telegraph, or radio stations) upon national or regional maps of sovereign territories, constructing networked infrastructures as a set of distinct and isolated yet connected parts. The maps typically used simple arrangements of dots or circles (connoting a fixed site of activity) connected by lines (connoting dynamic movements or flows). Though railroad, telegraphy, and radio infrastructures were new in the nineteenth and early twentieth centuries, the cartographic template used to represent them arguably dates back centuries to celestial charts, tree of life diagrams (Harley and Woodward 1987), or medieval diagrams of pilgrimage routes (Connolly 2009). Nevertheless, network maps were significant in the nineteenth and early twentieth centuries as they not only documented infrastructural developments, but also gave them a concise visual form. Network infrastructures were dispersed across vast distances and operated at speeds and scales that were impossible to photographically record or perceive in their entirety (Kern 2003; Schivelbusch 1987; Warf 2008). Network cartographers abstracted these processes, enabling viewers to comprehend the spatial organization of new technologies of transportation and communication by implanting them within familiar cartographic spaces. In this sense, historical network maps were both crucially instructive and highly reductive: they offered static and remote overhead projections of massive and dynamic systems.

In addition to making new infrastructures legible, historical maps gave new meaning to and tested concepts such as sovereignty, national community, and locale as they inscribed new routes and connections within and between the boundaries of sovereign national territories. The network map was a highly contradictory discursive space. On the one hand, it projected a visual rhetoric of technological integration and unification, inscribing the trajectories of emerging systems upon maps of sovereign national boundaries, which were, in some cases, still being contested. On the other hand, as the network map transposed a series of new lines upon already existing national and state boundaries, it mobilized a visual logic of transection, division, and reorganization. The network map at once played a role in discursively securing or reinforcing sovereign boundaries by showcasing the telecommunication and transportation infrastructures that tethered distant sites together and challenged this integration by delineating an array of new boundaries and modes of organization. In this way, network maps articulated what James Hay (2012) has described as a *liberal democratic regime of communication*, one that celebrated the new freedoms of mobility afforded by modern transportation and communication technologies while reserving the right to use those very technologies to patrol, secure, and defend its sovereign boundaries (also see Chun 2008).

To provide a clearer sense of the function of these historical network maps, let's examine a few U.S. telegraphy, railroad, and radio maps from the late nineteenth and early twentieth centuries. These maps can be understood as historical precursors to the more contemporary Google Earth–FCCInfo interface since they employed similar cartographic conventions.

An 1853 map by Chas. B. Barr of Pittsburgh, for example, which showed the locations of telegraph stations in the United States, the Canadas, and Nova Scotia, represented the telegraph system as a series of black lines connected to black dots. These lines and dots, which represent transmission routes and telegraph stations, are layered onto a map of eastern and southern territories in North America to provide a sense of where telegraphic communication could or could not have happened on the continent during the middle of the nineteenth century. For instance, the map shows limited access in the Canadas and in southern parts of the U.S. and, in doing so, reveals the infrastructure to be limited and partial in its reach – as a ***differential infrastructure*** rather than a total one. Even as the map foregrounds telegraphy infrastructure's partiality, it unveils expansionist ambitions, for remarks in the map's legend indicate that 27,000 miles of U.S. telegraph line was in operation in 1853, with another 10,000 miles under construction. Other remarks highlight the planned expansion of the system across the American South and into Mexico and Cuba. Finally, details about ownership are conveyed: the legend indicates private party Morse owned 17,500 miles of the existing telegraph line and the U.S. House of Representatives owned the rest. Long before Google Earth, then, network infrastructures were layered onto territorial maps to reveal systems owned and operated by multiple corporate and government stakeholders.

A railroad map from 1876 by G. W. and C. B. Colton & Company used similar cartographic conventions to indicate the routes of the Southern Pacific Railroad Company. Southern Pacific's two main routes were layered onto a regional map of the western U.S. and are color-coded as blue and red lines. The routes of two other companies – Central Pacific and Texas and Pacific – appear in brown and yellow, respectively, conveying the multiple competing railroad companies in the American West. Remarks in the legend indicate the map was presented to the Judiciary Committee in connection with Southern Pacific's application for rights to pass through federal lands under Congressional Acts passed in 1866 and 1871. Thus as the map reveals Southern Pacific's routes, it also puts into visual discourse questions about land ownership, access, and regulation that are vital aspects of infrastructure development. Like the telegraphy map, this map foregrounds the limited reach and partiality of this emergent infrastructure, as most areas are untouched by the tracks. It shows Southern Pacific's tracks extending from south to north through the agricultural corridor of California's central valley, with interstate connections into Oregon and Nevada via the Central line and into Arizona via Texas and Pacific. As lines are inscribed on a map of the Western U.S. to signify tracks, they rewrite existing state boundaries, emphasizing the railroad's capacity to support interstate movement and commerce.

A third and final example brings us into the era of broadcasting. A 1937 map of the National Broadcasting Company's radio network used uniquely patterned black lines to indicate the locations of NBC's red and blue radio network facilities as well as "supplementary legs" that could be used with either network. The lines representing network transmission routes were layered onto an abstract map of the U.S. that was shaded in orange. Like the telegraphy map, the lines connect to dots that represent stations scattered across vast distances. While this map showcased NBC's national expansion, it offers less geographic detail than either of the other maps discussed, signaling a turn toward greater abstraction. Since this map featured the infrastructure of one privately owned radio network – NBC – and none of its competitors, it functions as a document of strategic corporate planning and/or promotion as it delineates and showcases the network's extensions and enterprises across the country. At the same time, however, like the other maps discussed earlier, this map implicitly reveals the partiality and unevenness of NBC's infrastructure, since vast swaths of the country remain beyond the network's reach. Although areas along the east and west coasts, in the upper Midwest, and in the southern U.S. were interlinked via NBC facilities in 1937, those in the West were less trafficked by the network's signals. What the map does not represent are the localized patterns of coverage surrounding each affiliate station, which vary from site to site and are contingent upon the position, design, licensing, and strength of the transmitter.

Long before the emergence of Google Earth, then, cartographers designed graphics and icons to signify network nodes and routes, devised practices for layering graphically rendered networks onto territorial maps, and used color-coding and other visual techniques to differentiate systems with unique owners or routes. These earlier maps circulated information about the location, ownership, expansion, and regulation (or lack thereof) of telegraphy, railroads, and radio and generated discursive spaces for deliberating and assessing the design and political, economic, and cultural effects of infrastructural developments. Historical maps of network infrastructures are instructive in several other ways as well. First, by inscribing emergent networks of telecommunication and transportation within cartography, these maps helped to evolve a visual language for representing national network systems. While today such systems can be observed with one satellite's pass, in the nineteenth century massive, dispersed systems that stretched across an entire continent in some cases were drawn by one person's hand. This fusion of an extensive, material infrastructure with an individual's perceptual and creative capacities speaks to the incredible challenge of infrastructural representation. While telegraphy and railroads helped to augur new perceptual modes and aesthetics articulated with "the annihilation of space and time" (Carey 1989; Innis 1951; Kern 2003), the map or diagram became the only visual discourse that could represent the vastness of these new national systems in a single frame.

Second, and relatedly, historical maps provided a discursive space for articulating infrastructural specifications. As telecommunication and radio networks expanded and grew more complex, a standardized visual language for representing their internal circuitry emerged so that engineers could consistently convey the structure, function, and dynamism of different network nodes and operations. As Edward Jones-Imhotep observes, "Drawings were not just sites where concepts and ideas were worked out – they were instruments through which materials and objects gained meaning and acted back upon the drawings themselves" (2008, 449). He continues, "Drawings were the places where electronics were first (imaginatively) assembled, erased, operated, and reconfigured, and therefore a key site for contest over the meaning of the devices that went into them" (2008, 450).

By the mid-1950s networks were no longer only projected onto territorial maps, they were also increasingly splayed open, so to speak, and given their own semi-cartographic practice as electronic engineers – who also had to be trained as creators and readers of such diagrams – invented a language for delineating their internal dynamics. This meant that physical objects and processes were translated into standardized sets of symbols and icons that were designed to enable quick understandings of the structure and dynamism of these systems. Like the historical network map, the circuit diagram privileged abstraction over realism, resonating with Joe Milutis's observation that "[a] network, in a sense, is a pure abstraction, no longer determined by topography. It is a system of etherealized signs" (2006, 153).

Third, and finally, historical network maps signaled their own proprietary character, which was encoded through the inscription of the cartographer's name in the map's visual field. As cartographers visualized emerging infrastructures owned by competing parties, they were at the same time enacting their own property claims in an economy of signs – staking out intellectual property. While in the nineteenth century individuals or small companies produced network maps, by the late twentieth century the mapping of telecommunication and broadcasting systems had become a full-fledged industry. Today, large private firms such as Choisser, Geospatial Broadcasting Network, Analytic Graphics, Inc., and Telegeography are contracted by media and telecommunication corporations and regulatory agencies to produce local, national, and transnational maps of systems around the globe. Such maps are not only used to specify network locations and configurations, but are also instrumental in corporate planning and strategizing (Dodge and Kitchen 2004) and, as a result, have become increasingly proprietary and inaccessible to most people. As the privatization and abstraction of network mapping intensifies, it arguably becomes more challenging for citizens to gain access to information about the locations, ownership, operation, and regulation of infrastructures, which is problematic given that citizens subsidize, use, and are surrounded by infrastructures in everyday life. This is one of the reasons that Google Earth is a provocative space for thinking about infrastructural intelligibility: it has the potential to extend public access to and knowledge of network cartographies.

Unearthing U.S. broadcast infrastructure

When Google Earth first emerged in 2005, geographers suggested that the virtual globe would have the potential to catalyze greater public involvement in mapping and celebrated it as bolstering practices of participatory or volunteer geography that had begun with geographic information systems (Elwood 2009; Goodchild 2007). At the same time, however, since Google Earth relies on an international user community to produce content known as *layers* – geo-referenced datasets accompanied by graphics and icons formatted as kmz files that can be viewed in the platform – it also relies upon the *free labor* of Internet users – the uncompensated expenditures of human energy/time/attention, which, Tiziana Terranova argues, have become a defining condition of network culture (2004). Although some have lauded Google Earth's participatory structures, others have critiqued the platform's implicit disregard for national sovereignty, highlighting the opposition of countries such as Australia, India, Morocco, and South Korea to Google's release of high-resolution geospatial imagery of their sovereign territories, including sites deemed critical to national security (Kumar 2010; Parks 2012). Still others have discussed Google Earth as an Apollonian eye in the sky or as part of a neo-Baroque aesthetic. As Leon Gurevitch observes, "The digital globe interface communicates with renewed vigour the centrality of the human agent, elevating the scopic powers of that agent through an interface that deploys a 'code of spectacular vision' inherited from Renaissance perspective" (2013).

Rather than approach Google Earth in broad brushstrokes, let's focus on one layer called FCCInfo. We can explore how this layer structures and communicates information about contemporary U.S. broadcast infrastructure. Furthermore, we can assess whether FCCInfo has the potential to extend technological literacies and materialist understandings of signal distribution practices beyond a community of experts. FCCInfo was created by the private consulting firm Cavell, Mertz, & Associates and was made available as a free download in 2009. Based in Manassas, Virginia, Cavell, Mertz, & Associates' mission is "to assist industry leaders in navigating the complexity of today's broadcast and information platforms," and the company took on this project for the FCC to promote its mapping and consulting services (2015).

The FCCInfo layer generates an interactive cartographic display of all registered and licensed radio and TV stations, antennas, towers, and microwave broadcast facilities in the United States. Color-coded balloons are used to represent different parts of the broadcast system. AM radio stations are represented in purple balloons, FM radio stations in green, TV stations in red, and registered towers in orange. Microwave links are represented in light blue, lavender, and pink. The layer also provides pop-up windows offering detailed information about each structure and site, including the type of structure, height above ground level, height above mean sea level, the channel, and the owner of the structure. Through the pop-up window the user can click on a hyperlink to an FCC website with even more data about the particular structure and site and its licensing history. The user can also zoom in on specific network nodes or facilities and acquire aerial and, in some cases, street-view perspectives of broadcast infrastructure sites.

Never before have U.S. citizens, or members of the international community, for that matter, had such direct and immediate access to information about U.S. broadcast infrastructure, in both well-known urban media hubs and smaller, rural media markets.

To explore the FCCInfo layer in greater detail, we'll consider the representation of broadcast infrastructure sites in my hometown media market of Santa Barbara, California. Using Google Earth's navigation features, I zoomed from a national perspective to a local overview of this relatively small media market of 80,000 situated on the central coast of California, sandwiched between the denser signal territories of Los Angeles to the south and San Francisco to the north. Santa Barbara has two main transmission facilities located on the mountains above the city, which are in or adjacent to the Los Padres National Forest. One is located to the northeast and one to the southeast. Both of these facilities transmit signals to radio and TV stations in Santa Barbara and to other nearby towns (such as Solvang, Santa Ynez, and Ventura) via microwave links.

By zooming in on one of these facilities, it is possible to obtain a more detailed understanding of the signal traffic in this market as icons draw attention to different structures and transmissions. A close analysis of the facility on Gibraltar Road reveals there are twenty FM radio transmissions, twelve TV transmissions, eight microwave, and three registered towers. Clicking on any of the Google Earth balloon icons allows the user to hyperlink to FCCInfo.com, where further data about the licensee and the licensed structure can be found. For instance, by clicking on KJEE, we find a commercial FM radio station based in Montecito, California, that has been operating since 1994. The station also has a microwave link that connects to its parent facility on West Carrillo Street in Santa Barbara.

By isolating different broadcast systems (radio, TV, microwave), facilities (stations, towers, links), sites (urban, rural), and processes (transmission, repeating, linking), the FCCInfo layer compels a site-specific, object-oriented, and ecological approach to the study of broadcasting. If integrated within media studies courses, the layer could help students conceptualize and research broadcasting not only in relation to what appears in the frame or through the speaker, but also as property claims, transmission processes, spectrum and resource allocations, maintenance labor, and signal traffic. Approaching a location as a signal territory requires an investigation of the multiple signals being transmitted through the air in a location of any given moment, the technological and natural resources that are required to do so, and the spatiotemporal dimensions of transmission. Signal territories exist across urban and rural, wealthy and poor, local and national, terrestrial and circumterrestrial domains. They are fields shaped by human and nonhuman actors, perceptible and imperceptible activities. Signal territories cannot be seen with the naked eye; rather, they must be produced discursively or through phenomenological inquiry. In general, their presence must be inferred rather than observed. By examining the Google Earth–FCCInfo interface, it is possible to perceive Santa Barbara not only as a city with a particular location, population, and climate, but also as a particular kind of signal territory.

Just as the Google Earth and FCCInfo can be thought about as producing signal territories, it is important to consider the multiple industrial and governmental entities whose interests are transparently embedded within the interface, including broadcasters, transmission facility owners, satellite and aircraft operators, geospatial imaging firms, cartographers, software developers, Internet service providers, and regulatory agencies. Indeed, the Google Earth–FCCInfo interface interweaves multiple corporate and governmental entities (broadcasters, digital corporations, satellite operators, regulators), technologies (remote sensing, broadcasting, cartography, Internet service), and discursive strategies (Earth observation, market development, and public education) and, in the process, produces maps of broadcast infrastructure in a highly proprietary fashion.

Even though Google Earth offers the basic version of its virtual globe platform as a free download, clearly none of this is free. To access the Google Earth–FCCInfo interface, users must own or have access to a computer and an Internet connection. Once this access is established, the user can navigate public domain data (the locations of all licensed broadcast facilities) gathered by a federal governmental agency (the Federal Communications Commission). This information has been restructured as a layer by a private third party (Mertz, etc.) and can only be accessed and viewed on a privately owned yet publicly accessible web-based platform (Google Earth), which is composited from geospatial data that has been acquired by satellites historically subsidized by taxpayers. When this public domain FCC data is accessed and viewed in Google Earth, it becomes the privately owned intellectual property of Google, despite the fact that it is layered upon geospatial imagery and distributed through Internet networks that have historically been funded by taxpayers and consumers.

Although all U.S. broadcast facilities are now fully displayed in Google Earth, interestingly, the array of facilities, data centers, and server farms that makes Google Earth possible is *not* organized as a layer, hinting at the proprietary and strategic nature of this information – and the risks that such a layer might pose to Google's security, particularly given the world's growing dependence on Google's search engines, clouds, mapping, file sharing, and email services (Hillis, Petit, and Jarrett 2012). Google Earth is generated through an assemblage that includes aerial and satellite imaging technologies, transmission facilities, data storage centers, computer processing, software and applications, high-speed Internet networks, lands, spectrum, and myriad forms of labor.

Though Google Earth's infrastructure has not been organized as a layer, it is possible to view some of Google's data centers in Google Earth. Overhead views of facilities in Lenoir, North Carolina, and Council Bluffs, Iowa, resemble military installations enclosed by security gates, echoing the

"*closed world*" discourses that characterized visions of networked computing during the Cold War (Edwards 1997). In 2012 Google opened up some
of these sites and released a series of lustrous, color photographs of its data
centers' interiors. These photographs enable viewers to peer inside Google's
infrastructure sites in Iowa, Oregon, Georgia, South Carolina, Oklahoma,
Belgium, and Finland and vibrantly showcase the blocs of servers, fiber
optic cables, LED lights, and color-coded cooling systems that support platforms like Google Earth. Not unlike the historical map of NBC's radio network facilities, these photos function first and foremost as publicity shots.
They construct Google's infrastructure as a sleek, perfectly lit, machinic
playground, but offer scant detail about its historical development, costs,
and/or resource requirements.

Another important dimension of Google Earth's infrastructure is the
constellation of remote-sensing satellites orbiting the Earth. In 2008 AGI
Analytics released a Google Earth layer (kmz file) that maps all known satellites in orbit and refreshes their position in real time. While navigating
this layer, a user can locate the very satellite(s) that acquired the image data
used to constitute the Google Earth interface. In this context, Google Earth
functions as a kind of overview mirror that exposes and directs attention
to the orbital infrastructure that enables users to observe and navigate the
world in this way (Parks 2013). To acquire a comprehensive understanding
of Google Earth's infrastructure, then, it is necessary to piece together its
various pieces and parts, which extend from data centers on the ground to
satellites in orbit and from sites in Oregon to others in Finland.

While the FCC gathers data on all broadcast facilities because it licenses
and ostensibly regulates them, the Commission's authority over Google
is less pronounced. The FCC has asserted very little regulatory authority
over Google as the company has established monopolies over the Internet
search engine and the virtual globe. A Google search of the terms "FCC
and Google" turns up a handful of articles about Google having its hand
slapped by the FCC after the company was discovered to have gathered private data from households via Wi-Fi during data collection for Street View
between 2007 and 2010. Even though Google flagrantly violated privacy
laws, the FCC fined the company a mere $25,000 for impeding a federal
investigation by not producing information that had been requested (Streitfeld 2012). As Vaidhyanathan suggests, "Google insists on being regulated
at the lowest level, specifying a one-size-fits-all prescription to regulate its
complex interactions with real human beings and their diverse needs. . . .
Through its remarkable cultural power, Google has managed to keep much
regulatory action at bay around the world" (2011, 48). To be sure, Google
has risen to dominance in a media environment characterized by massive
deregulation that began during the Reagan era and has only intensified in
recent years (Holt 2011). One could read the FCCInfo layer as symptomatic
of Google's symbolic absorption of broadcasting and the diminishing power
and authority of the FCC, or as the FCC's struggle for relevance during an

era in which the digital behemoth threatens to transform everything from broadcast facilities to the FCC into intellectual property that is only accessible through Google.

Infrastructure, fieldwork, and creative mediation

While the Google Earth–FCCInfo interface provokes a consideration of various proprietary and regulatory issues, it also enables users to glimpse the thousands of individual physical installations that make up the U.S. broadcast system and compels phenomenological investigations. In this section, I present findings based on a visit to a transmission facility I first encountered in Google Earth. The results of the site visit are intended to infuse the Earth-observing platform with situated knowledge and affective engagements – to "unfreeze" infrastructure (Star 1999) using a *node-centric approach* (King 2006) that explores the material conditions that support and surround a single broadcast infrastructure site.

Inspired by the recent work of Sarah Kember and Joanna Zylinska, I set out to develop a *"creative mediation"* – a form of "media analysis" that is "simultaneously critical and creative" (2012, xvii) and that *"seeks to promote the invention of different forms of engagement with media"* (2012, 203). In their 2012 book *Life After New Media*, Kember and Zylinska challenge conventional forms of media analysis and call for "a more dynamic, networked, and engaged mode of working on and with 'the media,' in which critique is always already accompanied by the work of participation and invention" (203). Rather than approach media as static objects, they urge us to reflect upon the vital processes of mediation, which we, as critics, are always already implicated within. They argue for "envisaging and enacting playful, experimental, yet rigorous cross-disciplinary interventions and inventions that will be equally at home with critical theory and media practice and that will be prepared to and able to make a difference – academically, institutionally, politically, ethically, and aesthetically" (2012, 201).

Beginning with a printed screenshot of the Google Earth–FCCInfo interface (see Figure 8.1), I drove into the hills above Santa Barbara along the curvy Gibraltar road to the transmission site turnoff. There I found an open gate with a sign that read NO TRESPASSING! VIOLATORS WILL BE PROSECUTED!! If I drove down the road I would apparently be breaking the law, which was ironic given that the site is owned by an organization called Community Radio, Inc. Since the gate was open, I drove half a mile down the very narrow recently paved road and parked my car so that I could walk up the rest of the driveway to the facility. As I walked up the final stretch of the road, I encountered a series of signs on the fence warning "Radio frequency fields beyond this point may exceed the FCC general public exposure limit." Other signs indicated CAUTION – HIGH LEVEL RADIO FREQUENCY ENERGY AREA – NO TRESPASSING in English and Spanish. I continued to the end of the road and discovered a second gate (see Figure 8.2), this one closed and locked,

Figure 8.1 Creative mediation of broadcast infrastructure site.
Source: Photos by the author.

with posted information about the site administrator and more warning signs. I also found a wooden box next to the fence with a white notebook inside used by site workers to sign in and out during their visits. The sheet was empty. Since I could not get in the main locked gate, I started to return to my car. As I was walking I noticed a side fence had been left open (see Figure 8.3, top left) and decided to venture inside to get a closer glimpse of the medley of towers, antennas, and dishes on site. They appeared in different shapes and sizes and were painted matte gray or white or were aluminum so that they camouflaged in with the area and were difficult to see from a distance, calling forth the kinds of complex plays of visibility and invisibility that Hanna Rose Shell explores in her cultural history of camouflage, *Hide and Seek* (2012). A rickety wood scaffolding supported some of the antennas, suggesting that the site's elevation was not high enough for some transmission needs. I also noticed jumbled debris and unused material strewn about the site, including piping, bricks, and metal parts (see Figure 8.3).

While walking around I acquired a more proximate, physical sense of the site. I could hear the buzz of electrical equipment, feel the burning heat of the mid-afternoon sun baking the pavement, smell the scent of warm chaparral bush mixed with ocean air, and see massive power lines stretching across the hillsides and three large transmission towers farther up the

Figure 8.2 Creative mediation of broadcast infrastructure site showing fence and
warning signs.

Source: Photos by the author.

mountain. While approaching the facility, I was not entirely sure whether I
was on private or public land, what the penalties for trespassing would be,
and whether there were serious health hazards linked to being close to transmission sites. My wandering led me to think about broadcast infrastructure
very differently than when I viewed it in Google Earth. Rather than a massive system that could be seen from above, infrastructure became something
that could be sensed, felt, and mediated by my own body. Mapping the
signal territory in this more affective and physical way required recognizing
that the site, which looked quite orderly in Google Earth, was actually quite
eclectic and messy on the ground (Figure 8.3), a scattered archaeology of
transmission equipment that was more akin to "high-tech ramshackle" or
"twenty-first-century hillbilly." The visit also challenged me to think about
the biotechnical dimensions of broadcasting. This infrastructure site is not
only made of metals, plastics, rubber, and electromagnetic fields, but also of

Figure 8.3 Creative mediation of broadcast infrastructure showing open fence and materials on site.

Source: Photos by the author.

soil, rock, vegetation, insects, lizards, birds, and animals, organic materials and life forms that cannot be perceived in Google Earth and are not typically thought of as part of a media ecology.

As my fieldwork around the site tuned me in to the biotechnical dimensions of this tiny sliver of U.S. broadcast infrastructure, it also enabled me to think about issues that I would never have considered by examining this site only in Google Earth. Some key aspects of the site were completely invisible in Google Earth. The series of gates and trespassing signs I encountered in geophysical space, for instance, contrasted with unfettered access to the site in digital space. The pieces of hardware represented by color-coded balloons in Google Earth were camouflaged at the site so that they blended in with the local environs, and since they were fenced off, they were more difficult to see and identify. High-voltage currents and electrical radiation were announced as human health hazards at the site (yet were apparently safe for other wildlife in the vicinity), but were absent in Google Earth. The contingency of this facility's operations upon other infrastructures (see Figure 8.4) such as the electrical grid, water sewer system, and fixed telephony was not evident in Google Earth but became clear during the site visit. And, finally, the sound of broadcast infrastructure – the persistent

Figure 8.4 Creative mediation of broadcast infrastructure site showing environs and
          water and electrical infrastructure.

Source: Photos by the author.

ambient buzz of electrical activity – which provides an acoustic sense that
something dynamic is happening, is altogether missing from the Google
Earth–FCCInfo interface. While I was there I could not help but imagine the
initial installation of equipment at the site, the upgrading of that equipment,
and physical manipulation of transmitters and antennas that make broadcasting possible. In this sense, the site visit also evoked a history of labor –
electrical engineering and maintenance – that is increasingly being replaced
by sensors and computers that can be used to monitor such sites remotely.

Most of all, the site visit led me to consider the importance of *fieldwork* as
a vital method for investigating media technologies. In an era in which the
world can be navigated in Google Earth and seen in Street View, accessed
through Google's search engines, or streamed from YouTube's archives,
media researchers seem to spend more time than ever at screen and computer interfaces, and less and less time venturing out in the field, wherever
it may be. It is worth thinking carefully about how our critical practices
and methods are shaped and informed not only by our social subjectivities,
technological literacies, and intellectual training, but also by the geophysical
positions we are willing to engage with, occupy, or explore. How often do
we move beyond what Mark Andrejevic calls the **digital enclosure** (2009)
or what Nick Couldry calls the mediated center (2003)? If we are willing

to take seriously the fusion of the biological and the technological, it is important to consider not only how consumer electronics become human prostheses but also how automated facilities on the outskirts of cities that are dug deep into the dirt and surrounded by plants and wildlife – seemingly in the middle of nowhere – are integral to broadcasting in the digital age. In this sense, my project is invested in what Diana Coole and Samantha Frost refer to as *"new materialisms,"* which, as they explain, bring "biopolitics, critical geopolitics, and political economy together with genealogies and phenomenologies of everyday life" (2010, 28). By thinking and moving between historical network maps, the Google Earth–FCCInfo interface, and a specific infrastructure site, we can begin to recognize and investigate the ways in which resources such as lands, water, electricity, heavy metals, and other materials are organized to transmit signals and, in the process, turn the Earth's surface into signal territories. As Maxwell and Miller insist, "[U]nderstanding media requires studying them up, down, and sideways" (2012, 17).

Conclusion: Infrastructure resocialization

Though infrastructures have become part of the built environment and surround us in daily life, the public is socialized to know very little about their development, operations, and resource requirements. By highlighting multiple modes of infrastructure mapping, I hope to encourage *infrastructure resocialization* – a technological literacy project that urges the public to notice, document, and ask questions about infrastructure sites and become involved in discussions and deliberations about their funding, design, installation, operation, and use. Most people in the U.S. are familiar with commercial television and radio, but relatively few have ever visited a TV or radio station, attended municipal hearings to comment on cable operator franchises, or followed FCC proceedings on spectrum auctions and allocations. There is a serious disjuncture between the amount of public time and attention dedicated to screened entertainment and the amount of public time and attention dedicated to understanding the facilities and sites that distribute the signals that become entertainment. In public life and critical media studies alike, we need a firmer understanding of where and how media distribution has historically occurred in the U.S. and beyond (Sterne 1999). This will involve studying media technologies in relation to a wider array of industrial sectors such as real estate, energy, electrical engineering, architecture, design, public health, and security.

In addition, rather than approach Earth-observing practices only as *representing* infrastructure sites and processes, we need to understand these practices as *performative acts* that have different relations to time, which need to be specified and considered. That is, the drawing of a map of telegraphy stations, the compositing of aerial and satellite images and layering of icons to construct broadcast infrastructure in a digital Earth, or the visiting and photographing of an infrastructure site are all performative acts in time that are aimed not only at "representing" but also at enabling certain capacities and potentials. As such, they are what Kember and Zylinska refer to as *vital mediations*. As Kember and Zylinska explain, "[M]ediation becomes a key trope for understanding and articulating our being in, and becoming with, the technological world, our emergence and ways of interacting with it, as well as the acts and processes of temporality stabilizing the world into media, agents, relations, and networks" (2012, xv). The more ways in which infrastructures can be perceived, sensed, felt, and understood as part of life, the more potential there is for the public to reflect upon and intervene in their complex materialities and temporalities. This article closes, then, with a call for further creative mediations of the infrastructures that surround us.

Keywords

Closed world or mediated center
Creative mediation
Differential infrastructure
Infrastructural intelligence
Infrastructure resocialization
Layers and free labor

Materialist ecology
New materialisms
Node-centric approach
Performative acts
Signal territory

Discussion questions

1 Trace the signal territory of your cell phone provider. Discuss what such a territory would include and what research you would do to track down its characteristics.
2 Explore Google Earth's FCCInfo layer to learn more about your hometown's broadcast infrastructure. If possible, conduct fieldwork to explore the nearest infrastructure site – does this fieldwork add or alter your online experience? Explain how your understanding of infrastructure might be changed by fieldwork.
3 What do the similarities and differences between the telegraphy, railroad, and radio maps from the late nineteenth and early twentieth centuries and twenty-first-century Google Earth maps suggest about ways we think about or ignore the material impacts of these mediated technologies? Consider the aesthetics of the cartographic conventions Parks discusses as you respond.

Note

This chapter is an updated and condensed version of an article that originally appeared in the *Canadian Journal of Communication*, Volume 38, 2013.

References

Andrejevic, Marc. 2009. *iSpy: Surveillance and Power in the Interactive Era*. Lawrence, KS: University Press of Kansas.

Batchen, Geoffrey. 1997. "Da(r)ta." *Afterimage* 24.6: 6–7.

Bowker, Geoffrey C., Karen Baker, Florence Millerand, and David Ribes. 2010. "Toward Information Infrastructure Studies: Ways of Knowing in a Networked Environment." In *International Handbook of Internet Research*, edited by Jeremy Hunsinger, Lisbeth Klastrup, and Matthew Allen, 97–117. Netherlands: Springer Science.

Bozak, Nadia. 2011. *The Cinematic Footprint: Lights, Camera, Natural Resources*. New Brunswick, NJ: Rutgers University Press.

Carey, James. 1989. *Communication as Culture*. New York: Routledge.

Castells, Manuel. 1996. *The Rise of the Network Society*. Cambridge, MA: Blackwell.

Cavell, Mertz, & Associates website. 2015. Accessed February 14, 2015. http://www.cavellmertz.com/index.php?action=M

Challis, David Milbank, and Andy Rush. 2009. "The Railways of Britain: An Unstudied Map Corpus." *Imago Mundi: The International Journal for the History of Cartography* 61.2: 186–214.

Chun, Wendy. 2008. *Control and Freedom: Power and Paranoia in the Age of Fiber Optics*. Cambridge, MA: MIT Press.

Connolly, Daniel K. 2009. *The Maps of Matthew Paris: Medieval Journeys through Space, Time and Liturgy*. Woodbridge, UK: Boydell Press.

Coole, Diana, and Samantha Frost. 2010. *New Materialisms: Ontology, Agency, and Politics*. Durham, NC: Duke University Press.

Couldry, Nick. 2003. *Media Rituals: A Critical Approach*. London: Routledge.

Cubitt, Sean. 2005. *EcoMedia*. Amsterdam, Netherlands: Rodopi.

Dodge, Martin, and Rob Kitchen. 2004. "Charting Movement: Mapping Internet Infrastructure." In *Moving People, Goods and Information in the 21st Century: The Cutting Edge Infrastructures of Networked Cities*, edited by Richard E. Haley, 159–185. New York: Routledge.

Edney, Matthew. 1999. *Mapping an Empire: The Geographical Construction of British India, 1765–1843*. Chicago: University of Chicago Press.

Edwards, Paul. 1997. *The Closed World: Computers and the Politics of Discourse in Cold War America*. Cambridge, MA: MIT Press.

Elwood, S. 2009. "Geographic Information Science: New Geovisualization Technologies – Emerging Questions and Linkages with GIScience Research." *Progress in Human Geography* 33: 256–263.

Fischer, Claude S. 1994. *America Calling: A Social History of the Telephone to 1940*. Berkeley, CA: University of California Press.

Fuller, Mathew. 2007. *Media Ecologies: Materialist Energies in Art and Technoculture*. Cambridge, MA: MIT Press.

Goodchild, M. 2007. "Citizens as Sensors: The World of Volunteered Geography." *GeoJournal* 69: 211–221.

Gurevitch, Leon. 2013. "The Digital Globe as Climatic Coming Attraction: From Theatrical Release to Theatre of War." *Canadian Journal of Communication* 38.3: 333–356.

Harley, J. B., and David Woodward, eds. 1987. *The History of Cartography: Vol. 1. Cartography in Prehistoric, Ancient, and Medieval Europe and the Mediterranean*. Chicago: University of Chicago Press.

Hay, James. 2012. "The Invention of Air Space, Outer Space, and Cyberspace." In *Down to Earth: Satellite Technologies, Industries, and Cultures*, edited by Lisa Parks and James Schowch, 19–41. New Brunswick, NJ: Rutgers University Press.

Headrick, Daniel R. 1981. *The Tools of Empire: Technology and European Imperialism in the Nineteenth Century*. New York: Oxford University Press.

———. 1988. *The Tentacles of Progress: Technology Transfer in the Age of Imperialism, 1850–1940*. New York: Oxford University Press.

———. 1991. *The Invisible Weapon: Telecommunications and International Politics, 1851–1945*. New York: Oxford University Press.

Hillis, Ken, Michael Petit, and Kylie Jarrett. 2012. *Google and the Culture of Search*. London: Routledge.

Hilmes, Michele. 2011. *Network Nations: A Transnational History of British and American Broadcasting*. New York: Routledge.

Holt, Jennifer. 2011. *Empires of Entertainment: Media Industries and the Politics of Deregulation, 1980–1996*. New Brunswick, NJ: Rutgers University Press.

Hughes, Thomas. 1993. *Networks of Power: Electrification in Western Society, 1880–1930*. Baltimore: Johns Hopkins University Press.

Hugill, P. 1999. *Global Communications since 1844: Geopolitics and Technology*. Baltimore: Johns Hopkins University Press.

Innis, Harold A. 1951. *The Bias of Communication*. Toronto, ON: University of Toronto Press.

Jones-Imhotep, Edward. 2008. "Icons and Electronics." *Historical Studies in the Natural Sciences* 38.3: 405–450.

Kember, Sarah, and Joanna Zylinska. 2012. *Life after New Media: Mediation as a Vital Process*. Cambridge, MA: MIT Press.

Kern, Stephen. 2003. *The Culture of Time and Space, 1880–1918*. Cambridge, MA: Harvard University Press.

King, J. J. 2006. "The Node Knows." In *Else/where Mapping: Mapping New Cartographies of Networks and Territories*, edited by Janet Abrams and Peter Hall, 44–49. Minneapolis, MN: University of Minnesota Design Institute.

Kumar, Sangeet. 2010. "Google Earth and the Nation State: Sovereignty in the Age of New Media." *Global Media and Communication* 6.2:154–176.

Marvin, Simon, and Stephen Graham. 2001. *Splintering Urbanism: Networked Infrastructures, Technological Mobilities, and the Urban Condition*. London: Routledge.

Mattelart, Armand. 2000. *Networking the World, 1794–2000*. Minneapolis, MN: University of Minnesota Press.

Maxwell, Richard, and Toby Miller. 2012. *Greening the Media*. Oxford: Oxford University Press.

Milutis, Joe. 2006. *Ether: The Nothing That Connects Everything*. Minneapolis, MN: University of Minnesota Press.

Parks, Lisa. 2012. "Zeroing In: Overhead Imagery and Infrastructural Ruins in Afghanistan and Iraq." In *The Visual Culture Reader, 3.0.*, edited by Nicholas Mirzoeff, 196–206. London: Routledge.

Parks, Lisa. 2013. "Mapping Orbit: Toward a Vertical Public Space." In *Public Space, Media Space*, edited by Chris Berry, Janet Harbord, and Rachel O. Moore, 61–87. New York: Palgrave Macmillan.

Parks, Lisa. 2015. "'Stuff You Can Kick': Toward a Theory of Media Infrastructures." In *Between Humanities and the Digital*, edited by David Theo Goldberg and Patrik Svensson, 355–373. Cambridge, MA: MIT Press.

Peters, John Durham. 1999. *Speaking into the Air: A History of the Idea of Communication*. Chicago: University of Chicago Press.

Price, Monroe. 2002. *Media and Sovereignty: The Global Information Revolution and its Challenge to State Power*. Boston, MA: MIT Press.

Schiller, Herbert. 1969. *Mass Communications and American Empire*. New York: Augustus M. Keeley Publishers.

Schivelbusch, Wolfgang. 1987. *The Railway Journey: The Industrialization and Perception of Time and Space*. Berkeley, CA: University of California Press.

Shell, Hanna Rose. 2012. *Hide and Seek: Camouflage, Photography and the Media of Reconnaissance*. New York: Zone Books.

Star, Susan Leigh. 1999. "The Ethnography of Infrastructure." *American Behavioral Scientist* 43.4: 377–391.

Sterne, Jonathan. 1999. "Television under Construction: American Television and the Problem of Distribution, 1926–62." *Media, Culture & Society* 21.4: 503–530.

Streitfeld, David. 2012. "Google Is Faulted for Impeding U.S. Inquiry on Data Collection." *The New York Times*. Accessed November 1, 2012. http://www.nytimes.com/2012/04/15/technology/google-is-fined-for-impeding-us-inquiry-on-data-collection.html?pagewanted=all&_r=0

Terranova, Tiziana. 2004. *Network Culture: Politics for the Information Age*. London: Pluto Press.

Vaidhyanathan, Siva. 2011. *The Googlization of Everything*. Berkeley, CA: University of California Press.

Warf, Barney. 2008. *Time Space Compression: Historical Geographies*. London: Routledge.

Winseck, Dwayne R., and Robert M. Pike. 2007. *Communication and Empire: Media, Markets, and Globalization, 1860–1930*. Durham, NC: Duke University Press.

Part III
Convergence

9 Overview

Bert versus the Black Phoenix: an introduction to convergence and ecomedia

Anthony Lioi

Introduction

In the last decade, ecocriticism has gone "farther afield" from its founding concern with canonical national literatures and print culture (Murphy 2000, 1–11). The emergence of scholarship on film, music, and photography demonstrated the power of the environmental humanities as a mode of Green cultural studies, and coincided with a focus on environmental justice and eco-cosmopolitanism. Nonetheless, ecocriticism has been slow to theorize the *movement* of texts, images, and narratives through digital and other popular media. The concept of the literary work is itself part of the problem, because literary scholars are trained to work on objects, not processes. An analogy to the history of Western classical music is instructive. The philosopher Lydia Goehr (2007) argues that the concept of music as made of "works" solidified around 1800 as part of the Enlightenment reification of culture into discreet objects, both ideal and material (13). From this philosophy, it follows that performances are ephemeral, and therefore of lesser value than the work itself, which endures past any instantiation. Goehr demonstrates that the classical tradition is still dominated by this set of assumptions. In response, Christopher Small (1998) offers the concept of "musicking," which seeks to recover the value of *performance-in-community* as a framework for music analysis (1–18). The tension between work and event also appears in literary and media studies. Though one might argue about the exact moment the literary "work" turned into an object in North Atlantic cultures, such a moment had occurred by the time vernacular literary study emerged at the end of the nineteenth century. The literary work, not the act of reading or performing, became the center of literary study. This heritage proves a stumbling block for the understanding of cultural transmission in the era of digital media, and ecocriticism has suffered for it. As a discipline, we have failed to theorize the dynamics of ecomedia. We still imagine criticism as the installation of new masters at the eternal banquet, after T. S. Eliot's "Tradition and the Individual Talent," rather than considering ephemera. To remedy this problem, we should learn from the work of Henry Jenkins, a media studies scholar and a theorist of "*convergence culture*." According to Jenkins (2008), convergence culture has three components: *media convergence, participatory culture*, and *collective intelligence* (22). I will discuss each of these concepts and demonstrate that the movement of media content destabilizes the boundary between high and low culture, shifts the ground of interpretation, and expands the agency of activists.

Media convergence

By *media convergence*, Jenkins means "the flow of content across multiple media platforms, the cooperation between multiple media industries, and the migratory behavior of media audiences who will go almost anywhere in search of the kind of entertainment experiences they want" (Jenkins 2008, 2). This definition reflects a foundation in cultural studies and anthropology. Jenkins' earlier work investigated the behavior of fan groups relative to the pop-culture phenomena they follow, such as *Star Trek* or *Harry Potter*. Jenkins used ethnographic methods to record fan behavior in the manner an earlier generation of anthropologists had used to investigate non-Western cultures. Jenkins' work is descriptive and nonjudgmental in the style of the participant-observer. In doing so, he does not treat such cultural phenomena as separate from the global marketplace. However, unlike his predecessors in the Frankfurt School, he does not condemn the products of mass culture as ideological artifacts. Nor does he assume that fans and the media they consume can exist in a realm of high culture that transcends the philistine market. He conceives of media, industries, and audiences as part of a larger system of production and consumption with the potential for good and bad effects. He draws our attention to stochastic patterns of media content that travel in unexpected ways across borders of genre and nation.

His first example of convergence involves "Evil Bert," an image of the Muppet from *Sesame Street* that was uploaded to the Internet by Dino Ignacio, a Filipino-American student, in the fall of 2001. Ignacio posted images of Bert juxtaposed with terrorist leader Osama bin Laden among other figures, such as Hitler, the Unabomber, and Pamela Anderson (Jenkins 2008, 1). In the aftermath of the September 11 attacks on the World Trade Center, a publisher in Bangladesh searched for bin Laden images to print out for anti-American protests. Ignacio's images of Bert and bin Laden then appeared on posters throughout the Middle East during protests that were covered by CNN. Though the Children's Television Workshop (CTW), which owns the copyright on Bert, pursued legal action against this breach of intellectual property rights, Jenkins notes that it is not clear exactly which perpetrators they could sue (2). Other fans of *Sesame Street* mocked the incident by creating images of other Muppets consorting with terrorists. The Evil Bert example highlights the aspects of convergence culture Jenkins wishes to theorize: the agency of a solitary fan using a home computer; his ability to alter and distribute copyrighted content; the unintended use of that content in another country; the transformation of American culture into anti-American form; and the helplessness of the original owners to prevent any of it. To students of Internet culture, it is not surprising that digital media created the conditions for the Evil

Bert phenomenon. The way the images traveled from television to personal computer to website to printer and back to television is a familiar aspect of convergence culture. However, the inability of Sesame Workshop (the successor to CTW) to control its content is also identified as an element in a cultural process. This is controversial from several perspectives. From a traditional capitalist perspective, the loss of control over Bert's image is a violation of intellectual property rights. Sesame Workshop is situated inside a global market in which it competes for status to ensure the survival of public television itself. The elevation of an act of theft to the status of culture is suspect in such a context.

Box 9.1   High and low culture

In his seminal work *Culture and Anarchy* (1869), Matthew Arnold defined *culture* as the "best which has been thought and said in the world" (viii). In Arnold's sense, culture designates the finest artistic examples of humanity's quest for perfection. The arts should lead to spiritual improvement, because democracy requires ethical, not merely material, excellence. Culture is more than entertainment or commodity. This contrast between art that elevates and art that entertains is sometimes expressed as a conflict between "high" and "low" culture. High culture appeals to the intellect and spirit; low culture appeals to the senses and the emotions. These terms also carry a class connotation: high culture is associated with aristocrats and gentlemen, while low culture is associated with the poor. There is also a temporal component to the distinction. High culture evokes the classical past of ancient Israel, Greece, and Rome, while low culture connotes the present and its techniques of mass production. Many commentators after Arnold, including T. S. Eliot, have insisted that high and low culture nourish one another, that art can elevate and entertain at the same time. The Frankfurt School critics, however, extended Arnold's critique of low culture, fearing its influence as a vehicle for political propaganda. Digital media as low culture now provide another object of such concern, but some theorists believe that Arnold's distinctions have been rendered obsolete by the new technology.

Further reading

Gans, Herbert. 1999. *Popular Culture and High Culture: An Analysis and Evaluation of Taste.* New York: Basic Books.
Levine, Lawrence W. 1990. *Highbrow/Lowbrow: The Emergence of Cultural Hierarchy in America.* Cambridge, MA: Harvard University Press.
Parker, Trey. 2008. *Imaginationland: The Movie.* DVD. Directed by Trey Parker. Los Angeles: Paramount Pictures.

From a high-cultural perspective, the circulation of a Muppet's image as part of an American conflict with a terrorist enemy is a bathetic event. One might traditionally assume that grand political dramas would involve high, not popular, culture. The indictment of popular culture in Adorno and Horkheimer's *Dialectic of Enlightenment* predicted this subversion of politics by popular culture, as did Walter Benjamin's "The Work of Art in the Age of Mechanical Reproduction." Finally, the association of a beloved television character with a mass-murderer might strike many Americans as a puerile corruption, if not the endgame, of public education in a hypermediated age. Though Jenkins describes Evil Bert in neutral terms, this example demonstrates the potential of convergence to disrupt economic, political, and ethical norms.

Participatory culture

The next key term, *participatory culture*, signals a disruption in received ideas of audience, viewership, and the act of interpretation. For Jenkins, this term refers to the intervention of fans in the production of popular media (Jenkins 2008, 3). We can apply this idea of participatory culture to the 2013 Kickstarter campaign begun by fans of *Veronica Mars*, a television show about a young detective, to fund a film based on the show. To date, the Kickstarter campaign has raised over five million dollars after a starting goal of two million dollars. Fan intervention brought the show back to life financially, so the resulting film can no longer be regarded as a product of the entertainment industry offered for passive consumption. Participatory culture changes the nature of the audience as agent in a manner unanticipated by literary studies. Formalist theories of literature, such as the New Criticism, understood the text as an object that contains a stable meaning extracted by the act of reading. Louise Rosenblatt, a pioneer of reader-response theory, broke with formalism in her understanding of *Literature as Exploration* ([1938]1995). She argued that teachers should allow students to experience interpretation as an adventure with multiple outcomes. Stanley Fish, in *Surprised by Sin* (1967), understood the individual reader as a maker of meaning from moment to moment, such that the meaning of the work changes as the reader moves through it. Later, in *Is There a Text in This Class?* (1980), Fish moved toward a collective experience in which meaning is constructed in communities of interpretation. Feminist critics, such as Patrocinio P. Schweickart, contend that gender is foundational to interpretation and that the reader and community have been construed as normatively male (Schweickart 1986, 31). In each case, however, reading is conceived as a one-way flow from an origin (author, professor) to an end (reader, student). Participatory culture may begin in the traditional starting place, with an author, director, or producer, and result in a fan base that intervenes later in the process, as when a television show is cancelled. For instance, Joss Whedon's television show, *Firefly*, was cancelled in 2002 after only part of its first season had aired, but fan activism resulted in a feature film, *Serenity*, released in 2005, as well as a comic book that debuted in 2013. Participatory culture also includes activities such as fan conventions, zines, websites, cosplay (or costume play), and slash fiction that operate parallel to ongoing production. Works of literature, film, and television may extend beyond the medium of origin into the lives of fans who fashion lifeworlds out of them. However, as revealed by Evil Bert, participatory culture also generates an aleatory dynamic, creating unintended effects that may be transnational in scope. Images travel the Web like a beach ball at a concert, held aloft by brief moments of contact that send it in random directions. Participation, in this sense, is not the same as control.

Box 9.2   Talk about it: social media as convergence

Select a social medium that you use, such as Facebook, Tumblr, or Twitter. Then choose an image that appeared in your feed. Try to trace it back to its origin. How many times was it shared? Through which media did it pass? Did it originate in social media, or is it anchored by a website? Did it come from a professional, institutional source, such as an online journal, or did it originate with an individual? How have users commented on it each time it was posted? Was it subject to *trolling*, i.e., negative commentary with its own political agenda? When your investigation is complete, draw a flow chart that represents your results in graphic form.

Further reading and viewing

Ellison, N. B., C. Steinfield, and C. Lampe. 2007. "The Benefits of Facebook 'Friends': Social Capital and College Students' Use of Online Social Network Sites." *Journal of Computer-Mediated Communication* 12: 1143–1168.

Herring, Susan, Kirk Job-Sluder, Rebecca Scheckler, and Sasah Barab. 2002. "Searching for Safety Online: Managing 'Trolling' in a Feminist Forum." *The Information Society* 18: 371.

Parker, Trey. "You Have 0 Friends." *South Park* 14/4. April 7, 2010.

Collective intelligence

Neither is participation merely individual in convergence culture: the third term, *collective intelligence*, refers to the way convergence and participation allow us to combine our knowledge and skills in a network of action (Jenkins 2008, 4). Jenkins takes this idea of collective intelligence from the French sociologist Pierre Lévy. He adapts Lévy's idea as "consumption has become a collective process," and therefore "collective intelligence can be seen as an alternative source of media power" (4). It is here, however, that students of ecomedia should note that Jenkins takes for granted the socioeconomic structures of consumption as Lévy himself did not. Lévy's book, *Collective Intelligence: Mankind's Emerging World in Cyberspace* (1997), appeared in English at a moment when anarchist-utopian thinking about the Internet had not come to terms with the commodification of the Web. Lévy imagines collective intelligence as a force that is "less concerned with the self-control of human communities than with a fundamental *letting-go* that is capable of altering our very notions of identity and the mechanisms of domination and conflict, lifting restrictions on heretofore banned communications, and effecting the mutual liberation of isolated thoughts" (Lévy 1997, xxvii). Though Jenkins is deeply concerned with the implications of convergence culture for democracy, his ethnographic reach does not extend beyond liberal capitalist societies. Lévy, however, imagines collective intelligence as a force that transcends individualism without opting into the nation-state or the global economy. He describes collective intelligence in terms drawn from the work of Gilles Deleuze and Felix Guattari: it is nomadic, rhizomatic, and capable of direct and not just representative democracy (Lévy 1997, 63–69). Collective intelligence gives rise to a collective voice that is neither a fascist effacement of individual will nor a capitalist immersion in consumption for its own sake. With Lévy's utopian notion in view, it is possible to imagine media convergence and participatory culture unbounded by the marketplace. Given the way Web 2.0 has developed, it is clear that Jenkins and Lévy are both correct. Their accounts describe political uses of digital media that correspond to different political programs. Lévy's account anticipates Anonymous, the use of Facebook during the Arab Spring, and the culture of hacking. Jenkins's account favors the behavior of fan communities, flash mobs, and Twitter storm protests aimed at government reform. Because this contrast between reformers and anarchists also characterizes much of environmentalist culture in the period after World War II, students of ecomedia should not efface such tensions within collective intelligence, but take careful account of them.

The Black Phoenix

In order to see how convergence theory explains the movement of environmentalist content through media, consider the following example. The example comes from the "Reject and Protect" protest against the proposed Keystone XL oil pipeline, which, if completed, would carry a mixture of liquefied natural gas and tar sands bitumen from Alberta, Canada, to the Gulf of Mexico. The Keystone XL has been the focus of organized international protest because of the destructive strip-mining of the tar sands in Alberta; the potential of the pipeline to pollute the Ogallala Aquifer, which provides water to much of the American Midwest; and the burning of fossil fuels as a driver of climate change. This combination of problems has led to an alliance among Canadian First Nations, Nebraska farmers and ranchers, American Indian nations, and climate change activists. From April 22nd to April 27th, 2014, the Cowboy Indian Alliance of Nebraska staged ritual protests on the National Mall in Washington, DC, culminating in a ceremony in which a tipi was presented to President Barack Obama to remind him of his responsibility to protect indigenous nations and the planetary biosphere itself. A rally was held on the Mall on Saturday, April 26th, in advance of the presentation of the tipi. The protest sign shown in Figure 9.1 appeared at that rally.

Figure 9.1 The "Black Phoenix," a *Mockingjay*/Deepwater Horizon Mashup.
Source: Photo by the author.

This Black Phoenix image is an example of convergence culture at work in environmental politics: a "mashup," or combination of two media objects that had nothing to do with one another in their original form. Fans of Suzanne Collins's popular novel trilogy *The Hunger Games* (2008–2010) will recognize the Black Phoenix image as a transformation of the mockingjay, the personal symbol of Katniss Everdeen, the hero who leads Appalachian coal miners in a revolt against Panem, a totalitarian state set in a future North America. The mockingjay is a wild hybrid of the mockingbird and the "jabberjay," a weaponized, genetically modified bird capable of human speech. In *The Hunger Games*, the mockingjay becomes a symbol of the revolution. It represents Katniss's personal rebellion, the miners' political rebellion, and the species-rebellion of an avian drone that escapes its fascist creators to assist the hero. The third book of the trilogy, *Mockingjay* (2010), features a cover in which the bird breaks the circle that had trapped it and rises, phoenix-like, into the air. This cover image has been reproduced in movie posters and other merchandise associated with the *Hunger Games* franchise. The image on the protest sign visible in Figure 9.1 appears to be a fusion of the rebellious mockingjay and the oil-covered pelicans that featured prominently in media coverage of the Deepwater Horizon oil spill in the Gulf of Mexico in 2010. In those pictures, however, the pelicans appear curled up on themselves in a futile gesture of self-defense from the oil that saturates their wings. This protest sign combines the image of real birds threatened by a petro-catastrophe with the image of a fictional bird that frees itself from a coal economy to suggest a black phoenix flying free of a pipeline dystopia.

Though the interpretation of the image is important, because it creates an icon of environmental justice, convergence theory prompts us to investigate the process by which it was created, the media that were employed, and the transformations involved in its metamorphosis. Which media converged? As opposed to Evil Bert, which radiated from a single starting point, the Black Phoenix emerged from two distinct ancestors. The mockingjay image began as a character in a print book and became the cover of another print book, a sequel whose story was adapted into a film. The oil-soaked pelican emerged from the television, newspaper, and print periodical coverage of the Deepwater Horizon spill. In an interview with the author, the protestor carrying the sign at the demonstration indicated that he had not created the image himself and did not know the creator. There is a gap in our knowledge between the appearance of the Black Phoenix and the circulation of the source material through the Hollywood advertising industry and the coverage of the Deepwater Horizon. This gap highlights a moment of participatory culture that is occluded from our vision that must have occurred: the moment when an artist, or a group of collaborators, combined a fictional image of political resistance with an actual image of the struggling pelican. The resulting hybrid combines the virtues of political resistance and witness to environmental destruction. By intervening in the flow of media, the participants exhibited a collective intelligence that included attention to ecological disaster, a sensitivity to icons as expressions of political will, an understanding of the ideological and historical content of popular culture, and a willingness to restructure received media content for their own purposes. At the same time, it is important to note what participation did not accomplish: none of the media produced for the protests by the Cowboy Indian Alliance, the Reject and Protect homepage, or the 350.org media network included images of the Black Phoenix. The official image of the event became, instead, the circle of tipis erected on the Mall surrounded by signs that carried political messages in writing. A decision was made by the remediators of the event to transmit more traditional images of protest that did not require knowledge of popular culture to be understood. Another possibility is that the producers of official event media content did not themselves understand the image of the Black Phoenix, or the concept of the mashup, or the notion that popular culture contains political content relevant to the network of anti-Keystone activists. The work of fan culture appears to have been stymied. Though it is tempting to conclude that the life of the Black Phoenix stopped at the moment it was not remediated, such a judgment misunderstands the aleatory nature of convergence. The Black Phoenix may be ephemeral, or it may recur at unpredictable moments, including future protests, as the global circulation of media continues beyond official channels of production.

The application of convergence theory to a protest sign has revealed a complex entanglement of mass media, popular culture, and environmental activism. Perhaps the most provocative aspect of this discovery is the use of the mockingjay at a moment when ecocriticism and global climate activism struggle to explain the significance of nonhuman beings as "bodies that matter," both ethically and politically (Butler 1993, 27). The Black Phoenix points to the potential of art as an agent of environmental justice as culture moves past a convergence bound by neoliberal structures of slow violence and ecocide (Nixon 2013, 2). Global capitalism also provides the context for understanding the movement of media content through advertising, video games, and earth imaging, topics discussed in the essays that follow. Convergence is at work when the advertising industry adapts images of environmental concern to the task of selling a product. For example, with rising concern at the turn of the century about the effects of climate change, the polar bear became a symbol of the melting Arctic ice cap. Knut, a baby polar bear from the Berlin Zoo, then appeared on the cover of the 2007 Green Issue of *Vanity Fair*, Photoshopped into the picture next to Leonardo Di Caprio. Convergence allowed a cub who had never been to the Arctic to sell magazines. There is no greater example of participatory culture in virtual environments than that of Massively Multiplayer Online Games (MMOGs), such as *World of Warcraft*, where the fate of landscapes and races depends on the behavior of gamers across the world cooperating in a digital space. Earth mapping, a technology that allows us to trace the flow of radiation from Fukushima as readily as we access the street view of Google Maps, is an example of collective intelligence as Lévy imagined it. The extension of digital mapping techniques into projects of citizen science and political activism suggests that media convergence is environed but not limited by the economic logic of the global marketplace.

Convergence culture in ecomedia performs both a pragmatic, market-based function and a liberatory, political function in the digital public sphere.

Keywords

Collective intelligence	Participatory culture
Convergence culture	Performance-in-community
High culture	Reader-response theory
Low culture	Trolling
Mashup	Works
Media convergence	

Discussion questions

1   Find one example of media convergence and trace it from origin to end-point. What, if any, environmental content does it have? How was the content transformed by convergence?
2   Is Dino Ignacio responsible for the uses to which others put Evil Bert? What are the ethical ramifications of media convergence?
3   To what extent should aesthetic considerations affect our understanding of media convergence? Can traditional qualities of beauty, depth, and excellence be causes of convergence? If so, choose one example and explain it.
4   What do you think of Lévy's idea of "collective intelligence"? Is it not possible to see the Web as a medium of collective stupidity as well? If so, find one example of collective stupidity on the Web and determine its relationship to media convergence.
5   To what extent can participatory culture promote direct democracy? Are convergent media tools for democratic populism? To what extent are they also tools that allow for government or corporate propaganda?

Further reading

Adamson. Joni. 2012. "Indigenous Literatures, Multinaturalism, and *Avatar*: The Emergence of Indigenous Cosmopolitics." *American Literary History* (ALH) Special Issue: Sustainability in America. 143–162.

Boellstorff, Tom. 2010. *Coming of Age in Second Life: An Anthropologist Explores the Virtually Human*. Princeton, NJ: Princeton University Press.

Coleman, Beth. 2011. *Hello, Avatar: The Rise of the Networked Generation*. Cambridge, MA: MIT Press.

Dobren, Sidney I., and Sean Morey, eds. 2009. *Ecosee: Image, Rhetoric, Nature*. Albany: SUNY Press.

Galloway, Alexander, Eugene Thacker, and McKenzie Wark. 2014. *Excommunication: Three Inquiries in Media and Mediation*. Chicago: University of Chicago Press.

Heise, Ursula K. 2008. *Sense of Place and Sense of Planet: The Environmental Imagination of the Global*. Oxford: Oxford University Press.

Horkheimer, Max, and Theodor W. Adorno. 2002. Orig. 1947. *Dialectic of Enlightenment: Philosophical Fragments*. Edited by Gunzelin Schmid Noerr. Translated by Edmund Jephcott. Stanford, CA: Stanford University Press.

Jenkins, Henry, Sam Ford, and Joshua Green. 2013. *Spreadable Media: Creating Value and Meaning in a Networked Culture*. New York: New York University Press.

Landow, George P. 2006. *Hypertext 3.0: Critical Theory and New Media in an Era of Globalization*. Baltimore: Johns Hopkins University Press.

Lioi, Anthony. 2012. "Teaching Green Cultural Studies and New Media." In *Teaching Ecocriticism and Green Cultural Studies*, edited by Greg Garrard, 133–143. New York: Palgrave MacMillan.

Morton, Timothy. 2010. *The Ecological Thought*. Cambridge, MA: Harvard University Press.

Stein, Rachel, ed. 2004. *New Perspectives on Environmental Justice: Gender, Sexuality, and Activism*. New Brunswick, NJ: Rutgers University Press.

Turkle, Sherry. 1997. *Life on the Screen: Identity in the Age of the Internet*. Reprint edition. New York: Simon & Schuster.

Waldrip-Fruin, Noah, and Nick Montfort. 2003. *The New Media Reader*. Cambridge, MA: MIT Press.

Works cited

Arnold, Matthew. 1869. *Culture and Anarchy: An Essay in Political and Social Criticism*. London: Smith, Elder and Co.

Benjamin, Walter. 1969. "The Work of Art in the Age of Mechanical Reproduction." In *Illuminations: Essays and Reflections*, edited by Editor Hannah Arendt, translated by Harry Zohn, 217–252. New York: Schocken Books.

Butler, Judith. 1993. *Bodies That Matter: On the Discursive Limits of "Sex"*. New York: Routledge.

Collins, Suzanne. 2010. *Mockingjay*. New York: Scholastic Press.

Fish, Stanley. 1967. *Surprised by Sin: The Reader in* Paradise Lost. New York: St. Martin's Press.

———. 1980. *Is There a Text in This Class? The Authority of Interpretive Communities*. Cambridge, MA: Harvard University Press.

Goehr, Lydia. 2007. *The Imaginary Museum of Musical Works: An Essay in the Philosophy of Music*. Oxford: Oxford University Press.

Jenkins, Henry. 2008. *Convergence Culture: Where Old and New Media Collide*. New York: New York University Press.

Lévy, Pierre. 1997. *Collective Intelligence: Mankind's Emerging World in Cyberspace*. Translated by Robert Bononno. New York: Basic Books.

Murphy, Patrick D. 2000. *Farther Afield in the Study of Nature-Oriented Literature*. Charlottesville, VA: University of Virginia Press.

Nixon, Rob. 2013. *Slow Violence and the Environmentalism of the Poor*. Cambridge: Harvard University Press.

Rosenblatt, Louise. [1938]1995. *Literature as Exploration*, 5th ed. New York: Modern Language Association.

Schweickart, Patrocinio P. 1986. "Reading Ourselves: Toward a Feminist Theory of Reading." In *Gender and Reading: Essays on Readers, Texts, and Contexts*, edited by Elizabeth A. Flynn and Patrocinio P. Schweickart, 31–62. Baltimore: Johns Hopkins University Press.

Small, Christopher. 1998. *Musicking: The Meanings of Performing and Listening*. Middletown, CT: Wesleyan University Press.

10 Selling with Gaia
Advertising and the natural world

Joseph Clark

Introduction

You've seen the commercials. In fact, you can hardly avoid them. A rugged SUV turns off the pavement and charges off-road, splashing across mountain streams and climbing hills to reach a scenic wilderness vista; passengers step out of the vehicle and, smiling, take in the view, while a voiceover tells you in no uncertain terms that this kind of natural escape is only available to drivers and passengers.

In another common advertisement one might see on television or the Internet, an allergy sufferer reels away from pollen-clouded meadows, red-eyed, sniffling, and miserable – until an over-the-counter allergy medication kicks in and suddenly it's a sunny day outdoors, full of fresh scents, pastel colors, and smiling people.

Or maybe you've seen the print equivalents: ads featuring gorgeous stock photography of waterfalls and forest paths, advertising mutual funds or toilet paper. Leaping whales and talking lizards that sell insurance.

It's likely that you can easily think of several such advertisements and find plentiful examples in magazines, on television, and on YouTube and other Internet sites. Such ads are common because the natural world – in the form of animals, plants, waterways, cloudscapes, and other iconic visual imagery – is a regular component of TV and print advertising, even when the product or service being advertised has nothing to do with the environment we live in. Sometimes the connection is clear, as when the "green" features of an economical hybrid car or recyclable container are being described. Other times, the connection is less clear.

And there's not always a flattering portrait of Nature in these ads. After all, the out-of-doors can be a dangerous place, full of storms, floods, germs, and myriad other threats that can surely be mitigated if you purchase the recommended product or take the recommended action. Advertisers know we have a kind of ambivalence about the natural world; most of us love flowers and cuddly baby polar bears, but tend to flee in horror from mosquitoes and roaches. We're willing to pay large sums of money for expensive machinery to take us off-road, away from all the crowds and noise and all the other unpleasant side effects of the very technological civilization necessary to produce the complex SUVs that can bring our 4-channel Blue-tooth sound system and leather seats with us into the woods.

At least that's what the advertisements tell us.

In this chapter, we take a closer look at such advertisements and the way they depict the natural world and make it their spokesperson. Advertising companies spend huge amounts of money in the creation of appeals that will reach the largest possible audience with the greatest effect. Knowing this, we can use such ads as windows into contemporary culture and the complex relationship between culture and the natural environment that both supports it and, in many cases, is being destroyed by it. These ads reflect our view of "Nature" and, at the same time, they shape the way we view it, often in ways that have more to do with commerce than environmental sustainability. Advertising and marketing can also be prosocial, encouraging audiences to conserve resources or support environmental-protection legislation, for example. However, this chapter is primarily concerned with advertisements that promote consumption. As the examples cited here suggest, such ads often contain the most memorable and dynamic Nature imagery.

We'll look at different definitions of "Nature" and how these definitions are then used to connect commercial products with some positive or beneficial aspect of the natural environment or as a remedy for some environmental threat from "wild nature." We will also unpack buzzwords like "green" and *"eco-friendly"* and show how nonverbal, visual elements create impressions with different kinds of viewers and audiences. The chapter will also describe some of the research on this "eco-advertising" conducted over the past couple of decades, examining the theories being developed and the research methods used to test and extend those theories. And we'll examine a few case studies – from parody SUV ads to "bleeding-edge" augmented reality toys – that show how "Nature advertising" has begun to respond to new media developments that allow audiences to interact more directly with the message and create immersive and realistic depictions that are evolving from visual scenes (like magazine ads) to inhabitable spaces (like virtual reality).

Throughout this chapter, we'll be adopting a critical stance: Does the way the natural world is represented in these ads help us better deal with pollution, climate change, threats to water supplies, extinctions, toxic wastes, and other contemporary concerns – or does it sweep them under the rug, or worse yet, does it exacerbate the problems? Do these representations challenge structural and cultural practices, such as consumption-driven economies, that harm the very nature depicted in these advertisements? How are audiences engaging with these messages and challenging them? What would "ecologically friendly advertising" look like – assuming it's even possible?

A natural question: what is "nature"?

As mentioned earlier, **Nature** is a complex concept with many connotations. In this chapter, uppercase *Nature* is generally used to refer to human concepts and myths about the natural environment. When not capitalized, *nature* refers more directly to the natural world: forest, oceans, ecosystems, life forms, and so on. Understandably, these two meanings – what one might call "cultural" and "biological" – are not always distinct from one another.

The range of possible meanings of nature is important even within the realm of scientific research on advertising effects. For example, Hartmann, Apaolaza, and Alija's (2013) study of the effects of "natural imagery" on audience attention operationalizes "pleasant nature scenery" (185) as "pleasant natural landscapes with vegetation: a beech tree on a meadow, Mediterranean coastline, African savannah with trees, a mountain stream, lakes and forests, and an oak forest" (187). The contrasting images in the study – "unnatural imagery," as it were – included a cityscape and a sandy desert. One only has to reflect for a brief moment to consider the cultural understandings of "natural" embedded here: while it might be easy to think of a city as (by some definitions) not natural, any biologist will tell you that deserts – while perhaps not romantically scenic – are delicate and complex ecosystems. In other words, entirely within the realm of what one might consider natural.

Box 10.1   Defining nature

Just think for a moment about the many meanings of "natural." These meanings might refer to what is ordinary and expected – a synonym for "normal." Or natural might refer to something healthy, like fruit juice. It might refer to the unbuilt environment – all those places not directly touched by cities, roads, and other signs of human presence. Any one of these meanings might be at play when someone claims this or that is "natural." Raymond Williams (1983) says "nature" is one of the most loaded words in the English language. Environmental scholars like William Cronon (1995) and Roderick Nash (2001) have identified a complicated range of meanings to include:

- a dangerous, uncivilized place
- an unspoiled realm untainted by human contact
- a system of resources that support human civilization
- a place of spiritual restoration and scenic beauty
- a place distinct from and ultimately alien to human culture

Any of these shifting and overlapping views of Nature may be tied to particular threads in ideology, history, and culture. Further, any of these views has practical, physical implications for sustainable ecosystems.

To learn more about how "Nature" has been defined, see:

Cronon, William, ed. 1995. *Uncommon Ground: Rethinking the Human Place in Nature.* New York: W. W. Norton & Company.
Nash, Roderick F. 2001. *Wilderness in the American Mind,* 4th ed. New Haven, CT: Yale University Press.
Williams, Raymond. 1983. *Keywords: A Vocabulary of Culture and Society.* London: Flamingo.

Hansen and Machin (2008) describe the way advertisements decontextualize elements of the natural world, stripping them from the ecosystems from which they cannot exist apart. Natural imagery generally appears in a sanitized and romanticized fashion in advertisements. Nature is serene, distant, or majestic – a kind of postcard image – or it is photogenic, removed from its context, like a vividly colored frog or bird clinging to a tree branch. The authors' detailed analysis shows how Getty Images – a stock photography company widely used as a source of high-quality images for many print advertisements – systematically uses only the most generic images possible because they are likely to have the broadest possible market. The result is a glut of generic images that are never associated with a specific locale, and thus any specific ecosystem; the very specific and concrete habitats, ecological niches, and animal species that might be threatened around the world are never depicted (particularly if they are iconic, such as the habitats in which spotted owls live that might evoke unwanted "tree-hugging" associations). Instead, the natural environment is "transformed into something that can be useful for marketing purposes" (Hansen and Machin 2008, 784) before it is even selected for use in an advertisement.

In Hartmann, Apaolaza, and Alija's (2013) experimental study of responses to natural imagery in advertising, this decontextualization is further demonstrated. They found that such imagery aids message retention even when it is completely unrelated to the subject of the advertisement, suggesting that advertisers can benefit from including all manner of visually pleasing, generic, greeting-card-type images of Nature, because doing so will help sell the product. As a result, images of harm, pollution, habitat loss – and particularly any depictions of things harder to visualize, such as ozone depletion – are nowhere near as common in our media environment as aesthetically pleasing photos of happy animals and breathtaking vistas, reinforcing our notion that all is right with Nature and thus also often sending the message that all those pesky environmentalists are just unfounded alarmists.

Why study nature in advertising?

A large portion of our planet is awash in televised and print messages delivered by broadcast and Internet media, and we spend an enormous amount of time viewing advertisements, particularly on television. The huge popularity of Super Bowl ads is one sign that commercials have become their own genre of entertainment; since the advent of online channels like YouTube, memes like Dos Equis's "most interesting man in the world" and others become viewable at any time and can be embedded in blogs and tweeted again and again for repeat viewing. Advertisements are an integral part of contemporary culture; see, for example, Wharton (2013), Berger (2011), Ewen (1976), and Hovland and Wilcox (1989).

Quite a lot of material resources – time and money – are expended on these ads by people who believe the results are worth the expense. Catherine Roach's study of "godlike" imagery in Nature advertising sums this up well:

> Corporate marketing departments and their advertising agencies invest millions of dollars in careful research to ensure their advertisement campaigns have the broadest appeal. Advertising is thus a particularly telling forum precisely because it is designed to connect with very widespread popular feelings, anxieties, and desires.
>
> (Roach 2007, paragraph 25)

As Roach and many others have pointed out, when these advertisements deploy nature imagery or otherwise describe the natural world in some way, they reflect our ideas about Nature – but they also shape them, sometimes creating knowledge and attitudes where none existed (imagine the level of popular awareness of geckos prior to their use in ads by GEICO Insurance, for example). And the ideas of Nature that are shaped and created emerge from a context in which we are being exhorted to consume more – that is, extract natural resources, build factories, generate waste, and engage in any number of other behaviors that threaten Nature.

Kilbourne's (1995) analysis of the various kinds of "greenness" in advertising provides a framework for understanding how *commodity culture* (a culture organized around practices of production and consumption wherein nearly everything is reduced to its material cost) influences our perspective about the natural world. He identifies two axes of difference, the first of which he calls *political*: whether the perspective offered is reformist or radical. For Kilbourne, an "environmentalist" position suggests that things like habitat loss and climate change can be solved by modifying the existing system (through laws and regulations, for example). For those with an "ecological perspective," on the other hand, lasting change is only possible through a major overhaul of the dominant paradigm of capitalism. The other dimension he calls *positional*, referring to the presumed place of human beings. At one end of the scale, *ecocentrism* argues that the natural world has its own inherent value, apart from what use humans might put it to, and that human beings are just one more species in the animal kingdom, no more valuable than insects or fish. At the other end – which Kilbourne says is the *dominant* view – notions like *conservationism* and *wise use* value sustainable, environmentally friendly practices mainly for their anthropocentric value.

One of the primary reasons the dominant paradigm is anthropocentric, Kilbourne argues, is that radical ecocentrism is a direct challenge to the modernist valuation of industrialization. Instead, addressing environmental problems is almost always expressed in terms of technological fixes rather than political change: "The solution set derived from this mode of analysis always lies within technological rationality motivated by unlimited economic growth and consumption" (Kilbourne 1995, 10).

Advertisements that urge consumption in the name of environmentalism illustrate an inherent sustainability conflict within commodity capitalism, the economic system that spans the globe today. Schnaiberg (1993) describes the impact of such economic systems, not just on the environment, but on environmental consciousness itself. Those who own and manage capital (land, factories, money, and other kinds of wealth) seek to maximize their exploitation of their environmental holdings – such as a forest containing timber or an estuary resting on top of oil deposits – by either explaining the exploitation as somehow inherently "natural" or a "wise use" of the land – that is, not simply an attempt to maximize profits – or by claiming that the exploitation will create jobs or otherwise stimulate the economy. Schnaiberg calls these tactics "*unconsciousness-making*" in the sense that they impair public consciousness and awareness about the ecosystems they rely on, shifting public attitudes and policies towards a *commodified logic* of resource extraction (Schnaiberg 1993, 25). According to Schnaiberg, advertising and other forms of communication "reinforce the perception of the treadmill [his term for a focus on markets and wealth] as a social and individual good" (56) that leads to an "enduring systemic bias towards the economic synthesis, and against the ecological synthesis" (35).

This "*treadmill culture*" not only alienates us from Nature (Schnaiberg 1993, 6), but can also serve as an instrument of social control that preserves unjust power relationships among human beings, who are surely part of the natural world even if we don't always think of ourselves as such. In this way, not only Nature but also human beings – often the marginalized poor – feel disproportionate impacts of the treadmill. For Jhally, as with Schnaiberg, culture reproduces the economic system that surrounds it, creating a "*consciousness industry*" – what we often call "*the media*" – that benefits those with economic power and helps them preserve that power without resorting to physical force. Media products like nature-filled advertisements can thus reinforce attitudes toward the natural world that help maintain the "consent of the dominated" (Jhally 1989, 67; see also Jhally 2000).

Thus, no matter how many mountain ranges or rainforests they celebrate, advertisements often participate in a process that is anything but ecofriendly, because the process of treadmill culture sees the natural world as a resource to be exploited for gain. And as several scholars have pointed out, it does so even when purporting to encourage "green" purchases like low-wattage light bulbs or recycled paper towels. According to Smith, the usual green product purchase is more likely to be a way to make consumerism seem compatible with environmental sustainability, perpetuating the industrial system that "being green" is supposedly resisting (Smith 1998). That is, the most sustainable practice might simply be to not purchase anything at all, rather than use more recycled paper towels.

Advertisements that promote ecocentrism simply don't make sense in a consumer culture because they lead to the purchase of fewer goods (Winett et al. 1985). The effects of this bias ripple outward, impacting not only advertisements but the programming they frequently support. For example, no petroleum company that is fiscally responsible to its shareholders is likely to spend money sponsoring programs that blame climate change on energy consumption. It's just not a logical move within the framework of a capitalist economic system.

Explicit claims vs. implicit references

To some degree, audiences seem to recognize this conflict by casting a wary eye on "green" advertising, at least regarding fact claims. Fisk (1974) observed that even when advertisers make verifiable claims of environmental friendliness that consumers can understand, audiences have become so accustomed to hearing bogus "green" claims that viewers tend to mistrust them. They feel that advertisements from major companies are the least credible source there is for environmental information (Iyer and Banerjee 1993). This further reduces the motivation for advertisers to use factual information about how their product might have a smaller carbon footprint than a competitor's. It's much easier to dress up the advertisement with charismatic animals and spectacular scenery.

Parguel and Benoit-Moreau's (2013) experimental study of "*claims greenwashing*" vs. "*executional greenwashing*" helps us understand the complexity of the problem. "*Greenwashing*" refers to messages that create an aura of environmental friendliness not supported by facts but designed to make buyers feel good about purchasing. It's derived from the broader term "whitewashing" (that is, covering with a thin veneer of paint) that is often applied to political cover-ups and other forms of rhetorical damage control. When an advertisement makes verbal statements about the environmental benefits of a product, it is making *explicit claims*: higher gas mileage, more post-consumer ingredients, fewer phosphates, and so on. But Parguel and Benoit-Moreau also identify an "executional" channel, which refers to the presence of colors, imagery, and other design or even decorative elements that are designed to evoke Nature. A given advertisement may contain no explicit claims but still associate its product with environmental concerns through executional elements, such as a background image of the beach or a design theme that uses iconic blues or greens typically associated with seashores and oceans. Parguel and Benoit-Moreau found that nonexpert audiences, who barely recalled the claims made in the advertisements, were generally persuaded by the executional elements. Unexpectedly, however, they also found that expert audiences – though they recalled the verbal claims – were also swayed by executional elements. This lends even greater support to Hartmann, Apaolaza, and Alija's (2013) point that advertisers can't go wrong by adding a cute koala or majestic coastline to their ads.

Mommy dearest: disciplining nature

As noted earlier, within most commercial advertisements, threats to the environment simply don't exist. Instead, pleasant associations with the natural world are tied to a product or service. If there is an unpleasant side to the environment, it's almost always something that the advertised product can mitigate or make disappear.

Box 10.2   Talk about it: feminizing nature

In ecofeminism, the most commonly cited example of a problematic dualism is the way Western culture – since the days of Aristotle and made more prominent by the work of Descartes – creates totalizing bifurcations like man/woman and civilization/nature and then creates linkages that allow women to be associated with nature, and vice versa, thereby permitting their exploitation under similar logics of oppression. That is, women are seen to be mindless, wild, uncivilized, embodied reproductive functionaries, while the natural world is inscribed as weaker, feminized, to be dominated, and so on. These associations are then used to exploit both women and nature. Ecofeminists such as Greta Gaard, Carolyn Merchant, and Vandana Shiva have argued for a revalorization of the nondominant half of the classic dualist pairs. That is, they want to retain the connection between women and nature but flip things over so that these are properly valued. Women are still "closer to nature" in this formulation of ecofeminism, it's just that the patriarchy has distorted and subverted the value of both, and this needs correction.

Can you find examples of advertisements that feminize nature in order to control it or exploit it? How about examples that connect women and nature in positive, empowering ways?

To learn more about ecofeminism and the feminization of nature, see:

Gaard, Greta. 1997. "Toward a Queer Ecofeminism." *Hypatia* 12.1, 114–137.
Merchant, Carolyn. 1980. *The Death of Nature – Women, Ecology and the Scientific Revolution*. San Francisco: Harper Collins.
Mies, Maria, and Vandana Shiva. 1993. *Ecofeminism*. Halifax, Nova Scotia: Fernwood Publications.
Plumwood, Valerie. 1993. *Feminism and the Mastery of Nature*. London: Routledge.

Roach (2007) uses the folk trope of "Mother Nature" to describe these views as either "good mother" or "bad mother" Nature. Sometimes the product is a portal to the Good Mother. Perhaps the most literal example of this is a mid-2000s magazine ad for Bass Pro Shops. Under a headline enticing readers to gear up (buy things) for great adventures, a photo of the storefront – a stone-and-log fascia recalling the grand lodges and rustic cabins of national parks in the American West – was modified such that visible through the entry arch was not the store itself but a view of snow-dusted mountain peaks against a clear sky, above forested slopes and an unspoiled mountain lake. Below this composite photo were the prominent logos of eight outdoor-gear manufacturers. The implication was clear: the Bass Pro Shops' Outdoor World store is a portal to nature – perhaps the most important portal there is.

Gunster (2004) shows how SUVs are not only described (without apparent irony) as a means of escaping technology, allowing their owners to demonstrate their rugged independence from civilization, but the vehicles are themselves described and depicted in ways that suggest they, too, are wild animals. Andersen's study found that SUV ads create "a symbolic world where SUVs not only can co-exist with nature, but are naturalized within the wild geographies of the places they inhabit" (Andersen 2000, 170). These advertisements depict the SUVs as not just ecofriendly, but, using wild-animal imagery and metaphors, as "natural" objects.

On the other hand, when Mother Nature is bad, the product becomes a solution – again making the product itself natural and reinforcing the idea that even the natural world cannot be faced or experienced without the mediation of commercial products. Gunster (2004) argues that SUV advertising has shifted towards depicting the vehicles as technological solutions to a kind of Bad Mother Nature – one that has begun to inhabit our cities, which are presented as urban jungles fraught with all the dangers of wild habitats. In addition to the not-so-subtle class and racial implications for wealthy urban SUV drivers traveling through ghettoes, Gunster's argument is that such depictions naturalize conditions of alienation and disempowerment that are very much the result of very human policies. The result reinforces a spiral of fear that leads to more privatized security, weaker governments, and more dangerous cities – generating a need for more powerful and secure vehicles in these wild places.

Green advertising meets the prosumer

Emerging forms of advertisements invite audiences to participate more directly in the message, like interactive web contests and mixed-reality stunts. Henry Jenkins (2004) uses Michel de Certeau's concept of *"textual poaching"* to describe how audiences and consumers use new forms of media to appropriate content for their own uses, which may not be those of the dominant, commodity-oriented *culture industry* (a blanket term for the for-profit corporations that produce most of the books, films, and other media that we use to transmit our culture from one generation to the next). Through textual poaching, consumers can "archive, annotate, appropriate and recirculate media" (Jenkins 2004, 33) to resist the gatekeepers that traditionally controlled messaging in advertisements on television and in print. The result "alters the relationship between existing technologies, industries, markets, genres and audiences" (34) and leads to emergent knowledge cultures that will resist and channel the forces of *commodification* in ways that the designers of advertising messages may not have intended. Empowered by the audience agency that new media permits, audiences participating in knowledge cultures are using them as the nexus of new social relations at a time when existing social ties and communities are on the decline (in part because of new media and global capitalism).

Jenkins helps us see that participating in the dominant commodity culture doesn't just have to be a one-way process whereby green impulses are co-opted into greenwashing. In fact, he recommends participation as a way for audiences to work from the inside, "actively shaping the flow of media" (Jenkins 2004, 36). The online fan communities described by Halverson (2007) are one instance of this insider work. She shows how these fans *remix* and repurpose media clips from the TV shows they admire and, in the process, "master the design grammar" (1) of new media. These audiences are thus participating in the culture-production experience rather than simply learning how to comprehend messages. Knobel and Lankshear (2008), echoing Laurence Lessig, also see these remixes and *mashups* as entertaining and engaging ways for audiences to insert themselves into the process of cultural production. In fact, they argue that culture is a remix:

> At the broadest level, then, re-mix is the general condition of cultures: no remix, no culture. At this general and mundane level, we remix language every time we draw on it and remix meanings whenever we take an idea, artifact, or a particular stretch of language and integrate it into what we are saying and doing at the time.
>
> (23)

Halvorson and Knobel and Lankshear argue that the process of remixing media seen so commonly in blogs, YouTube videos, and websites is a new kind of cultural literacy activity, wherein people use technical and discursive skills as they evaluate messages and remix them in ways specific to a community (29). These new knowledge communities may cluster around media narratives (such as *Twilight* or *Harry Potter*, for example), technologies, or genres (such as the meme-oriented website *I Can Haz Cheezburger*).

That is not to suggest that these knowledge communities are immune to co-optation by the forces of commodity culture. Jenkins notes that many computer game companies have not only tolerated but even actively participated in the construction and maintenance of fan communities as a way of building long-term relationships with consumers (Jenkins 2004). In fact, Andrejevic (2005) argues that online fan communities and producers of fan fiction are just providing free labor to help sell the original product. Rather than truly interacting with audiences, he says, the media companies simply use fan activity as a form of surveillance, "deputizing" fan communities even when fans believe they are operating only for themselves and their knowledge communities. And as Grimes (2006) argues, in many cases of user-created content, a focus on marketing and sale of the remixes to other members of the community simply reinscribes commodity culture.

Even so, Andrejevic (2007) observes that audiences who, for example, use the Internet to create new forms of entertainment from old TV episodes are participating in cultural (re)production. In fact, as Jenkins has observed:

> Fans respond to [the] situation of an increasingly privatized culture by applying the traditional practices of a folk culture to mass culture, treating film or television as if it offered them raw materials for telling their own stories and resources for forging their own communities.
>
> (Jenkins 1992, 6)

In other words, despite the continual threat of co-optation, a vigilant and information-literate prosumer community that includes a wide range of local, everyday, amateur voices can still help fulfill the promise of new media and participatory culture.

Remixing SUVs

Corporations seeking to exploit fan communities in advertisements are not always successful. In fact, advertisers eager to capitalize on the interactive and participatory character of new media have found their strategies blowing up in their faces more than once, demonstrating one path by which audiences can generate counternarratives that expose the contradictions in green marketing. One of the most striking demonstrations of this was a web advertising campaign for the Chevrolet Tahoe SUV, which invited audiences to invest themselves in the product by creating their own versions of a Tahoe commercial, using interactive tools on the company's website:

> To create a video, users can choose from video clips depicting the Tahoe in natural settings, like driving through snowy mountain ranges or perched at the edge of a rushing waterfall, pick one of eight soundtracks and add text to narrate the commercial.
>
> (Bosman 2006)

The results were such that the campaign is included in a number of "top marketing failures" lists circulating on the web today. Rather than create glowing tributes or excited testimonials about the vehicle, many environmentalists used the tools as an opportunity to criticize the vehicle and its gas-mileage rating, ironically using Chevy's SUV-in-Nature video clips to highlight the message. The resulting creations showed that at least some audiences were not buying. One parody included the message "Our planet's oil is almost gone. You don't need G.P.S. to see where this road leads." Another said, "Like this snowy wilderness? Better get your fill of it now. Then say hello to global warming" (Bosman 2006). Although the website is no longer online, examples of the parody ads can still be found on YouTube, such as one that features the following text over images of the Tahoe in a variety of "extreme nature" settings – perched on an inaccessible peak, etc. – that strain credulity:

> We paved the prairies. We deforested the hills. We strip-mined our mountains and sold ourselves for oil. To bring you this beautiful machine so you can finally drive to see what's left of our wilderness. And now that we're here, we can't get out of the car. America 2006: the ultimate padded cell [over a shot of the Tahoe's comfortable interior].
>
> (Vinh 2006)

The Tahoe advertisement's selection of clips are classic examples of using "executional" elements to associate the vehicle with the natural world and show it as both a means of accessing that world and mastering it at the same time. The irony was not lost on viewers, many of whom have clearly mastered what Halverson (2007) calls the "design grammar" of advertising slogans and the visual vocabulary of SUV advertising. Not all of these parodies were spontaneously generated by a public fed up with gas-guzzling vehicles, of course. Many of the parody ads were initiated by members of the Democratic Underground community: a post by the user Lars39 in the site's web forum lists well over a hundred variations ("DU's Chevy Tahoe Entries" 2006), though only the ones uploaded to sites like YouTube are still available today.

The very existence of "viral marketing gone bad" episodes like this then becomes a familiar element in popular culture, more recently exemplified in a series of Twitter "hashtag fails" (q.v.). Following the Macondo well blowout in the Gulf of Mexico in 2010, several parody Twitter accounts were created to mock the public-relations spin being generated by British Petroleum. One of these accounts, BPGlobalPR, continued producing parody tweets – such as "ATTN Smokers: Do you love messing with carcinogens, but you hate the taste? Eat gulf shrimp!" (Mascarenhas 2010) – up to two years after the event, satirizing BP's attempts at image management and deconstructing the greenwashing present in the company's advertising.

The environmental group Greenpeace showed their adroitness with this new cultural meme – the bungled new media advertising campaign – by creating a fictitious version of Shell Oil's "Let's Go" marketing campaign in 2012. The capstone was a faked press conference satirizing the technological fetishes of commodity culture in which a scale-model oil well malfunctioned and sprayed guests with black liquid. A corresponding series of web advertisements were designed to appear as if something like the Tahoe SUV debacle had occurred, though in this case Greenpeace was the host, not Shell. Using photographs of iconic wildlife like polar bears and arctic foxes along with the Shell logo and a "Let's Go" slogan, the ads featured tag lines like "You can't run your SUV on cute," and "If we show you pretty pictures, it must mean we care about the environment" (Iezzi 2014). The latter comment is an explicit reference to the power of nonverbal, executional elements described by Parguel and Benoit-Moreau (2013) and shows that environmentalists are finding ways to resist them through parody and satire, which foreground these elements in ways that may make them less effective forms of greenwashing. If SUVs perched on mountaintops and oil-company images of cute arctic wildlife become the butt of jokes, they lose their power to persuade – at least for some audiences. Advertising's use of the natural world as a selling tool may have to evolve in the participatory, "prosumer" culture that Jenkins and others describe. This is especially true as greater literacy in cultural production leads to even more consumer skepticism about advertisers' environmental claims and their manufactured, pseudo-viral social media campaigns.

Immersive advertising

There is also an ongoing evolution of mediation itself as it moves from observed-from-without (in the case of magazines and TV commercials) to the lived-from-within phenomenal immersion of computer games, virtual worlds, and *augmented reality* (see below). Using these technologies, we participate in the creation of convincingly ontological realities that are just as rhetorical as a TV commercial. Computer games and multiuser virtual environments (MUVEs) like *Second Life* continue to become more immersively realistic, with users inhabiting the virtual space in the form of embodied avatars. The result is what Stewart and Nicholls (2002) refer to as "one phenomenal body" (87) that blurs the line between media and reality. Although in one sense gamers and MUVE users are simply watching displays on a computer monitor, at a subjective and phenomenological level they are "inside" these spaces, treating them as if they are real spaces and places, responding to components within them (dragons, spaceships, animals, landscapes) as if they have material existence, projecting themselves into their avatars. Gaming chairs that rumble under a player when a landslide occurs, haptic-feedback controls that resist player movement, and wraparound headgear like the Oculus Rift expand the "screen" to include other senses. Such spaces thus become "virtual reality" as they approach a state of being virtually indistinguishable from material reality. When such media are used as conduits for green advertising that depicts aspects of the natural world, the implications are potentially troubling. Romanticized, highly rhetorical depictions, as well as impossible-but-convincing executional juxtapositions of products and "real" Nature, can become harder to distinguish from the real world they purport to represent.

Box 10.3   Nature in virtual reality

An emerging area within cultural studies explores the way the natural world is represented in computer simulations, electronic games, virtual reality, and other related technologies. This approach takes elements from earlier scholarship on visual rhetoric as well as the rhetoric of memorials, parks, and other spaces. Theory spans the tradition of landscape painting and English gardens from the eighteenth and nineteenth centuries, contemporary three-dimensional landscape and architectural modeling, and speculation about near-term developments in computer simulations in order to better understand and interpret changes in our reproductions and simulations of Nature. Useful readings include:

Opel, Andrew, and Jason Smith. 2004. "ZooTycoon™: Capitalism, Nature, and the Pursuit of Happiness." *Ethics & the Environment*, 9.2, 103–120.

Dickinson, Gregg, Carole Blair, and Brian L. Ott, eds. 2010. *Places of Public Memory: The Rhetoric of Museums and Memorials*. Tuscaloosa: University of Alabama Press.

Stewart, Robert S., and Roderick Nicholls. 2002. "Virtual Worlds, Travel, and the Picturesque Garden." *Philosophy & Geography*, 5.1, 83–99.

Also, see an entire journal volume devoted to this subject:

"Our Visual Landscape: Analysis, Modeling, Visualization and Protection." 2001. Special issue of the journal *Landscape and Urban Planning*, Volume 54.

Two relatively early forays into the medium of gaming environments demonstrate some of the potential for environmental misinformation: Chevron's *Energyville* game and BP's collaboration with the *Sims* franchise. In the former, players must select from various energy sources to power a small city shown in the kind of aerial, isometric view common in games like *Civilization* and *Age of Empires*. Springer argues that *Energyville* presents itself as a realistic simulation, yet greatly oversimplifies energy options. Players have no petroleum-free option, for example, which ignores the range of solar and wind technologies available in the nonvirtual world. Even when players make errors with energy choices, the environmental impacts are not visually evident at all. The game is touted as authoritative, having been "designed by the Economist group," a reference to a supposedly impartial party. Instead of simply reading about energy options or viewing presentations about them, the medium encourages players to believe that they have engaged in a realistic depiction of dynamic forces at play in the physical environment, rather than a limited, rhetorical subset of them (Springer 2012).

Similarly, BP's collaboration with the *Sims* is marketed as a "more nuanced" simulation that realistically (and, thus, by implication, impartially) presents the "tradeoffs" among energy options. As Schiesel (2007) notes, the BP game is more accurate than *Energyville* in its depiction of environmental and human impacts of energy choices, but even so, the presentation is partial and rhetorical: "One wrinkle in the game's marketing is that relatively clean systems like wind farms, natural gas plants and solar farms are branded with the BP logo, while the dirty options like coal are not" (Schiesel 2007). This allows the advertiser to present a world in which its products are always the more environmentally friendly choices; the more immersive and complete the virtual world presented, the greater the sense that this reality maps directly onto the physical one we inhabit, because we have "been there."

Colonizing reality with the virtual

Just as virtual reality in computer games and MUVEs "imports" real Nature into a virtual space, newer technologies collectively referred to as "augmented reality" (AR) deploy computer-generated images onto images of the real world on devices like portable smartphones. When a tourist aims her smartphone camera at a city street, AR technology can add information to the view – from labels and travel directions to entire computer-generated buildings and fanciful animated creatures. As technology advances, this artificial "skin" over the image can make the real and the representation difficult to separate. If you already know the street you're seeing on the phone's screen is real, since the real and the computer-generated image appear to be occupying the same real space, it's as if the virtual world has "escaped" to join you in the real world.

Realism is enhanced when the viewer can manipulate virtual objects by manipulating a real object, such as a sheet of paper imprinted with a distinctive QR code. For example, the "Plug into the Smart Grid" campaign from General Electric lets users interact with a virtual energy-technology demonstration that appears to exist in the real world if they view it through their computer monitors. When a user holds a sheet of paper with a special code on it in front of a webcam, the software shows the webcam's view on the computer screen and overlays it with an interactive and realistic toy windmill landscape:

> You can interact with the model – By blowing into the microphone, you actually cause the wind turbines to spin, which encourages you to interact with the experience and experiment with what's possible. You

can also tilt the Solar Energy model back and forth to move the sun and
cause the solar panels to follow. . . . it actually looks like it has become
a part of the page, and that you're holding a whole little world in your
hands.

(O'Brien 2014)

O'Brien's description aptly captures the "reality" of augmented reality:
this "whole little world" that magically appears before your eyes both acti-
vates the technological-fix obsession that Kilbourne (1995) warns about
and gives you a sense that you are directly experiencing – in this case –
real energy technologies in operation. GE can thus "teleport" its products
right into your home, in other words, in a carefully crafted sales presentation. The convincing realism of these images can mask the fact that they are
most decidedly not complete. They are just as partial and rhetorical as the
sanitized choices in *Energyville* or the SUVs that we're told will connect us
with Nature without harming it. And they are perhaps even more powerful
because these "whole little worlds" are under viewer control, implying a
similar control over the natural environment.

An even more immersively persuasive form of AR with both promising
and potentially disturbing application from an environmental perspective is
not yet widespread, though simplified versions of it can be found in smartphone travel apps like Layar and Yelp! These programs can be used while
traveling in an unfamiliar city: you can "scan" the surroundings with your
smartphone camera, and, as you pan around, the locations of nearby restau-
rants and coffee shops are superimposed over the video display – in effect
augmenting reality with additional information that appears to be a part of
the real world.

Of course, looking through a small smartphone screen makes the artifice
readily apparent – but consider the potential persuasiveness of executional-
element "rose-colored glasses" in existing technologies like Google Glass or
proposed ones like contact lens–embedded heads-up information displays.
There is potential for masking real-world problems by filtering out unpleasant views and replacing them with comforting greenery, for example, or
embedding virtual products and technologies into the visual landscape while
concealing their impacts. Technologies such as these make the world of *The
Matrix* – in which human beings are completely unaware of the desolation
of the planet they live on – seem much less like dystopian science fiction and
more like tomorrow's consumer electronics showcase.

Because the graphics and computing requirements of highly realistic
games and augmented realities place them beyond the means and abilities
of many to participate in their construction, these new technologies currently allow less participation than blogs and YouTube, returning us in a
sense to the controlled messages of the television, magazine, and film industries – with dramatically higher potential for powerful "executional greenwashing." On the other hand, if the means arise for audiences to contribute

content with these "new realities" in the way they could resist and parody the Chevy Tahoe ads, they can continue to challenge the persuasive realism of virtual and augmented reality as well as the commodity culture they propagate. This is especially critical as such media become deployed as new forms of advertising that continue the long tradition of utilizing both verbal and executional "Nature" in their messaging.

One promising approach is suggested by the Findery website, a tool that allows users to "tag" any point in the real world with commentary that is then visible to other users via maps or augmented-reality views as they move through the corresponding landscape. This creates a kind of crowd-sourced markup of the real world, with messages that can improve environmental awareness. As one user reports, "I've learned the names of plants I'd never noticed before. Someone has grafted branches from fruit trees onto the trees in the park near my office, and you can forage fruit from them" (Madrigal 2013). Thus, while advertisers may be able to layer a skin of visual appeals over everything we see, crowdsourcing apps and other technologies can also continue to provide opportunities for audiences to participate in the conversation and ensure that multiple voices and alternatives are not obscured.

Conclusion

In this chapter, we've examined research and theory focused on the ways advertisers have connected their products with the natural world – either to tout environmental claims or, more often, to simply make associations with preexisting human ideas about the value of Nature. As we've seen, in many cases the language is visual, which means that scholars must employ methods that help us understand design grammars as well as verbal claims. And we've looked at some new media theories and applications that help lay a foundation for understanding new advertising languages and forms of public participation emerging in websites, game worlds, and augmented reality.

The critical perspective adopted here is important, because we live in a finite world whose resources are under ongoing pressure from population growth, development, and in some cases, short-sighted practices, and we are thus well-advised to pay close attention to our cultural practices to learn their environmental ramifications. As many scholars have noted, advertising by its very nature tends to reproduce an ethic of consumption, with at most only a thin veneer of greenwashing. In the worst cases, it exploits our affinity for the natural world while simultaneously helping us destroy it. And as new developments like augmented reality suggest, advertising may help us blind ourselves to this danger. Finally, although we caution against uncritical evangelism regarding new participatory media, these emerging forms of public participation hold promise as tools of resistance as well.

Keywords

Augmented Reality
Commodification, commodity
   culture
Culture industry

Greenwashing
Nature
Remix, mashup

Questions for discussion

1   Is it possible to advertise in an ecologically direct and beneficial way?
2   Governments frequently regulate the kinds of verbal claims that advertisers can make about the "greenness" of a product. For example, automakers may have to measure fuel economy via specific means, or terms like "organic" may be limited to food grown in a particular, well-defined fashion. Can the same kind of regulation and standard definitions be applied to "executional" elements?
3   In your lifetime, have advertisements changed (or not changed) in the way they acknowledge threats like climate change, water shortages, habitat loss, or other environmental threats that have become newsworthy in the last decade?
4   If, as Fisk (1974) argues, audiences don't believe explicit, factual environmental claims that advertisers make about products, how do consumers gain the information needed to make informed purchasing decisions?
5   What would an ecocritical, crowdsourced web application look like? How would it work?
6   What are some of the environmental costs involved in advertising itself? For example, how much energy do web servers and game servers use?

Further reading

Andersen, Robin, and Lance Strate. 2000. *Critical Studies in Media Commercialism.* London: Oxford University Press.
Hansen, Anders. 2002. "Discourses of Nature in Advertising." *Communications: European Journal of Communication Research* 27.4: 499–511.
Jenkins, Henry. 1992. *Textual Poachers: Television Fans and Participatory Culture.* New York: Routledge.
Kilbourne, William E. 1995. "Green Advertising: Salvation or Oxymoron?" *Journal of Advertising* 24.2: 7–19.
Petty, Richard E., and John T. Cacioppo. 1981. *Attitudes and Persuasion: Classic and Contemporary Approaches.* Dubuque, IA: William C. Brown.
Roach, Catherine E. 2007. "Thinking Like a God: Nature Imagery in Advertising." *Reconstruction* 7.2. Eco-Cultures: Culture Studies and the Environment. http://reconstruction.eserver.org/072/roach.shtml
Smith, Toby. M. 1998. *The Myth of Green Marketing: Tending Our Goats at the Edge of the Apocalypse.* Toronto: University of Toronto Press.

Works cited

Andersen, Robin. 2000. "Road to Ruin: The Cultural Mythology of the SUV." In *Critical Studies in Media Commercialism*, edited by Robin Andersen and Lance Strate, 158–172. London: Oxford.

Andrejevic, Mark. 2005. "Cybernetic TV." *Flow*, October 21. http://flowtv.org/2005/10/cybernetic-tv/

———. 2007. "Watching TV Without Pity." *Flow*, April 5. http://flowtv.org/2007/04/watching-tv-without-pity/

Berger, Arthur A. 2011. *Ads, Fads, and Consumer Culture: Advertising's Impact on American Character and Society*, 4th ed. Lanham, MD: Rowman & Littlefield.

Bosman, Julie. 2006. "Chevy Tries a Write-Your-Own-Ad Approach, and the Potshots Fly." *The New York Times*, April 4. Accessed April 23, 2014. http://www.nytimes.com/2006/04/04/business/media/04adco.html

Cronon, William, ed. 1995. *Uncommon Ground: Rethinking the Human Place in Nature*. New York: W. W. Norton & Company.

"DU's Chevy Tahoe Entries: Democratic Underground." 2006. Accessed May 11, 2014. http://www.democraticunderground.com/discuss/duboard.php?az=view_all&address=364x812060

Ewen, Stuart. 1976. *Captains of Consciousness: Advertising and the Social Roots of the Consumer Culture*. New York: McGraw-Hill.

Fisk, George. 1974. *Marketing and the Ecological Crisis*. New York: Harper & Row.

Grimes, Sara M. 2006. "Online Multiplayer Games: A Virtual Space for Intellectual Property Debates?" *New Media & Society* 8.6: 969–990.

Gunster, Shane. 2004. "'You Belong Outside': Advertising, Nature, and the SUV." *Ethics & the Environment* 9.2: 4–32. doi:10.1353/een.2005.0003.

Halverson, Erica. 2007. "Reality Television, Fan Behavior, and Online Communities of Practice." *Proceedings of the 8th International Conference on Computer Supported Collaborative Learning*. International Society of the Learning Sciences, 244–246.

Hansen, Anders, and David Machin. 2008. "Visually Branding the Environment: Climate Change as a Marketing Opportunity." *Discourse Studies* 10.6: 777–94.

Hartmann, Patrick, Vanessa Apaolaza, and Patxi Alija. 2013. "Nature Imagery in Advertising: Attention Restoration and Memory Effects." *International Journal of Advertising* 32.2: 183–210.

Hovland, Roxanne, and Gary Wilcox. 1989. *Advertising in Society: Classic and Contemporary Readings on Advertising's Role in Society*. New York: McGraw-Hill.

Iezzi, Teressa. 2014. "See Shell's (Not Really) Crowd-Sourced Arctic Drilling Campaign." *Co.Create*. Accessed May 12, 2014. http://www.fastcocreate.com/1680935/see-shells-not-really-crowd-sourced-arctic-drilling-campaign

Iyer, Easwar, and Bobby Banerjee. 1993. "Anatomy of Green Advertising." In *NA – Advances in Consumer Research*, Volume 20, edited by Leigh McAlister and Michael L. Rothschild, 494–501. Provo, UT: Association for Consumer Research.

Jenkins, Henry. 1992. *Textual Poachers: Television Fans and Participatory Culture*. New York: Routledge.

———. 2004. "The Cultural Logic of Media Convergence." *International Journal of Cultural Studies* 7.1: 33–43.

Jhally, Sut. 1989. "The Political Economy of Culture." In *Cultural Politics in Contemporary America*, edited by Ian Angus and Sut Jhally, 65–81. New York: Routledge.

————. 2000. "Advertising at the Edge of the Apocalypse." In *Critical Studies in Media Commercialism*, edited by Robin Andersen and Lance Strate, 27–39. London: Oxford.

Kilbourne, William E. 1995. "Green Advertising: Salvation or Oxymoron?" *Journal of Advertising* 24.2: 7–19.

Knobel, Michele, and Colin Lankshear. 2008. "Remix: The Art and Craft of Endless Hybridization." *Journal of Adolescent & Adult Literacy* 52.1: 22–33.

Madrigal, Alexis C. 2013. "How Augmented-Reality Content Might Actually Work." *The Atlantic*. February 20. Accessed March 23, 2014. http://www.theatlantic.com/technology/archive/2013/02/how-augmented-reality-content-might-actually-work/273348/

Mascarenhas, Alex. 2010. "BP's Global PR vs. BPGlobalPR." *Newsweek*, June 3. Accessed August 13, 2014. http://www.newsweek.com/bps-global-pr-vs-bpglobalpr-73125

Nash, Roderick F. 2001. *Wilderness in the American Mind*, 4th ed. New Haven, CT: Yale University Press.

O'Brien, Cory. 2014. "GE Plugs into the Smart Grid with Augmented Reality." *The Future of Ads*. Accessed May 12, 2014. http://thefutureofads.com/ge-plugs-into-the-smart-grid-with-augmented-reality

Parguel, Beatrice, and Florence Benoit-Moreau. 2013. "The Power of 'Executional Greenwashing': Evidence from the Automotive Sector." Accessed March 29, 2014. http://www.cerog.org/lalondeCB/CB/2013_lalonde_seminar/program/papers/parg.pdf

Roach, Catherine E. 2007. "Thinking Like a God: Nature Imagery in Advertising." *Reconstruction* 7.2. Eco-Cultures: Culture Studies and the Environment. http://reconstruction.eserver.org/072/roach.shtml

Schiesel, Seth. 2007. "Game Maker Joins Forces With Energy Company." *The New York Times*, October 10. Retrieved May 10, 2015. http://www.nytimes.com/2007/10/10/arts/10sims.html

Schnaiberg, Allan. 1993. "The Political Economy of Environmental Problems and Policies: Consciousness, Coordination, and Control Capacity." In *Advances in Human Ecology*, Volume 3, edited by Lee Freese, 23–64. Greenwich, CT and London: JAI Press.

Smith, Toby. M. 1998. *The Myth of Green Marketing: Tending Our Goats at the Edge of the Apocalypse*. Toronto: University of Toronto Press.

Springer, Michael. 2012. "Greening Games: Chevron's 'Energyville'." *Playing with Rhetoric*, September 9. Retrieved May 10, 2014. http://findingagap.wordpress.com/2012/09/09/greening-games-energyville/

Stewart, Robert Scott, and Roderick Nicholls. 2002. "Virtual Worlds, Travel, and the Picturesque Garden." *Philosophy & Geography* 5.1: 83–99.

Vinh, Khoi. 2006. "Chevy Tahoe Parody Ad." Accessed May 10, 2014. https://www.youtube.com/watch?v=SiE4FXO8nDs

Wharton, Chris, ed. 2013. *Advertising as Culture*. Bristol: Intellect Ltd.

Williams, Raymond. 1983. *Keywords: A Vocabulary of Culture and Society*. London: Flamingo.

Winett, Richard A., Ingrid N. Leckliter, Donna E. Chinn, Brian Stahl, and Susie Q. Love. 1985. "Effects of Television Modeling on Residential Energy Conservation." *Journal of Applied Behavior Analysis* 18.1: 33–44.

11 Where the wild games are
Ecologies in Latin American video games

Lauren Woolbright and Thaiane Oliveira

Introduction

Digital games have a unique ability that other media do not necessarily boast: they require the audience to participate directly in the action rather than passively observe events. Actively taking part in the development of characters and advancement of plot – even the simplest of plots – makes for a unique media experience, one that immerses players in digital worlds, exposes them to diverse characters with varied perspectives, and puts them in situations where their choices determine the outcome of the story. Mostly, game designers are concerned with selling games, but as games become more mainstream, they get more diverse in form and content. The *indie games* market (small companies and individuals/small teams of developers) in particular allows for design experimentation that can create the same depth of meaning we find in what is considered "great" film and literature. Games are fast becoming accepted as art and have even been recognized as such by august bodies like the U.S. Supreme Court (Sutter 2011). Specifically, when the state of California made the claim that the immersive nature of games sets them apart, disqualifying them from First Amendment protections, the court maintained that choice in media is nothing new, and as an expressive medium, games deserve protections, a ruling that legitimizes them as art. Like all art forms, video games communicate meaning, and we will be focusing on their relevance as meaning-makers of environments and purveyors of environmental themes.

Narratology vs. ludology

As narrative art, video games – like film, comics, and other storytelling forms – often include plot and character development. However, they also include *mechanics* specific to their form: rules, restrictions, and control buttons a player must push in a particular sequence to accomplish an action or goal. Scholars such as Rick Adams (2014), Greg Costikyan (2002), and Jesper Juul (2013) suggest that mechanics are what make interactive games unique. Valuing games not for meaning-creation, but for the challenge and fun they provide, such scholars propose a theory known in game studies as *ludology* (from the Latin "ludens" meaning "play"). *Narratology*, by contrast, focuses on plot and character development. Narratologists such as Janet Murray – who tend to come from literary and film studies backgrounds – feel that video games work best as a new storytelling medium, and when the story is strong, the game is strong (Murray 1998). Media theorist Henry Jenkins reminds us that both these views are valid, that both deserve equal attention, and that ludologists would benefit from a greater appreciation of narrative in games (Jenkins 2004).

Importantly, mechanics help frame meaning-making because how one physically can play a game helps shape our sense of its communication. Games scholar Ian Bogost (2007) writes that since most game designers cannot program with all possible themes in mind, the player is left to decode meaning from the story, the characters, and the mechanics – what he calls a game's *procedural rhetoric*. When Bogost refers to "procedures," he means the "core affordances of computers: running processes and executing rule-based symbolic manipulation" (Bogost 2007, cover). Translation: computers operate by rules, which can be interpreted by users as meaningful because of *how* they work. When Bogost says "rhetoric," he means effective persuasion, thoughtful argument, and thinking about perspective and audience. In short, the rules of games and how players work within those rules are ways of making arguments, whether intended by designers or not. One might ask, what environmental arguments do video games make?

Scholars such as Alenda Chang suggest that video games commonly share flaws in accurately or ethically representing the nonhuman natural world: "relegating environment to background scenery, relying on stereotyped landscapes, and predicating player success on extraction and use of natural resources" (2011, 58). Like Chang (2011), Espen Aarseth (2008) points out such flaws in widely popular games such as *World of Warcraft*, *The Legend of Zelda*, and *Minecraft*; however, games also have the potential to positively engage environmental arguments.

The following sections of this chapter introduce game studies terms that are especially relevant for grounding analysis of representations of environmental ethics in games. In the final sections, we then turn our ecocritical attention to the two fastest growing game industries in the world – Mexico and Brazil.

Is this the real life?

The distinction between the physical world and *gamespace* is one that is increasingly perceived as illusory. Jan Rune Holmevik asserts that "what we have previously believed is a boundary between the real and the virtual is an illusion we constructed in order to privilege the material or 'real' world over an immaterial or 'virtual' world" (Holmevik 2011, 93). Holmevik is responding in part to McKenzie Wark, who seeks to dissolve the binary between real and virtual. In *Gamer Theory* (2007), Wark writes: "You are a gamer whether you like it or not, now that we all live in a gamespace that is everywhere and nowhere. . . . You can go anywhere you want in the gamespace, but you can never leave it."

The act of playing a video game is an experience that involves the trading of two spatial constructions. The first relates to the game itself, which Jesper Juul (2005) defines as the *game world* based on considerations of Johan Huizinga, an early twentieth-century gaming visionary who considered the social and cultural characteristics of in-game environments (Huizinga 1950). Huizinga called the separation of what is ordinary world and what is game world a *magic circle*, since games usually have their own spatial and temporal universe that is distinct from the ordinary world (210). According to Huizinga, play is a voluntary activity within fixed limits of time and place with rules freely accepted, but absolutely binding, which help create feelings of tension, joy, and awareness "different" from those inspired by the ordinary world, where we eat, sleep, and work. Katie Salen and Eric Zimmerman further develop the concept of magic circle (2006). More than a separation between the real and the game world, the magic circle has been employed to describe the way users create boundaries between the real and fantasy, between the ordinary world and the game world.

These discussions raise some crucial questions: how do ordinary and game worlds intersect, and what are their ecological repercussions? While it is obvious that there is a material footprint in the creation and maintenance of game systems, we can also ask, how do their narrative and mechanical designs affect our environmental imaginations? What messages about environments might we carry from games into our ordinary worlds, and vice versa? Below we briefly consider a variety of popular video games to help answer some of these questions.

Into the cave

Early video games were often text based. Players would be given information about the world in text form and based on textual commands they could explore the game's world. *Colossal Cave Adventure,* designed by William Crowther and Don Woods in 1976, was a popular example of such a text-based game with a digital landscape based on a real place – Mammoth Cave in Kentucky (2004). Cave enthusiasts reported that a player familiar with the game could successfully navigate the actual cave system from the game's descriptions (Chang 2011).

Whether a game like *Colossal Cave Adventure* deepens environmental understanding or appreciation depends on the player, and a wide range of responses to any given game are possible. As with any medium, when many interpretations are possible, the ethical approaches to the content reside not only with designers (the writers) but also with players (readers/viewers). Through this game, players could reflect on the destruction human visits to caves can cause or might even recognize the disturbing ecological footprint of technologies that make gameplay possible. Might this spur them to *do* something? As of yet, we can only speculate that it could.

Box 11.1   Going wild

What can players realistically learn about cave environments or other geologically, biologically, and geographically diverse ecosystems from playing a game like *Colossal Cave Adventure*? Do they gain an appreciation for or want to visit the real cave system, or would this potentially give them a reason to stay home (why leave when you can experience a cave from the safety of your living room)? What game mechanics might encourage or discourage players to consider environments?

World of Warcraft ecologies

While *Colossal Cave Adventure* is an older, text-based example of video games that suggest environmental possibilities, one example of a more recent and advanced game that can similarly be explored is Blizzard's *World of Warcraft*, launched in 2004. *WoW* (as it is colloquially known) is the most successful *massively multiplayer online role-playing game* (MMORPG) in history, boasting over eleven million players at its peak in 2006 (*WoWWiki* 2014). As of 2014, it boasts over seven million players worldwide.

World of Warcraft features idyllic, stereotyped scenery, which often serves only as backdrop to the action. However, as analyzed by Aarseth (2008), there are also various ecological themes. Players can deforest and strip mine or try to stop these environmentally destructive actions; they can put out a forest fire and observe regrowth; and one common justification for killing to level up is to control invasive species. There are over forty quests that use the term "ecology" and plenty more that mention "environment." Certain races are nature oriented; the tauren as well as the night elves exhibit ethics of eco-holism, maintaining balance in the natural world (*WoWWiki* 2014). *WoW*'s environmental disasters are typically not natural, but caused by sentient races. For example, goblins are a highly tech-dependent, playable race that see harvesting resources as necessary to their advancement. Their starting zone overflows with garbage, they drive smoke-spewing cars, and their Venture Co. Mine near the tauren starting zone destroys the mountains and pollutes the water.

The variety of possible environmental interactions and the choices players make about whether and how to participate means the players must engage with in-game ethics, which they define for themselves. While a player can play both sides of these conflicts as multiple characters, Miguel Sicart writes that *WoW* has ethical limits; because of the game rules, it is impossible to level up an environmentally ethical goblin or a tauren industrialist, just as it is ineffective to level up *any* character without killing (Sicart 2009). Pacifist characters simply cannot advance, thus every player determined to succeed in the game must put their character in constant conflict with the natural world.

Minecraft-ing

Mojang's **sandbox game** *Minecraft* depicts yet another type of environmental interaction. Sandbox games are not structured around leveling, narrative, or quests; they drop players into a world meant for building, exploring, and manipulating. *Minecraft* has enemies to fight and villagers to defend when night falls, but only if the player chooses. Its main appeal lies in controlling the game's natural resources, which do not regenerate over time as they do in *WoW*. Most of *Minecraft*'s gameplay consists of digging, chopping down trees, building with harvested resources, and raising crops and livestock to survive. Players choose how many trees to chop and how many to plant, where to dig and how deep or wide, and how many buildings to make. While the game is realistic in that often resources do not regenerate and all changes made by players are permanent, there is no industry or pollution, and game mechanics allow for things like putting two sheep in a pit and having them breed thousands of sheep to happily coexist in the pit. There is no measure of in-game success except accomplishing personal resource goals; environmental ethics are thus not part of the design but are instead player motivated and severely limited in the game world.

Games like *Colossal Cave Adventure*, *WoW*, and *Minecraft* are America's video gaming legacy to the world and thus useful starting points for ecocritical analysis. However, in the remaining sections of this chapter, we leave America's monolithic game industry to explore the ecocritical nature of games developed in the fast-growing game markets of Mexico and Brazil. Turning our attention here helps shed light on the environmental attitudes of Latino cultures as presented through their gaming expressions.

Mexico's game industry

Mexico has the fastest growing game industry in the world. Analysts attribute this to a number of factors, including the fact that over fifty percent of the population of the country is under the age of twenty-five ("Latin American Game Market" 2013), and games are popular with a young audience. This generation grew up with arcades down the street and with the earliest available in-home consoles; they have been around games their entire lives.

The arcade market stayed strong in Mexico much longer than in the United States, right through the 1990s (Cervera and Quesnel 2013). The 2000s have seen Mexican gamers picking up in-home gaming consoles such as the Microsoft Xbox and Sony PlayStation. American games are popular with Mexican gamers, but game design and production is also growing in Mexico (*LAI* 2014). American titles that represent Mexico or Mexican culture tend to portray stereotypes or negative subjects like drug trafficking and cartels (first-person shooters like *Uncharted: Drake's Fortune* [2007] and *Tomb Raider: Underworld* [2008] are classic examples). In such games, Mexico often serves simply as an exotic backdrop to the action and gameplay experience. In contrast, many Mexican-designed games point to untapped eco-potential in their depictions of and gameplay with the unique landscapes and cultures of Mexico. These games represent only a small portion of the indie platformer and mobile games markets and have yet to find the enormous audience triple-A American titles have in Mexico. Because of their local focus and affordability, however, they have been rising in popularity; we are likely to see more games like these.

Mexico's mobile market

While the Mexican console games market has yet to pick up steam, the mobile and online games market is strong in Mexico. Companies such as Slang Studios, Ricardosoft, and Phyne Games have developed a variety of apps and Facebook games mimicking successful U.S.-developed games in the same genre (*Farmville* and *Plants vs. Zombies*, for example); some do offer content dealing with the environments and cultures of Mexico. Phyne Games, for example, developed the mobile game *Mictlan* (2012), which follows the design model set by *Plants vs. Zombies*, but uses a *Dia de los Muertos* (Day of the Dead) theme.

Box 11.2 Talk about it: festivals and video games

Dia de los Muertos: In Catholic Mexican culture, the Day of the Dead is a time to honor those who have passed on. People clean relatives' gravestones and decorate them with offerings of food, flowers, and religious objects. In doing so, they celebrate life and what the earth has to offer those who are alive. For example, *pan de muertos* (semisweet breads) are baked in the shape of bones and dusted with sugar (to represent the soil from which life springs). In recent years, the holiday has evolved to become similar to American Halloween with industrially manufactured candy and costumes and similar consumerist valences. By researching the evolution of *Dia de los Muertos* or the festival rituals of other cultures (for example, *Diwali* in the Hindu tradition), consider how ordinary world cultural practices might become relevant in game worlds in terms of narrative and mechanics. If you were to design a game about a contemporary festival, how might you inform the game's environmental attitudes?

In *Mictlan* (the Aztec word for the underworld), protagonist Luno – a recently deceased boy – must placate spirits with traditional offerings to keep them from advancing into the mortal world and presumably wreaking havoc on the living. Developers at Phyne were deeply conscious of the meaning behind each element of game design and play, celebrating Mexican culture and bringing it to a wider audience (Icarus1806 [YouTube persona] 2012).

At first, this game might seem entirely human focused, but Luno serves as the caretaker – the steward – of the rest of humanity and the world. The damage the dead might wreak on the living – that death can wreak on life – has decidedly environmental overtones. If Luno fails and is not a diligent steward maintaining the natural order of life and death, the repercussions can be overwhelming. This interpretation is one that resides with the players rather than being intentionally designed.

Jane Bennett and other object-oriented theorists trouble the arbitrary boundaries we draw between the living ("vibrant things") and the inert ("dull things"). Bennett argues that objects are active forces in our lives, using examples like the "lively" flow of chemicals and air pollutants from our supposedly disposed-of garbage (2009, viii). She develops the concept of vital materiality to illustrate how seemingly lifeless things actually have lives that affect ours, ecologically speaking (Bennett 2009). The dead rising to threaten the living in games can be read as a metaphor for these processes. In a natural cycle, death is essential, and the decay of dead material means new life for other creatures – a vital materiality. However, when this cycle is disrupted, as suggested by the rising of the dead to threaten the living in the game, such transcorporeal materiality can become toxic (see Alaimo 2010). *Mictlan* also acknowledges the importance of honoring the dead with candles, bread, and bones, all essential items in the traditional practices of *Dia de los Muertos* and important "inert" signifiers of the vitality of life. If the player wins the game, they succeed in holding the natural balance of life and death in order, and they do so using these significant cultural symbols that blur the boundaries between humans and their relationship to the nonhuman.

Guacamelee!: between worlds

Another Mexican-themed game, the Indie **platformer** (side-scrolling, often 2-D games with running, jumping, climbing mechanics) *Guacamelee!* was produced by a Canadian company and developed by a Mexican-Canadian programmer. Though the game was not developed in Mexico, it is set in Mexico and the game stars a *luchador* – a Mexican wrestler.

The plot is a stereotypical damsel in distress situation where the player must rescue the kidnapped beloved, navigating perils along the way. This heavily gendered plot is complicated by the player being able to choose to play a male or female character. While playing a female, nonplayer characters still refer to this *luchador* character as Juan and the villainess flirts with Juan referring to Juan's size and strength in ways that can be read as either reinforcing traditional feminine–masculine roles or queering it, depending on one's perspective. Environmentally speaking, most of the gameplay takes place in small, traditional Mexican villages and the desert and forest landscapes between them. The player fights adversaries from the spirit world, and the player must move between the living world and the Underworld. Like *Mictlan*, this game has a spiritual awareness worked into its mechanics. The game's art style keeps Mexican culture firmly in the player's mind, and even in landscapes that might be anywhere (see figure), players often run across well-kept shrines and Aztec ruins as well as *Dia de los Muertos*–themed enemies.

Ecological themes do not figure prominently in *Guacamelee!*, but the bulk of the gameplay involves navigating dangerous environments: sliding safely past thorny vines, avoiding watery traps, fighting off man-eating plants and other creatures, and smashing through rocks to practice new abilities that are crucial to success in combat. While the player might mindlessly move through these areas, s/he is exposed to adversarial environments for the majority of the game, and that is the main experience s/he takes away from it. The game is full of undead monsters, most notably a giant *alebrije* (fantasy creature in Mexican folk art style) sleeping in one of the temple ruins. The beast is coded to attack the player, so it is "okay" to destroy it, and there is no way to advance without doing so, even though the beast is beautiful and is being made to attack by the game's antagonist; this is thin justification for killing common to such games. While adversarial, the

Figure 11.1 Alebrije monster from *Guacamelee!*
Source: Courtesy of DrinkBox Studios, Inc.

natural world also facilitates the character's progress toward his goal. The terrain can be used strategically against enemies in combat through the players' movements to higher or lower ground (up trees and cliffs) or their use of natural elements such as large stones as weapons or tools to progress through an area.

Like *Mictlan*, *Guacamelee!* depicts passage from the living world to the Underworld and back, exploring the permeability of that boundary (enemies can reach up from the Underworld to harm the player, but the player must go through a portal into the Underworld to defeat them). The presence of the undead in the living world along with the monsters and the portals portray an ecosystem out of balance, and while the game is upbeat and humorous, the undead invasion is constantly at odds with the player, who must accomplish the "real" goal of saving the beloved. As with *Minecraft*, environmental themes are thus available for interpretation, even though they are not foregrounded in the narrative.

Papo & Yo: fear and loathing beyond Mexico

Anxiety has a prominent place in our next game. Mexico has a history of environmental problems. In the 1990s, air pollution in Mexico City was so bad experts claimed it was the most dangerous city in the world for children (Hibler n.d.). Although a number of policies have been passed to improve the situation, air pollution is still a serious problem (Hibler n.d.). Every Mexican lives with this awareness, so games designed in Mexico do reflect such consciousness, if not on the surface, then as a subtext. Brazilian indie puzzle/platformer *Papo & Yo* (2013) is a good example of a game popular in Mexico, so we will mention it here, even though it is not Mexican. The main content of the game is a metaphor for child abuse, but the mechanics and scenery are deeply rooted in environmental disturbances unique to Latin America.

Papo & Yo's protagonist, a young boy named Quico, navigates himself and a monster representing his father through the *favelas* (overcrowded slums) of a Brazilian city. The player must flee Quico's alcoholic father into a dream world and use the monster he meets there to move heavy objects and progress from one level to the next. Though not part of the game's explicit point, playing through that dilapidated landscape coupled with the game's dark social message of the pain caused by child abuse communicates the environmental and economic problems the poor in the *favelas* face every day. The challenge of moving from one level to the next, never knowing when the monster will turn from helper to attacker, creates a sense of unease and fear, which the environmentally alert player then can associate with the broken urban landscape they navigate. Such landscapes recall the thick scholarship of environmental justice, which Latin American scholars such as David Carruthers (2008) remind us help draw attention to toxic materialities that arise from the tightly enmeshed web of socioecological disadvantages.

The Brazilian uncertainty zones of alternate reality games

In all, the platformer games discussed so far and popular in Mexico are ones that allude in metaphorical ways to environmental themes in the ordinary world, maintaining a more or less explicit magic circle that keeps gameplay contained in the virtual sphere. Now let us consider alternate reality games from the growing game market of Brazil, as these articulate environmental themes in interestingly different ways as the game design blurs the magic circle, enabling ordinary and game worlds to collide more fluidly.

Originating from the experience of role-playing games (RPGs), ARGs or *alternative reality games* are considered a subcategory of pervasive games, as this is a game genre that uses both Internet spaces and ordinary world spaces as a large board where players everywhere are looking for solutions to the puzzles of the game.

Box 11.3   The first ARG

The ARG emerged as game genre in 2001 as the promotional campaign of the film *Artificial Intelligence* directed by Steven Spielberg. This game was named *The Beast*. During the course of the three months of the campaign, the game incorporated thirty diverse in-game websites, with information fundamental for the game event.

Gamers speculated that there were 666 puzzles in the game. Examples of some the puzzles were the three entry points called rabbit holes. The Rabbit Hole (recalling Lewis Carroll's famous story, *Alice in Wonderland*) refers to the strategy used by Puppetmasters (a term for game developers) to hook the audience in such a way that reality and fiction become fluid. The three rabbit holes were: 1) some trailers and posters that included a credit line for Jeanine Salla as Sentient Machine Therapist; 2) one of the trailers encoded a telephone number. If the player called this number, a message reported that "Jeanine is the key"; and 3) a promotional poster was sent to some technology and entertainment media outlets; it included a code stating "Evan Chan was murdered. Jeanine is the key." Such clues and puzzle game engaged thousands of members and generated over 40,000 messages amongst players.

ARGs have a fragmented narrative and tend to be used on various platforms and devices, including landscape spaces, such as urban settings, where puzzles and riddles of the game are distributed. ARG structure involves different communication tools – such as email, social media, SMS, websites, mobile – that are used to connect characters in a fictional universe. To advance in this universe, the player must solve puzzles and investigate mysteries, among other challenges (Oliveira 2012; 2013). Dan Provost further explains:

> All of the players are intensely involved in the story, which takes place in real-time and cannot be replayed. The narrative evolves based on players' interactions with it, and everything is designed and controlled by humans, rather than a computer or some artificial intelligence (as would be the case in a traditional computer or console game).
>
> (Provost 2008, 2)

Because of this blurring of reality and fiction and the use of collaboration to solve the game's puzzles, Provost considers the ARGs as the first metafictional narrative art form on the Internet. An interesting phenomenon of this game genre is *This Is Not a Game* (TINAG), which consists in pretending that the game is real to enhance the experience.

Jane McGonigal reports that moments after the attack of 9/11, many players of *The Beast*, a game developed in conjunction with Steven Spielberg's film, *Artificial Intelligence* (see Box 11.3), approached the event as if it were a game. Even though they were fully aware that 9/11 was not a game and instead reality, they hoped to together unravel its mysteries because the game had "profoundly affected their sense of identity and purpose, to the point that a game mentality was a natural response to real-world events" (McGonigal 2003, 1). They believed they would be able to assist federal agencies resolve the attacks on the World Trade Center, as their successful previous experiences with solving complex mysteries in the game happened a few months before the tragic event in the United States. After two days of insistence from the players, the moderators of the group had to intervene in discussions, reminding them that 9/11 was not a game. In general, TINAG serves as a mantra for ARG games. Part of the fun of participating in ARGs is facing challenges of the experience as if it was not a game.

Since 2001, at least 200 ARGs have been developed in various countries, including Turkey, Greece, Sweden, Germany, Belgium, El Salvador, and the United States. Brazil is the second largest producer and, consequently, the largest consumer of non-English language ARGs (DENA, 2009, 206). ARG success in Brazil can be largely attributed to *Zona Incerta*, our next case study.

The national identity of the Amazon rainforest in the game *Zona Incerta*

Zona Incerta, which roughly translates to "Uncertain Zone," refers to the game's geographical focus, the Amazon rainforest and river basin. It is an ARG made by the Youth Nucleus of Editora Abril in partnership with the multinational company AmBev. The game's purpose was to promote a Brazilian soda called Guaraná Antarctica. Guaraná Antarctica, since the early twentieth century, when it was created, always presents itself and has been appreciated as a part of national identity, as a genuine product of Brazil, in contrast to other competing soft drinks, like Coke.

The brand appropriates the Amazon as its iconography, not only because this is a region where the fruit guaraná grows, but also because the Amazon is an important element of cultural identity. It is a major South American biome that represents over half of the planet's remaining tropical forests and comprises the most tropical forest biodiversity in the world. The territory also contains significant mineral wealth for the nuclear industry, such as niobium and uranium, and thus is valued not just ecologically, but also for its economic promise. The Amazon territory has been at the center of transnational politics since the Treaty of Tordesillas and territorial fights between Spain and Portugal for the region. Recognizing its unique characteristics, Brazilian society values its Amazonian territories as a symbol of national identity, collective memory and pride, and a region to be preserved against international greed. By branding itself with the Amazon, Guaraná Antarctica reinforces a positive image with its consumers who identify with the product as something that forms part of their "Brazilianness." The company's social and environmental rhetoric and actions, such as its program "AmBev Recycles" is also helpful in eliciting Brazilian support.

In general, in a country of prevalent multiculturalism, few cultural elements support national cohesion as much as the Amazon. Thus, one of Guaraná Antarctica's brand strategies was the production of the ARG *Zona Incerta*. The ARG gained notoriety not only because of the number of Brazilian players engaged (approximately 70,000), but also for garnering visibility for a controversial and costly topic for Brazilians: the preservation of the Amazon. The company created nine websites. Dozens of videos were released on the Internet strategically. Blogs and pages of fake profiles for significant characters were published on Orkut, the top social network in Brazil at that time. In one of the videos, the character Allen Perrell, Senior Director of Marketing for Arkhos Biotech and the game's villain, announced to the world that the Brazilian government would no longer be able to protect the Amazon region. (The video can be accessed on YouTube.) His foil, the "hero" of the game, Miro Bittencourt, is a fictional scientist who works at Guaraná Antarctica; he has discovered the secret archives of the company. Through the Internet, he is able to launch various puzzles, asking the netizens to help him decode the riddles and save the Amazon. Despite not being the first, this was the most controversial ARG launched in Brazil.

Many Brazilians believed the videos were real and shared them via social media and word of mouth. Some even organized protests virtually through emails demonstrating their anger at the company Arkhos Biotech (which did not exist outside the game). For example, on YouTube, it is still common to find some of the outraged comments, such as this one *"[%$&]!!! They end up with their forests and want to take the others . . . yes! Amazon has an owner, which they certainly are not, nor will it be!"*

Along with everyday citizens, then-Senator Arthur Virgilio spoke out strongly in the senate calling for appropriate action by the federal government against the company, all without realizing that it was part of a game (Senate News Portal 2007). Because of this episode, Senator Virgilio was invited to become the "poster boy" of the Guaraná Antarctica's campaign. The senator publically accepted, but this partnership was not pursued. Instead, the videos of Virgilio's speech were taken off the network under allegation of copyright infringement.

The senator was not the only one to commit the gaffe of believing *Zona Incerta*'s game content to be real. Another public figure, State Deputy Perpetua Almeida, made the same speech against Arkhos Biotech, as did Roberto Requião, the ex-governor of Paraná. Through the political and journalistic failures to check news sources and through an extensive viral marketing of the games' videos, it is obvious that the barriers that separate reality from fiction are more fluid than the contemporary imagination tends to believe. They are complementary forces in our lives – not mutually exclusive ones.

Our ecological perspective on ARGs recognizes that we must pay attention to the game as an environment that not only reproduces existing social discourses, but also speaks on its own, reverberating both in game and in society. We understand that the game in question, which has a transience between reality and fiction, is an environment that blurs the boundaries of the magic circle, one that falls in line with Wark's discussion of how everything in life is a game that, ultimately, we find hard to leave. Confused by *Zona Incerta*'s realism, politicians found themselves playing the game of politics over the issue of the Amazon, which is, in fact, a real-life concern. Thus, rather than seeing all of life as a game, we might acknowledge the reality of games and claim that games are, in fact, a kind of reality, one that does impact players in ways we have yet to fully understand.

Blurred boundaries

Beyond the dissolution of the borders of the real and the fictional that some people have encountered, there have been several times when the game itself has forced this break. Soon after *Zona Incerta* had launched, on March 17, 2007, during U.S. President George W. Bush's visit to strike a deal on Brazilian ethanol, thousands of Brazilians turned up to protest. One group of people dressed as trees with a huge banner reading: "Out Arkhos Biotech – The Amazon is ours!" The banner was signed by Parallax Effect, with the address of the website. Parallax Effect was a (fictional) group of environmental activists who saw the foreign researchers sent to the Amazon as a threat to national sovereignty. Bush's visit to Brazil was broadcast around the world, simultaneously advertising Parallax Effect. Through a link on the Parallax Effect website, players learned about the company Arkhos Biotech (also fictional and co-opted from the *Zona Incerta* ARG). Parallax Effect claimed that the forest is increasingly threatened and that its importance should be an international environmental concern.

This is a discourse very close to the heart for Brazil, since the Amazon is a place with not only territorial fights but symbolic disputes. Players came up with the idea to create a website against Arkhos Biotech in an effort to keep the issue of the Amazon from dissipating. In other words, they created new ways of fighting for environmental causes and for the preservation of the Amazon apart from traditional activist strategies. Fiction was used to propagate fact.

Conclusion: potential (under)growth

Whether platformers, MMORPGs, or pervasive games, all games have the potential to generate ecological themes, creating dynamic interactive player experiences involving environmental arguments and ethics. Though few games are doing this overtly and as yet few game scholars are calling for it, the possibilities are very promising. Games have the capacity to blur the lines between ordinary and digital worlds and call into question the "fakeness" of games that makes so many people write them off as an insignificant or even damaging medium. These rich and enriching worlds offer life at a different level, and it is well worth asking what kinds of environments we want to build in them. As much as game designers communicate via the mechanics, aesthetics, and narratives they develop, players hack, modify, and interpret for themselves, intertwining their own experiences with the game environments they co-create.

Video games have vast ecocritical potential in their game design and the code that dictates how players are permitted to interact with the nonhuman natural game world – not to mention how it might interact back! We hope to see more ecocritical game studies and games exploring these ideas more overtly in the future. We might design a few ourselves.

Keywords

Alternative reality games (ARGs)
Indie games
Ludology
Massively multiplayer online role-playing games (MMORPGs)
Mechanics

Narratology
Platformer
Procedural rhetoric
Role-playing games (RPGs)
Pervasive games
This Is Not a Game (TINAG)

Discussion questions

1   What specific aspects of the design, mechanics, and gameplay experience contribute to your definition of what counts as an environmental or environmentally conscious game?

2   Make a list of the main environmental problems around you. Come up with an idea for a game that is designed with environmental themes in mind (i.e., there are elements from ordinary worlds that can affect perceptions of the players during the game and after.) What design features will make for the best player engagement and experience in this game?

3   Overcoming the nonhuman natural world as an adversary is a common requirement in many games. We can speculate that such game mentality has an effect on out-of-game attitudes in players. Yet, no one has done any large-scale studies to determine such effects. What do you think some of the possible effects *could* be, if any? Survey your classmates and friends to see how they might bring their own gaming experiences to help answer these questions. Make a convincing argument for gaming's effects or lack thereof on the ordinary world.

Further reading

Bell, Mark W. 2008. "Toward a Definition of Virtual Worlds." *Journal of Virtual Worlds Research* 1.1. Accessed November 7, 2012. https://journals.tdl.org/jvwr/index.php/jvwr/article/view/283/237; DOI: http://dx.doi.org/10.4101/jvwr.v1i1.283.

Carruthers, David. 2008. *Environmental Justice in Latin America: Problems, Promise, and Practice.* Cambridge, MA: MIT Press.

Chang, Alenda Y. 2011. "Games as Environmental Texts." *Qui Parle: Critical Humanities and Social Sciences* 19.2: 57–84.

Hedron, Nassau. 2012. "MeXBox Rising: Mexico's Gaming Industry Turns into a Monster." *Once and Future Mexico* March 17. WordPress.com. Accessed August 30, 2013.

Martin, Adam, B. Thompson, and T. Chatfield. 2006. *Alternate Reality Games White Paper.* International Game Developers Association.

McGonigal, Jane. 2011. *Reality Is Broken: Why Games Make Us Better and How They Can Change the World.* New York: Penguin.

Meyers, Eric M., and Robert Bittner. 2012. "'Green Washing the Digital Playground': How Virtual Worlds Support Ecological Intelligence . . . Or Do They?" *iConference 2012*, February 7–10. Toronto, Ontario, Canada.

Szulborski, Dave. 2005. *This Is Not a Game: A Guide to Alternate Reality Gaming.* Lulu.com.

Works cited

Aarseth, Espen. 2008. *A Hollow World: World of Warcraft as Spatial Practice.* Boston: MIT Press.

Adams, Rick. 2014. *Colossal Cave Adventure Page.* Accessed May 12. http://rickadams.org/adventure/

Alaimo, Stacey. 2010. *Bodily Natures: Science, Environment and the Material Self.* Bloomington: Indiana University Press.

Bennett, Jane. 2009. *Vibrant Matter: A Political Ecology of Things.* Durham, NC: Duke University Press.

Bogost, Ian. 2007. *Persuasive Games.* Cambridge, MA: MIT Press.

Carruthers, David. 2008. *Environmental Justice in Latin America: Problems, Promise, and Practice.* Cambridge, MA: MIT Press.

Cervera, Humberto, and Jacinto Quesnel. 2013. "Video Games around the World: Mexico." *XGameBrainX.* Accessed May 12, 2014.

Chang, Alenda Y. 2009. *Playing the Environment: Games as Virtual Ecologies.* Digital Arts and Culture PhD Dissertation. Berkeley, CA: University of California.

———. 2011. "Games as Environmental Texts." *Qui Parle: Critical Humanities and Social Sciences* 19.2: 57–84.

Costikyan, Greg. 2002. "I Have No Words & I Must Design: Towards a Critical Vocabulary for Games." *Proceedings of Computer Games and Digital Cultures Conference*, edited by Frans Mäyrä. Tampere University Press. Accessed 8 July, 2015. http://www.digra.org/wp-content/uploads/digital-library/05164.51146.pdf

Dena, Christy. 2009. "ARGs Around the World – Part 2." In *Christy's Corner of the Universe.* Blog. 9 March. Accessed 8 July, 2015. http://christydena.com/online-essays/worldwideargs2/

Guacamelee!. Gold Edition. 2013. DrinkBox Studios.

Hibler, Michelle. n.d. "Taking Control of Air Pollution in Mexico City." *IDRC.* Accessed May 12, 2014.

Holmevik, Jan Rune. 2011. *Inter/vention.* Cambridge, MA: MIT Press.

Huizinga, Johan. 1950. *Homo Ludens: A Study of the Play-Element in Culture.* New York: Roy Publishers.

Icarus1806 [YouTube persona]. 2012. "Culturally-Focused Video Games: Part 1, Part 2, Part 3 – Mexico – LAI Meets Phyne Games." YouTube. July 5. Accessed 12 May 2014.

Jenkins, Henry. 2004. "Game Design as Narrative Architecture." In *First Person: New Media as Story, Performance and Game*, edited by Noan Wardrip-Fruin and Pat Harrigan, 118–130. Cambridge, MA: MIT Press.

Juul, Jesper. 2005. *Half-Real: Video Games between Real Rules and Fictional Worlds.* Cambridge, MA: MIT Press.

———. 2013. *The Art of Failure: An Essay on the Pain of Playing Video Games.* Cambridge, MA: MIT Press.

"Latin American Game Market (Mexico, Brazil)." 2013. *Language Automation, Inc.* April. Accessed April 5, 2014.

McGonigal, Jane. 2003. "This Is Not a Game: Immersive Aesthetics and Collective Play." *Melbourne DAC 2003 Streaming Worlds Conference Proceedings.*

Mictlan. 2012. Phyne Games.

Minority Media Presents: Papo & Yo. 2013. Accessed August 30, 2013. http://www.weareminority.com/papo-yo/

Murray, Janet. 1998. "Building Coherent Plots in Interactive Fiction, IEEE." *Intelligent Systems.*

Oliveira, Thaiane. 2012. "Mapeamento Cas Competências Cognitivas No Gameplay de Jogos de Realidade Alternada." *Contemporânea* 10.

———. 2013. "Arquitetura de Uma Narrativa Transmidiática: Análise do Jogo de Realidade Alternada Zona Incerta." *Revista Mediaçã* 15.

Oliveira, Thaiane, L. Carvalho, and E. Ferreira. 2013. "Ectodiegesis as Immersive Effect in Pervasive Games." *AcademicMindTrek '13 Proceedings of International Conference on Making Sense of Converging Media* 281, New York.

Papo & Yo. 2013. Minority Media.

Provost, Dan. 2008. "Metafiction and Web Based Story Telling." Parson School.

Salen, Katie, and Eric Zimmerman, eds. 2006. *The Game Design Reader: A Rules of Play Anthology*. Cambridge, MA: MIT Press.

Senate News Portal. 2007. "Laboratório norte-americano está propondo a privatização da Amazônia, alerta Arthur Virgílio." 27 March. Accessed 6 July, 2015. http://www12.senado.leg.br/noticias/materias/2007/03/27/laboratorio-norte-americano-esta-propondo-a-privatizacao-da-amazonia-alerta-arthur-virgilio

Sicart, Miguel. 2009. *The Ethics of Computer Games*. Cambridge, MA: MIT Press.

Sutter, John. 2011. "Supreme Court Sees Video Games As Art." CNN.com. June 27. Accessed August 13, 2014.

Tomb Raider: Underworld. 2008. Eidos Interactive.

Uncharted: Drake's Fortune. 2007. Sony Computer Entertainment.

Wark, McKenzie. 2007. *Gamer Theory*. Cambridge, MA: Harvard University Press.

WoWWiki. Wikia. Accessed May 14, 2014.

12 New media, environmental NGOs, and online-based collective actions in China

Aimei Yang

Introduction

The emergence of a global information society increasingly draws attention to the role of media and communication technology. Around the world, information communication technologies (ICTs) have been utilized by for-profit companies, governments, and nonprofit sectors to reach audiences in this new media environment. The new media environment differs from traditional mass media environment in terms of the characteristic of content, modes of transmission and reception, and pattern of use (Barabási 2014). The *new media environment* features multimedia, user-generated content, and a mix of one-to-many and many-to-one communication, and information can be disseminated virtually around the world regardless of the time zone and geographic distance. Among various types of organizations, many nongovernmental and nonprofit organizations (NGOs) changed their traditional outreach approach to include new media endeavors, while others have moved entirely online to capitalize on networking potential while keeping the operating cost low.

Some scholars conceptualize media as an indispensable part of civil society. *Civil society* can be understood as the structure and communication flows in networks of civil actors both online and offline. The new possibilities associated with new media and their implications for civil actors have invited considerable attention, speculations, and research (Hildebrandt and Turner 2009; Jenkins 2009; Yang and Taylor 2010). Civil society is formed by local civil actors (e.g., local communities, religious groups, grassroots organizations, labor unions, civic associations, etc.) who articulate and pursue social interests. In semi-authoritarian countries such as China, where civil actors have traditionally lacked access to information and channels of communication, the potential impact of new media may be especially important (Brook 1997).

Recognizing the value of civil actors' use of new media, this chapter is intended to introduce the new media landscape in China and discusses the situation facing Chinese NGOs and how their use of new media may affect their communication, advocacy, and collective actions both online and in the broader eco-sociopolitical world. ***Collective actions*** are defined as actions taken together by a group of individuals to advance a shared objective. As illustrated in this chapter, a proper understanding of Chinese NGOs' new media use has to be situated in the Chinese eco-sociopolitical media context.

In this chapter, special attention is given to Chinese environmental NGOs because this NGO community is exceptionally active in China and plays a significant role in China's environmental protection campaigns (Yang and Taylor 2010). Environmental protection refers to practices of protecting the natural environment. Environmental NGOs (***ENGOs***) are dedicated to environmental protection issues such as sustainable development, waste reduction, water and air protection, and animal rights protection. In China, environmental protection is among the few social issue areas that the government tolerates large-scale civil participation. The number of ENGOs has considerably increased since 1994 and now is the most active NGO sector in China (Ho 2001; Yang 2009).

New media in China: a public sphere with Chinese characteristics

Many communication scholars and commentators speculate about the potential social implications of the Internet and what it means for civil society and democracy in China (Bamman, O'Connor, and Smith 2012; Yang 2009; Yang and Taylor 2010). The Internet is not only a network of computers, but is also a network of human beings, organizations, and nation-states. For a country lacking a history of free expression, the Internet seems to present democratizing potentials, such as allowing citizens to express their opinion and form online communities. Over recent decades, the Chinese government has taken substantial strides in building communication infrastructure and developing information technologies (Donald, Hong, and Keane 2014). As a result, according to a recent study, there are over 500 million Internet users, about 100 million bloggers, and 300 million microbloggers in China (Sullivan 2014). The sheer number of users combined with the assumption that many of them could use the Internet to express, communicate, mobilize, and even organize collective actions and social movements, including those focused on environmental concerns, have invited the wildest speculations and prophesy of the future of the Internet in China.

Nevertheless, from the incipiency stage of the Internet, the Chinese government has been fully aware of and probably threatened by the potential consequence of the Internet on social stability (Chiu, Ip, and Silverman 2012). The government's monitoring has always existed and was tightened after the 2010 Arab Spring, during which waves of demonstrations, protests, riots, and civil war, effectively initiated on or facilitated through social media, brought down several authoritarian regimes in the Middle East. China has some of the most pervasive Internet surveillance in the world, and the Chinese firewall effectively blocked out many of the world's most popular social media including Facebook, YouTube, Twitter, and even search engines such as Google (Bamman, O'Connor, and Smith 2012; Yang 2009).

Despite tight government monitoring and regulation, the Chinese new media sphere is not a silent, sterile domain. The government has adopted a multifold approach to reach a delicate balance between avoiding suffocating communication and depriving the country's opportunities to develop in the age of the Internet (Bamman, O'Connor, and Smith 2012). First, externally, the government has not banned or blocked all communication between domestic citizens and the outside world. Rather, the government has taken a selective approach and mostly banned domestic access to outlets that are considered politically sensitive or troublesome. For instance, among social media platforms, YouTube and Twitter are banned in China. But LinkedIn is widely available and even launched its Chinese version.

Second, internally, the government has regulated and encouraged the development of a variety of indigenous social media outlets. For almost every Western social media platform, one can find its Chinese domestic clone (Chiu, Ip, and Silverman 2012). For instance, Weibo is similar to Twitter, YouKu and Tudou can replace YouTube, Uber's Chinese cousins include DiDiDaChe and KuaiDaChe, and the list goes on. Some social media even have unique services and features that are especially designed for Chinese culture. For instance, WeChat is a popular Chinese social media that combines some features of Facebook and Twitter, with additional features such as text messaging, hold-to-talk voice messaging, sharing of photographs and videos, and location sharing. These convenient features helped to bring down the cost of communication (many users choose WeChat's free service over traditional mobile text messaging and calls) and reached enormous success in countries, such as China and India, where mobile phones enjoy much higher penetration rates than does the Internet. By 2013, WeChat had 300 million users, among which 70 million live outside of China (Hui 2013).

Third, as Chinese citizens enjoy the abundance of choices of social media platforms, their communication is still censored both by the government and Internet service carriers who are regulated by the government. Some service carriers even hire designated staff to read and manually delete any potentially sensitive content and comments. The censorship is not strict in the sense that criticism of the government or its policy and officials cannot be expressed. In fact, many forums exist online to host debates and discussion about political issues (e.g., QiangGuo Forum) and the government even drew intelligence from some online sources in its anticorruption campaigns. The censorship is strict in the sense that it does not tolerate most attempts of civil organizations to engage in collective actions and social movements. Attempts to organize protests, sit-ins, and demonstrations are often met with repression. For instance, after the Arab Spring, some activists in China planned to organize a "Jasmine Revolution" in over a dozen cities in China. This attempt started with anonymous calls online but was immediately investigated by the state police. A number of arrests were made and some activists were charged with inciting subversion of state power. Further, state censorship causes self-censorship in society and among individual users. To avoid state sanction, many Internet users censor themselves and stay away from sensitive topics (Bamman, O'Connor, and Smith 2012).

Fourth, one should keep in mind that the Internet and associated new technology are ongoing development projects. The boundaries and rules of the Chinese cyberspace are still far from well-established (Chiu, Ip, and Silverman 2012). Government regulations are often challenged by ad hoc legal structures and emerging social norms. For instance, the government revised regulation policy for the Management of Computer Information Network International Connections several times since 1996 (See Box 1.). Additionally, rapid technology developments often generate communication flows that move faster than the censorship system can keep up with. There are indeed many blurry areas that allow netizens to negotiate power relationships despite restrictions (Yang 2009). How such negotiations may interact with the current political systems and what compromises can be made on both sides will continue to demand research and attention.

Box 12.1   Talk about it: Internet regulation policies

While China, as this chapter and the sample of regulations below suggest, is a country in which the Internet is strictly monitored, other countries similarly have important Internet regulations. These regulations are instituted for a number of reasons, from national security to telecommunication industry control to consumer protection including freedom of expression. Along with your classmates, research the Internet regulation policies of your country. Trace the history of these regulations and debate some of the current controversies.

A sampling of Chinese Internet regulation policies

1994: Ordinance of the People's Republic of China on the Protection of Computer Information System Security.
1996: Temporary Regulation for the Management of Computer Information Network International Connection.
1997: Security Management Procedures in Internet Accessing.
2000: State Council Order No. 292, "Measures on Internet Information Services."

Further reading

Deibert, Ronald J. 2002. "Dark Guests and Great Firewalls: The Internet and Chinese Security Policy." *Journal of Social Issues* 58.1: 143–159.

Zhang, Lena L. 2006. "Behind the 'Great Firewall': Decoding China's Internet Media Policies from the Inside." *Convergence* 12.3: 271–291.

Overall, the Chinese government has developed an Internet censorship system that is capable of controlling and channeling online sentiment and activities (Bamman, O'Connor, and Smith 2012). At the current stage, the goal of the system is not to suffocate civil communication, as doing so may trigger massive reaction and hinder China's economic development. It is necessary to note that in the twenty-first century, *ICT* (Information and Communications Technology) is a basic requirement for economic growth. ICT can enhance human capabilities through improving productivity. Human capabilities in turn contribute to technology innovation and development. The "virtuous circle" thus creates a critical foundation for nations to compete in today's global economic system.

The government believes that the Internet and communication technologies substantially contribute to the nation's economic prosperity. Such belief has led to supportive policy stimulation by the state, especially for infrastructure. However, ecomedia scholars such as Richard Maxwell and Toby Miller (2012) are critical of such economically driven ICT development. Steeped in Western models of economic growth, such development is inherently problematic as it compartmentalizes technology's production and disposal from its use. As such, it makes invisible the many environmentally harmful aspects of ICT's material presence and planned obsolescence (its e-waste) in favor of it being a symbolic driver of progress. Coupled with lax monitoring of environmental externalities in ICT production and disposal (Powell 2013), the Chinese government's censorship of the Internet environment to channel sentiments, encourage commercialized social media use, and monitor social trends helps propagate environmentally problematic models of consumerism.

Nonetheless, one can argue that there are opportunities for civil actors and certain types of collective actions and even social movements, as the Internet may support new ways for citizens to participate in nonpolitical or nonsensitive issues that have ecological resonances. While the media alone is insufficient to present substantial challenge to the state's authority and technology alone cannot accomplish or promote social changes, individuals and organizations can use the Internet in crucial and fundamental ways to seek change. In the following section, I will introduce an important type of civil actor, Chinese NGOs, and explore the social and ecological implications of NGOs' use of social media.

Chinese NGOs: struggle and survival

Since the 1990s, Chinese NGOs have grown rapidly both in their number and scope of activity. By 2004, there were 289,000 registered NGOs in China, and the number has continued to rise over the years (Yang and Taylor 2010). Many NGOs meet marginalized social demands (social demands ignored by both the government and the for-profit sector), which often include environmental concerns or address social issues and challenges. As such, many NGOs have gained social legitimacy at the local community level or have attracted some donors. Nonetheless, many of them still face daunting challenges regarding raising funds and legally registering, as they operate within restrictive boundaries defined by government authorities.

Before exploring details of Chinese NGOs, it is necessary to acknowledge that in examining civil society and civil actors, as reflected by numerous studies on the topic (see "further reading" at the end of the chapter), we must acknowledge that relationships between governments and civil actors are always complex and not necessarily a simplistic tale of control versus a struggle for autonomy. This is true not only in China but across the world.

In fact, the Chinese government does not simply see all civil actors as threats. Many governmental officials have readily acknowledged the beneficial social impact of NGOs. For instance, in 2008, after a devastating earthquake in Sichuang, thousands of NGOs collaborated and demonstrated great influence in disaster-affected areas. The prime minister of China acknowledged NGOs as offering solutions to pressing social problems (Yang 2014). In fact, besides government-sponsored NGOs, many grassroots NGOs also seek government funding and grants and work on government cosponsored collaboration projects. As an example, an NGO named Enpei was founded specifically to help and train grassroots NGOs to build connections with relevant government agencies, to obtain government grants, and to work with various institutions and media outlets. Enpei calls itself an NGO incubator because for an NGO to succeed in China, such social connections and governmental relationships can be advantageous and sometimes even vital. Enpei supported the early development and staff training of many environmental NGOs.

The Chinese government adopts different approaches towards different types of NGOs, depending on the size of the organization, the source of funding, and the type of mission. Generally speaking, small, provincial NGOs focusing on social services such as orphanages, rural children education, and animal shelters are less likely to experience governmental interference; whereas national, large NGOs, especially ones that work on sensitive social issues (religion, ethnicity, human rights, AIDS, etc.) are more likely to attract state attention and government control.

Chinese NGOs, when categorized by the type of organizers or founders, can be divided into four major types: government-run/official-organized/top-down NGOs; traditional grassroots/bottom-up NGOs; student NGOs;

and finally online-based NGOs (Yang and Taylor 2010). Specifically, official NGOs receive government subsidies, and personnel in the leadership positions are generally appointed by the government or filled by former government officials. Official NGOs often enjoy relatively stable financial support from the government and the protection from powerful allies in the party-state bureaucracy. For instance, organizations such as the China Youth Development Foundation can work on sensitive AIDS advocacy issues without strict government regulation and interference. In the recent decade, some official NGOs have become more independent in terms of program management and fundraising, but many still closely affiliate with the government. In recent years, some official NGOs have been challenged by credibility crises. For instance, in 2011, a young woman named Meimei Guo used Sina Weibo to show off her wealth and luxury possessions. Guo identified herself as a 20-year-old "General Manager of the Red Cross Society." Such an action infuriated millions of Internet users and many suspected that Guo's wealth was a result of stealing donations for disaster relief. The Red Cross Society in China is an official NGO. In the aftermath of the Guo incident, the Red Cross Society in China was criticized for its lack of transparency and the leadership's financial misappropriation. It has consequently suffered a severe loss of credibility. Such a public relations catastrophe, at the surface level, can be read as public suspicion about a specific official NGO. But to a certain degree, it also reveals distrust between the public and the government, and organizations or agencies closely associated with the government.

The second type of Chinese NGOs is traditional grassroots/bottom-up NGOs. This group of NGOs is most similar to their Western grassroots counterparts, and many of them are organized around marginalized interests, such as responding to HIV/AIDS; promoting labor rights, women's rights, and environmental protection; and taking care of senior citizens. Many grassroots NGOs seek resources and operate outside of state resources. Because they are unlikely to attract state support, grassroots NGOs often have difficulty in legally registering, fundraising, and preserving talent. For instance, a survey found that more than 60% of grassroots NGOs do not have permanent offices; about 50% lack access to computers and the capacity to disseminate information online.

Student NGOs are unique in the sense that most of them are initiated by college students. Student NGOs are often university based and mostly focus on environmental protection–related activities. Leadership positions in student NGOs are filled either by elected or appointed students. They participate in NGO-related activities during after-school free time and their activities are supervised by professors of their respective universities. Core personnel in the student NGOs usually serve 10–12 months. This service period on average is shorter than staff working in other types of NGOs. Student-run NGOs are often limited by funding (mainly supported by university funding, government grants, and other foundations), time, and experience, and therefore are limited both in scope and impact. Because these NGO founders generally lack social connections, they often do not have the competencies for navigating a social system that is the domain of former party-state bureaucrats or other seasoned social actors.

Finally, some NGOs are primarily online based (e.g., 1KG, Aibai, and VJoin). Such NGOs are often organized by geographically distant staff and members and draw volunteers from around the country. They are heavily dependent upon the Internet and are often adept in exploiting the power and resources of social networks. For instance, the geotourism NGO, 1KG, started off as a website, where the founder called upon hikers and travelers to carry 1KG books or other charity products (e.g., textbooks and study supplies) to rural and underdeveloped areas. Using this method, with practically no cost, the NGO (which at the beginning had no paid staff but a few volunteers operating virtually) was able to mobilize thousands of volunteers and help rural communities scattered around China.

Even though one can categorize Chinese NGOs into four major types, there is not necessarily a distinctive boundary between them. Further, new types of NGOs such as online-based NGOs are not replacing traditional ones. Instead, the NGO landscape in China is still evolving. Collaboration and alliances have brought together and reshaped many NGOs' organization structures and formats. Additionally, the negotiation between different power relationships continues to shape Chinese NGOs. Among Chinese NGOs, environmental NGOs are exceptionally active. Their collective actions and use of social media deserve special attention and are elaborated on in the next section.

Environmental issues and environmental NGOs in China

Unlike in the West, where the environmental movement has a tradition dating back to the nineteenth century, early Chinese environmental activists, mostly professionals and scientists, began to advocate for environmental issues in the mid-1980s (Ho 2001). China's modern environmental movements trace back to the 1990s. The first citizen-founded Chinese ENGO is the Friends of Nature, which publishes regularly and organizes conferences to gather domestic activists with international organizations.

Over the past three decades, China's rapid economic and social developments have had dreadful environmental consequences. The ICT sector is also a culprit in such environmental harm, as is apparent from the internationally covered stories of e-waste dumps in Guiyu, which lies across the border from Hong Kong and receives illegal influxes of waste from outside China (Powell 2013, also Rust in this volume). In general, public outcries over environmental problems have raised the public awareness of environmental issues, and many people are supportive of environmentally friendly activities. For instance, in May 2013, over two thousand citizens in the City of Kunming in Yunnan Province took to the streets to protest against the government's plan of building a petrochemical plant in the nearby city of Anning. Many citizens requested an open dialogue between citizens and the government on major decisions. The protest was one of the top trending news stories on the social media platform Sina Weibo, and photos were posted of protesters wearing masks and waving banners (Reuters 2013). Within the same week, in Shanghai, thousands also protested against another government plan to open a lithium battery factory. This factory (HeFei GuoXuan High-Tech Power Energy Company, Ltd.) manufactures lithium batteries, lithium power supplies, and lithium backup power supplies. While such protests aren't necessarily implicating ICT use in environmental degradation, it is worth noting that lithium batteries are commonly used in mobile devices such as smartphones on which users access the Internet, and, of course, the prevalence of petrochemicals in the production of ICT gadgets is a no-brainer.

To understand the social significance of these environmental issue–related protests, it is necessary to mention that in every country, political protests come with costs and personal consequences. Such consequences may especially be heavy for citizens living in semiauthoritarian countries such as China. Very few social issues in China have a strong enough appeal to the general public that people are willing to risk being repressed or charged by the state. Yet, people are willing to take action for environmental causes, because environmental issues have become so pervasive in China and many citizens feel their life and health are severely threatened by environmental problems.

ENGOs in China range from voluntary nonprofits registered as social organizations (*shehui tuanti*), nonprofit enterprises registered as business enterprises, research centers affiliated with higher education institutions, and student-run environmental groups. As a diverse community, ENGOs include most of the previously discussed NGO types. There are also a large number of online-based groups and voluntary associations that function as NGOs but are not registered. These ENGOs primarily use new media to coordinate their collective actions.

While some ENGOs, such as those that participated in the Shanghai and Anning protests, are engaged in protests and civil litigations, most established ENGOs engage in areas that are consistent with the interests of the government, such as promoting environmentally friendly lifestyles, organizing environmental awareness campaigns, and advocating species conservation. A number of ENGOs have actively engaged in and promoted campaigns and programs that engage citizens in various civil activities such as environmental awareness education events, power saving campaigns, and tree planting events.

In recent years, environmental NGOs were able to organize national level, high-profile campaigns. Even though Chinese ENGOs make it very clear that they are only interested in issues related to environmental protection (e.g., many ENGOs state in their mission that their sole concern is to protect the environment or to contribute to sustainable development), some recently formed ENGOs have been involved in issues that question the government's policies, for example, through anti-dam campaigns and advocacy for pollution victims. In cases such as the 2003 Nu River campaign, ENGOs had a clear political goal to influence public policy; they mobilized their constituency and carried out collective actions. ENGOs have also performed similar roles in the campaigns to preserve snub-nosed monkeys in Yunnan province and the endangered Tibetan antelope (Yang 2009). In recent years, some environmental activism even evolved into mass protest and demonstration and formed confrontations with local authorities and large corporations. New media and NGOs virtual collective actions have become prevalent in ENGO work.

Online-based collective actions in China

The new media landscape and the Chinese government's policies regarding virtual communication, the idiosyncratic nature of China's online public sphere, as well as the delicate role that many NGOs play, form the context in which Chinese ENGOs can utilize new media to advance their goals and objectives. In general, ENGOs can use the Internet for information dissemination, education, rising awareness, or even mobilization of mainly online-based collective actions. Though censorship and regulation are in place to ensure that sensitive topics have little chance to enter the virtual public sphere and any attempt to bring virtual collective action to the offline world is met with watchful scrutiny, it is impossible to completely filter every online message.

For most Chinese ENGOs, the Internet provides two major benefits: an *information benefit* and a *network diversity benefit*. The information benefit refers to the opportunities civil actors obtain because the Internet offers a cheap and fast medium of information distribution (Barabási 2014). Although the Chinese government closely controls and censors information flows, Chinese ENGOs can use new media for education and raising awareness. For instance, Yang and Taylor (2010) examined the website content and relationship-building functions of 151 environment Chinese NGOs. The majority of these ENGOs predominantly used their websites to provide educational information while downplaying their interaction and mobilization functions. For instance, many websites provide plenty of information such as how to lower individual carbon footprints, but most websites do not include a forum or any interactive sections. This study concluded that "today's ENGO websites are mostly used for educational rather than activation communication" (350).

The network diversity benefit refers to the penetration of the information technology infrastructure around the globe (Barabási 2014). Online, relationship development is less constrained by geographic boundaries and distance. The Internet supports both asynchronous and synchronous communication, and therefore allows communication to overcome the constraints of time. More importantly, the Internet facilitates loosely structured networks, weak identity ties, and campaigns organized around issues.

It is important to note that in today's China, many ENGOs interact with the state, media, foreign donors, and international NGOs working on similar issues. The Internet and new media help to facilitate communication and networking both at the organizational level and individual level. At the organizational level, facilitated by communication technologies, there has been increased networking, collaboration and alliance building among Chinese NGOs of various sorts, journalists, international NGOs, and local people affected by developmental projects.

Environmental collective actions are among the few social issue areas where the government tolerates large-scale, nationwide mobilizations. For instance, in 1999, the Save the Tibetan Antelope campaign was one of the first large-scale online-based environmental social movements. As the name suggests, Tibetan antelope are native to Tibet and now listed on the World Conservation Union endangered list. Poaching, to obtain their rich wool, which is woven into sought-after shahtoosh shawls, resulted in a drastic reduction in their population. In the late 1990s, their numbers were down from millions to around seventy thousand (Yang 2003). This campaign was organized by Greener Beijing, an online-based ENGO. Greener Beijing founded a website, Save the Tibetan Antelope, which attracted nationwide attention. A coalition network among several hundred organizations across China was formed to innovatively raise money and increase awareness of the plight of Tibetan antelope. Even though the organizers of the campaign were careful to not include any offline demonstrations (the organizers never organized offline events, but some individual members and volunteers voluntarily organized offline meetings), the campaign reached unprecedented success.

Similarly, in 2012, the Guizhentang Pharmaceutical Company's plan to be registered for public trade on the stock exchange market triggered nationwide outrage. This is because the company harvests Asian black bear bile, and if the company succeeded becoming a public company, it planned to triple the size of its bear-bile farms. This plan was publicized by a group of NGOs (a coalition between the international NGO, Animals Asia Foundation, and a group of Chinese NGOs and Chinese celebrities). They combined their online campaign with appearance on traditional mass media outlets (e.g., newspapers, TV talk shows, etc.). Thousands of Chinese citizens submitted online complaints and petition letters to the government and to the China Securities Regulatory Commission to stop Guizhentang's plan. The campaign successfully stopped the plan to increase bear farming. (See Box 12.2 for details of the case.)

Both of these examples suggest how, despite government surveillance, Chinese new media creates platforms that facilitate interaction among citizens. On an organizational level, eco-coalitions can be successfully built. On an individual level, the low-cost and easy-to-use new media makes participation available and feasible to a much broader range of citizens and gives netizens' motivations to take eco-actions, such as signing petitions and submitting online complaints.

Box 12.2   An animal rights controversy in China: a case study

On February 1, 2012, the China Securities Regulatory Commission published a list of companies to be registered for public trade on the stock exchange market. The list triggered a national controversy because one of the companies was Guizhentang Pharmaceutical Company, which harvests Asian black bear bile. If Guizhentang succeeded in going public, the company planned to triple the size of its bear-bile farms. Asian black bear bile is valued in traditional Chinese medicine for its alleged ability to relieve muscle aches, joint pain, fever, and hangovers. The World Conservation Union lists the Asian black bear (also called Asiatic black bear or Himalayan black bear) on the Red List of Threatened Animals (see http://www.iucnredlist.org). Not only are the bears vulnerable, but the process by which bile is extracted is considered cruel. Throughout their lives (normally 10–15 years), the bears are kept in crush cages where they cannot stand up. The daily extraction process results in severe physical problems ranging from excruciating pain, malnutrition, loss of hair, stunted growth, muscle mass loss, cancer, and, inevitably, a high mortality rate (Huo 2012).

Soon after publication of the list, Animals Asia Foundation (AAF) and a group of Chinese NGOs and 72 celebrities (e.g., the former NBA star Yao Ming) sent petition letters to the China Securities Regulatory Commission (Yang and Veil 2015, in press). Thousands of Chinese citizens submitted online complaints and petition letters to stop Guizhentang's plan. Guizhentang was negatively covered in the media as cruel to animals, and its application was halted.

Conclusion

Without any doubt, the Internet and online-based communication technologies are crucial to the development of Chinese ENGOs. The introduction of the Internet runs concurrent with the growth of Chinese civil society and NGOs. As argued by Yang (2009), the two trends have developed hand in hand. Many NGOs nowadays are either established online or have a virtual presence. Chinese ENGOs have been among the most active adopters of technological changes brought about by the Internet and social media. The availability afforded by mobile phone technologies and communication apps have presented new opportunities for collective actions.

For many Chinese ENGOs struggling with limited resources, the low-cost options offered by new media give them otherwise unimaginable access to stakeholders and the public. Nonetheless, it would be highly inappropriate to assume that Western models of online collective actions can be readily applied to the Chinese context, because there are substantial differences among these political systems. Similarly, we cannot expect that ENGOs' online presence will necessarily tackle the **materiality paradox** of ICT, which is, as Maxwell and Miller (2012) describe, the paradox that arises from believing that through technology we can solve our problems, and thus we tend to consume technology. Because the Chinese virtual space is generally nonpolitical, it does not necessarily question consumerism. Instead, it often involve goals, collective actions, and organizational characteristics that are adaptive to the political environment of China, which is strongly economically driven. Thus, ENGOs don't necessarily address the human and environmental costs of ICT use. However, the structure of government–NGO relationships has changed over the years and may continue to evolve. Importantly, China has been and still is experiencing substantial eco-social changes. Ultimately, discussion in this chapter mainly serves the purpose of introduction rather than prediction, for new and exciting trends may continue to emerge in the years to come.

Keywords

Censorship	Information benefit
Chinese environmental NGOs	Internet
Civil society	Network diversity benefit
Collective action	New media
Environmental protection	Online participation

Discussion questions

1   Visit an American ENGO online site. How does it employ social media? Visit a Chinese ENGO online site. Compare its use of social media to that of the American ENGO. Explain their similarities and differences by considering the broader contexts that frame media expression in both countries.

2   Consider the following scenario: You are a citizen of China and are concerned about environmental issues in your town. What are the advantages of using new media to express your concern? What are the disadvantages? Knowing these pros and cons, if you were to start an online ENGO, what would your site highlight and why?

3   To what extent can lessons learned in the American ENGO sector be applied to the Chinese ENGO sector? Explain why or why not some lessons may not be applicable.

Further readings

Economy, E. 2005. "China's Environmental Movement." Testimony before the Congressional Executive Commission on China Roundtable on Environmental NGOs in China: Encouraging Action and Addressing Public Grievances, 7.

Knup, Elizabeth. 1997. "Environmental NGOs in China: An Overview." *China Environment Series* 1.3: 9–15.

Schwartz, Jonathan. 2004. "Environmental NGOs in China: Roles and Limits." *Pacific Affairs*: 28–49.

Tang, Shui-Yan, and Xueyong Zhan. 2008. "Civic Environmental NGOs, Civil Society, and Democratisation in China." *The Journal of Development Studies* 44.3: 425–448.

Wu, Fengshi. 2002. "New Partners or Old Brothers? GONGOs in Transnational Environmental Advocacy in China." *China Environment Series* 5: 45–58.

Yang, Aimei. 2013. "When Transnational Civil Network Meets Local Context: An Exploratory Hyperlink Network Analysis of Northern/Southern NGOs' Virtual Network in China." *Journal of International and Intercultural Communication* 6.1: 40–60.

Yang, Guobin. 2005. "Environmental NGOs and Institutional Dynamics in China." *The China Quarterly* 181.1: 44–66.

Works cited

Bamman, David, Brendan O'Connor, and Noah Smith. 2012. "Censorship and Deletion Practices in Chinese Social Media." *First Monday* 17.3.

Barabási, Albert-László. 2014. *Linked: How Everything Is Connected to Everything Else and What It Means for Business, Science, and Everyday Life*. New York: Basic Books.

Brook, Timothy, ed. 1997. *Civil Society in China*. London: ME Sharpe.

Chiu, Cindy, Chris Ip, and Ari Silverman. 2012. "Understanding Social Media in China." *McKinsey Quarterly* 2. 2012: 78–81.

Donald, Stephanie Hemelryk, Yin Hong, and Michael Keane, eds. 2014. *Media in China: Consumption, Content and Crisis*. London: Routledge.

Hildebrandt, Timothy, and Jennifer Turner. 2009. "Green Activism? Reassessing the Role of Environmental NGOs in China." In *State and Society Responses to Social Welfare Needs in China: Serving the People*, edited by J. Schwartz & S. Shieh, 89–110. London: Routledge.

Ho, Peter. 2001. "Greening without Conflict? Environmentalism, NGOs and Civil Society in China." *Development and Change* 32.5: 893–921.

Hui, Tong. 2013. "Research on WeChat according to Communication Study and Its Influence." *Chongqing Social Sciences* 9: 11.

Huo, Yin Li. 2012. "The Blocked Way to Market? Was Guizhentang Co. Sabotaged?" *Business Review*: B13.

Jenkins, Henry. 2009. *Confronting the Challenges of Participatory Culture: Media Education for the 21st Century*. Cambridge, MA: MIT Press.

Maxwell, Richard, and Toby Miller. 2012. *Greening the Media*. London: Oxford University Press.

Powell, Daniel. 2013. "Assessing and Improving China's E-waste Problem." April 8. Accessed February 1, 2015. http://ourworld.unu.edu/en/assessing-and-improving-the-e-waste-problem-in-china

Reuters. 2013. "Chinese City Bans Anti-refinery Protests Ahead of Trade Fair. May 28. Accessed February 1, 2015. http://www.reuters.com/article/2013/05/28/us-china-protest-idUSBRE94R05720130528

Sullivan, Jonathan. 2014. "China's Weibo: Is Faster different?" *New Media & Society* 16: 24–37.

Yang, Aimei. 2014. "Framing Chinese Civil Actors: Earthquake Relief and Unintended Consequences on Media Coverage." *Chinese Journal of Communication* 7: 155–173.

Yang, Aimei, and Maureen Taylor. 2010. "Relationship-building by Chinese ENGOs' Websites: Education, Not Activation." *Public Relations Review* 36: 342–351.

Yang, Aimei, and Shari Veil. 2015 (in press). "Nationalism vs. Animal Rights: A Semantic Network Analysis of Value Advocacy in Corporate Crisis." *Journal of Business Communication.*

Yang, Guobin. 2003. "Weaving a Green Web: The Internet and Environmental Activism in China." Woodrow Wilson International Center for Scholars.

Yang, Guobin. 2009. *The Power of the Internet in China: Citizen Activism Online.* New York: Columbia University Press.

13 Earth imaging
Photograph, pixel, program

Chris Russill

Introduction

Al Gore, at the close of *An Inconvenient Truth* (Guggenheim 2006), asks us to look at a pixel.

It is perhaps the only pixel with a name, "pale blue dot," and it is described by Gore as "us," as "our only home," and as the site of all human significance: "all of human history has happened on that pixel" (see Figure 13.1).

The frame shown by Gore was envisioned originally as a piece of a broader image. It is one of sixty frames composed from recordings of light made in the 1990s by NASA's Voyager 1 as part of the "Solar System Family

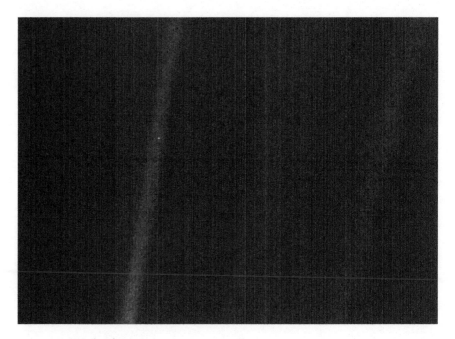

Figure 13.1 Pale Blue Dot.
Source: Courtesy of NASA (Public Domain).

Portrait" program. The plan was to image the earth by using a space probe exiting our solar system.

The goal of the "family portrait" was to depict the whole earth in its complete solar environs for the first time. It didn't work out. The brightness of the sun obscured some planets, others were too dimly captured, and the image was incomplete. The resulting mosaic of frames failed to attract popular interest.

The pixel shown by Gore was salvaged from the project and popularized by astronomer and public science communicator, Carl Sagan. For Sagan (1994), the pixel contained a revelation. It illustrated the obscurity of our world from a cosmological perspective and instantiated a principle known since ancient antiquity: "the Earth was a mere point in a vast encompassing Cosmos, but no one had ever *seen* it as such" (4). When seeing the earth in this way, as one pixel in a light-suffused universe, we are "revealing to ourselves our true circumstance and condition" (4).

The blue pixel stands in contrast to the planet's most widely reproduced photograph, "Blue Marble," a "whole earth" image depicting "us" from a vantage point located between the sun and earth (see Figure 13.2). The "whole earth" fills most of the frame and suggests the priority of the global in understanding our earthly condition. Sagan's dot, on the other hand, hints at a cosmic zoom by adopting the perspective of an interstellar machine probe. If we adopt the space probe's perspective, and if we pull back from the immediacy of a brilliantly lit "whole earth," the planet recedes in size until appearing as a mere point of light. For Sagan, this image rebukes the hubris of human exceptionalism to illustrate how fully dependent we are on a finite and fragile planet: "Our planet is a lonely speck in the great enveloping cosmic dark" (Sagan 1994, 7).

If that is a lot to see in a pixel, there is still more. Sagan overlooks the difference between a point and a pixel. Pixels are points of *programmable* light and illustrate just how intensely our imaging of the earth is programmed, enumerated, and brought into the ambit of what Paul Virilio once called, "***big optics***," or "the optics of lasers, radar, television, to which materiality is transparent, and which reduces the human world at first to a tiny globe spinning in empty space and finally to a point disappearing into unreality" (Cubitt 1999, 129).

Big optics

Big optics, for Virilio, dispenses with the configuration of space for embodied humans by organizing our imaging capabilities around the technical recording and use of the electromagnetic (EM) spectrum. This deployment of light has many significant consequences. Virilio (1994) often emphasizes how technical exploitation of electromagnetism allows information to move at the speed of light, or "***realtime***" transmission where the pacing of information flows exceeds the temporality of human perception, thought, and

Figure 13.2 Blue Marble.
Source: Courtesy of NASA (Public Domain).

judgment. Imaging delivered by computers connected at light speed – or very quickly, at any rate – confers strategic military advantage, one that permits rapid responses to conditions (enemy movement, meteorological change) observed from afar. It is a capability, however, that also forces "reliance on automated, preprogrammed plans" (Edwards 1996, 7). Why? The scale of the observations, the speed at which they are compiled, and the temporary advantage they afford tend to outstrip how quickly humans can process them.

A contemporary example can exemplify this logic: drone imaging. While more drone operators than pilots are trained by the U.S. military these days, the "targets" of drone observation have learned to exploit the "latency" of the system, or the time required for humans to process and act on the drone imaging of environments (Packer and Reeves 2013, 323–324). The desire to capitalize on realtime drone imaging for combat has led to the automation of execution orders, or the removal of humans from "kill" commands, thus speeding up how imaging becomes actionable for military strategy (Packer and Reeves 2013, 323). The politics and conduct of war now reflect the capabilities of the imaging system. A fundamental question of human judgment – the distinction between friend and enemy – is subject to technological programming.

While "programming" and "latency" are of central importance to earth imaging, as discussed below, it is not simply a question of how rapidly images can circulate in this case. Big optics also relativizes human vision as a mere slice of the broader EM spectrum. Humans only see and sense some of the light in this spectrum – the rest remains invisible and insensible. Our imaging of the earth, however, now encompasses this broader spectrum of light, and the organization of earth imaging on these terms signals a shift to the *"electromagnetic conditioning of territory"* (Virilio 1997, 12).

Box 13.1   The electromagnetic spectrum

The electromagnetic spectrum is the continuum of electromagnetic radiation as organized from shorter wavelength (higher frequency) to longer wavelength (lower frequency) and includes radio, microwave, infrared, visible light, ultraviolet, x-rays, and gamma rays. Electromagnetic radiation is composed of particles (photons) that move in wave patterns at the speed of light. Much of the electromagnetic spectrum is blocked from reaching the surface of the earth by its atmosphere. Detection and recording of electromagnetic radiation involves the use of sensors that are sensitive to specific wavelengths/frequencies of light. Humans can usually see electromagnetic radiation only in the visible light band of the spectrum and feel infrared light as heat. (See Feynman 1985, and Conway 1997.)

Let me explain. Our environments are livable because of solar radiation passing through and reflecting from the atmosphere. The technical understanding of atmospheric change is produced through recordings and simulations of how the earth processes such sunlight – not just the visible light we can sense, but the broader electromagnetic spectrum of light (see Feynman 1985; Kittler 2010). This is how many global environmental crises are known. We determine ozone holes and the threat of solar radiation exposure by comparing how different wavelengths of ultraviolet (UV) light pass through the atmosphere. We "see" the preconditions, development, and tracks of hurricanes through microwave and infrared (IR) imaging. Carbon concentrations in the atmosphere and global warming are also measured and known through IR sensing of the atmosphere and sea. In brief, our sense of environmental crisis is conditioned, in Virilio's sense, by big optics, and the global is thus constituted as a shimmering series of "data images," to use Paul Edward's phrase (2010, 431)

As the recording of invisible light (EM radiation) affords a broader sense of our environmental realities, our intuitive and place-based understandings of distance and space are challenged. Our senses are no longer the grounds for authoritative depictions of environmental change. The sense of distance, perspective, and space that orients our experience of the world dissolves into an "undulatory optics," according to Virilio, as our world becomes transparent to EM wavelengths that "see through" and disclose broader (yet invisible) realities of our environmental circumstances. "[W]e see only waveforms, not things: today we measure quanta of light" (Cubitt 2000, 57). Earth imaging, in brief, now depends on light recorded from sites that are uninhabitable or inaccessible to humans, at wavelengths we cannot perceive directly, travelling at speeds and in quantities we cannot handle.

Here then is the challenge of big optics for ecomedia: it imposes new techniques for abstracting, organizing, and programming light as culturally authoritative and displaces the priority of embodied and earthbound ways of sensing the world. It is a challenge that Virilio (1997) has long encouraged us to recognize in its multiple dimensions – even calling for a "grey ecology" to aid a "green ecology." Yet, it is especially pressing today. By changing the chemical composition of the sky, humans alter how solar radiation moves through the atmosphere, reaches the surface, and is retained as heat on the planet. We can discern the effects of these changes, as ozone holes and increases in global temperature, due to our technological sensing and imaging systems. The problem, however, is how we accord cultural priority to this way of imaging and knowing in order to act politically. For example, our inability to address the threat of climate change is often attributed to its invisible nature – to an inability to understand the necessity and workings of the "vast machine" that makes climate change observable (Edwards 2010).

Using Virilio as a guide, I elaborate these remarks by discussing several iconic images: the photographing of the whole earth in the 1960s, the pixelation of these photos in the 1990s, and the programming of Google Earth, 2005–2015.

Photograph

The origin story for the first color photograph of the whole earth involves an ex-Army photographer turned Northern California hippie dropping acid, having a "vision," and goading NASA into releasing the desired image. As Stewart Brand himself tells the story, he was hallucinating on a San Francisco rooftop, gazing downward, and noticed the buildings diverging slightly on the land below, an apparent indicator of the curvature of the earth. He projected himself higher, increasing the curvature of the horizon, until he acquired a "whole earth" vision.

It seems the first whole earth image was a drug-induced hallucination. How to disseminate this perception and generate a collective experience? The best means of collective hallucination, Brand reckoned, would involve a color photograph and mass media:

> And I figured a photograph – a color photograph – would help make that happen. There it would be for all to see, the earth complete, tiny, adrift, and no one would ever perceive things the same way. But how to accomplish this? How could I induce NASA or the Russians to finally turn the cameras backwards?
>
> (Brand 1977, 168)

Brand launched a goofy campaign asking "why haven't we seen a photograph of the whole earth yet?" a proto-tweet he attached to pin-back buttons, sold on university campuses, sent to celebrities, and otherwise used to garner attention for the liberation of a single photograph (an especially odd campaign when juxtaposed to efforts to emancipate a colonized territory or subjugated people, the more usual sites of 1960s protest).

In 1968, Brand got his photograph, "Earthrise," which displayed a partially illuminated earth (see Figure 13.3). Close enough, Brand figured:

> Those riveting Earth photos reframed everything. For the first time humanity saw itself from outside. The visible features from space were living blue ocean, living green-brown continents, dazzling polar ice and a busy atmosphere, all set like a delicate jewel in vast immensities of hard-vacuum space. Humanity's habitat looked tiny, fragile and rare. Suddenly humans had a planet to tend to.
>
> (Brand 1977, 168)

Brand finds in the perception afforded by the photograph a cultural revelation, an unfolding ecological consciousness able to reconfigure how humans inhabit the planet. The environmental movement, the first Earth Day, and the first United Nations Conference on the Environment seemed to confirm Brand's prophecy of the transformative effects of the image:

> The photograph of the whole earth from space helped to generate a lot of behavior – the ecology movement, the sense of global politics, the rise of the global economy, and so on. I think all of those phenomena were, in some sense, given permission to occur by the photograph of the earth from space.
>
> (Brand 1977, 168)

Four years later, the iconic "whole earth" photograph was acquired, the Blue Marble. As if to underscore the hallucinatory nature of his original experience, the object of Brand's campaign is often misidentified as this photograph. It is an understandable mistake. Blue Marble is more obviously "whole" in its depiction of the earth than Earthrise, and it structures how

Figure 13.3 Earthrise (rotated landscape view).
Source: Courtesy of NASA (Public Domain).

we expect the planet to look from space. As well, Brand's *Whole Earth Catalogue* featured an image similar to the 1972 Blue Marble – a color satellite image taken from NASA's ATS-III in 1967 (see Figure 13.4). Yet, as Sturken and Cartright (2009) conclude of the Brand story, "with the first photographic images of the whole earth, carrying with them the connotations of photographic evidence, a new embrace of the globe took place" (Sturken and Cartright 2009, 391).

Why, we should ask, the emphasis on photography? Whereas the ATS-III image scanned the earth as thin horizontal strips on each orbit, "as if peeling a single, continuous strip of rind from an orange" (Edwards 2010, 274), the astronaut photographs seemed more immediate, natural, and organically whole. There is something about photography – and a specific conception of photography – that is important to how Brand wished us to see the earth.

The Brand story affirms the role of individual initiative in using media to raise consciousness to instigate societal change. It reflects how countercultural advocates in the 1960s encouraged political change through the development of alternative mindsets. Yet, Brand reduces decades of imagery into an iconic expression, levels diverse environmental struggles into a general sentiment or feeling, and directs reflection on the imaging capacities of technical media to

Figure 13.4 ATS-3 Full Disk.
Source: Courtesy of NASA (Public Domain).

examples suggesting the priority of the human eye. We see, Brand suggests, just what the astronauts saw. The ability to envision the whole earth in a glance generates cultural authority for "the global," a conception reorganizing our sense of environment, politics, and economy. In this respect, Brand's tale is a tightly compressed historical account designed to convey a set of assumptions about the imaging of the earth in an uncomplicated manner.

The Brand story is compelling because it has a nemesis: rocket scientists. In his campaign to release a photograph, Brand challenged the "von Braun" paradigm that governed NASA's approach to space travel (see Poole 2008). In this paradigm, rocket scientists viewed the earth primarily as a prison rock or a cradle – in short, as a limitation requiring transcendence or escape. The goal was to literally leave the earth behind to inhabit outer space and other planets. All activities were obsessively organized around this goal. Or as contemporary rocket enthusiast and founder of SpaceX, Elon Musk, says, "Fuck Earth! Who cares about Earth!" (Anderson 2014).

On Brand's account, the earth is not a geophysical rock but composed of ecological systems. Whole earth photographs snapped by inspired astronauts challenged the dismal conceptions of the planet implied by a desire to escape it. The earth is a home demanding care, not a prison requiring escape. In short, the photos reconfigure the cultural politics of the earth around finitude and stewardship for our only home. They represent moments of human joy liberated from the strategic calculations of the Cold War. Countercultural inspiration trumps inhumane efficiency.

Brand's story illustrates how a war of perception developed over earth imaging. In doing so, however, he rooted earth imaging in a narrow history dominated by the episodic adventures of the space exploration paradigm. What would a fuller history disclose? If we follow Virilio, this history implicates the 20th-century evolution of earth imaging in the perpetual churning of environments by industrialized war.

During the world wars of the 20th century, Virilio observes, militaries hid their armies and weapons within the earth to escape the reach of increasingly destructive weapons (rooting men and weapons in trenches and bunkers). Military strategy became an elaborate game of hide and seek; landscapes were soon redesigned to anticipate threat and attack. The upshot, Virilio notes, was a shift in the nature of aggression – war increasingly attacked an environment to disable a threat. Entrenched armies were difficult to attack directly so weapons were designed to render their environments and earthly fortifications uninhabitable – alter the geophysics and geography to attack the biological. Arsenals developed to upturn the earth (trenches, bunkers, mines) and the result was to turn combat environments upside down in a rain of bombs, missiles, and other explosives, not to mention the occasional poisoning of the atmosphere (through the release of chemical gases) – all of which required still more intense earthly fortification (bunkers), atmospheric filtering (gas masks), and other forms of environmental modification. This baleful history, of course, escalates to the threat of nuclear armaments and it issues forth a military strategy predicated on making entire countries, if not the planet, uninhabitable as a consequence of war.

War, in Virilio's account, redesigns environments and suffuses earth imaging. Bombing churns the landscape; gas warfare alters the atmosphere – the organization of earth observing, in brief, is tied to a dynamic wherein environments are constantly churned, rendered unrecognizable, and threatened with regard to their habitability. It is the volatility of environmental change that drives the evolution of more advanced, systematic, and ubiquitous observing capabilities. The war dynamic is clearer still if we accept that one species has appropriated the earth's entire biosphere for its consumption, a process of environmental churn eliminating species at a rate some describe as the Sixth Extinction (Kolbert 2014).

Rocket science, in brief, traces a longer history than manned space exploration. Missiles churned combat environments in a rain of explosions, carried photographic equipment for imaging the earth beneath their flight paths, and placed observing satellites in orbit (Poole 2008; Russill 2013). The historical development of infrared sensing technology emerges from the tracking and guiding of missiles through the atmosphere – an understanding that would later inform the science of how carbon dioxide contributes to climate change (Weart 2001). Both matters involve tracing how heat moves through the atmosphere, a problem requiring that global atmospheric circulation (of missiles, of heat) becomes programmable. Spacecraft, as well, evolved from broadcasting units to programmed devices through the incorporation of "programmable sequencers" (O'Brien 2010, 3).

My point is that 20th-century earth imaging issues from a different history and evolutionary dynamic than we typically realize when gazing at whole earth images. Earth imaging records changes inaccessible to the eye, a point I will insist upon below in turning to the iconic photographs.

The first thing to emphasize is the logistics of rocket travel. Transporting human eyes to a vantage point for gazing at a "whole" earth involves lifting humans off the planet, positioning them 32,000 kilometers away (between the sun and earth), in a windowed craft oriented to target the earth through the window. Only three people have ever acquired the position to see the earth as depicted in the Blue Marble image (Belden-Adams 2008, 24; Reinart 2011). None of them did. The astronauts were confined in tight cabins, the windows small, and the cameras held at the hip of the astronaut, not in alignment with the human eye. As Underwood (2000) recounts, "you couldn't distort your body very well to look out the window of those spacecraft through a viewfinder, so they were taught to shoot from the hip, like 'Gunsmoke,' draw and shoot, get your target."

Second, the craft's navigation was tethered to the unmanned earth imaging system, which was used to program the schedule for acquiring desired views. As Richard Underwood, Chief of Photography at NASA, explains:

> I had access to all that equipment and all the weather satellites. I could even tell where weather was all over the world. These were rather rudimentary satellites compared to today's satellites, but you had the general idea. No point in saying, "Hey, we want you to get a picture of a certain area" when you know it's cloudy. There's no point in them either orienting the spacecraft and using fuel or staying awake or even looking out the window. And also we knew where the storms were and fronts and other weather things to tell them, "Hey, you're going to come up on a hurricane three hours from now," or something. "Try to get a series of pictures."
>
> (Underwood 2000)

Third, the cameras were preprogrammed based on previous earth imaging experience. Earth imaging involves how best to filter sunlight reflected from earth in order to accentuate a desired contrast, often that between clouds and the earth/ocean below. The necessity for this capability for satellite imaging was well understood and already incorporated into NASA's first weather satellite, TIROS 1, launched in 1960. The astronaut cameras had standard settings that were designed to capture light reflected from the earth into space in a particular way. According to Underwood:

> Well, we knew exactly the light conditions generally from those altitudes. You're above the clouds, so you're not going to get changes from clouds. We knew where the sun position was. We knew the dynamics of the film, the lens, the camera, and knew that with rather common settings, where they didn't have to play any games with cameras, we could go to general settings and they could get a great array of photographs.
> (Underwood 2000)

The ship, in many senses, is an extension of the broader earth imaging system. At any rate, once acquired, the photographs need to be made visual. This raises the question of temporality. The photographs, not unlike the ATS-III image discussed above, are composed of different moments in time. As Kris Belden-Adams (2008) put it, "N.A.S.A.'s Big Blue Marble then represents an image with an instantaneous relationship to time (thanks to the camera's quick shutter operations), but which actually depicts a duration of time and movement that transpired in the past" (24). Different moments in time and spatial position are congealed in the photograph. We usually fail to notice or care about this fact given the speed of the camera's operation and the approximation of the resulting image to what we see.

The temporality of the imaging process hints at the *latency* of the image, the quality of existing in a dormant or undeveloped state. The latency is best illustrated by the five-decade dispute over just *who* took the Blue Marble picture (see Figure 13.2). We know when, where, and how it was taken, yet each of the three astronauts on Apollo 17 insistently claimed to have taken the photograph. A similar dispute over Earthrise also emerged (Poole 2008, 30).

The disputes illustrate how partial the "triggering" of the camera is to the more widely distributed capacity to image the earth. It is latency and processing that define earth imaging, as Lisa Parks (2005, 91) suggests, not the moment of acquisition. Perhaps we should credit Richard Underwood, as he "discovered" the photograph when processing the film through a complicated chemically managed system:

> So the rolls came back and we gave them very tender loving processing in a very slow process . . . but it delivered perfect photographic processing, even though it was a slow process and some people complained about that. "You've got these machines to run the roll through in six minutes. Why are you taking five hours?"
>
> The imaging involved not only painstaking editing but the occasional chemical bath: "if anything goes wrong, you can cut the film at that point – we had rehearsed all this – and yank that piece out and put in a neutralizing chemical in vats that were all lined up there at that point to neutralize the film at that point, then recycle."
> (Underwood 2000)

Once made, the original photograph is then never seen again! We see a copy of a copy of a copy:

> Then they get developed. Then we would make a master, because we didn't want to fool around with the original. . . . We didn't want it handled, the original, but very seldom, so first a master was made and we looked at that, really. . . . Beyond that, you would print from the numbered master, but the original had no numbers on it and was never numbered, to this day. So what was released beyond that would be a third generation. Then we would make another series of a certain amount of unnumbered masters and then physically scratch the numbers into them so we would have some second-generation stuff to look at, *because no one's ever going to look at the original again.*
>
> (Underwood 2000, emphasis added)

These copies are then reoriented to align with cultural expectations for popular consumption (Poole 2008; Kelsey 2011). For example, Earthrise is usually shifted from *"portrait view"* (Figure 13.5) into *"landscape*

Figure 13.5 Earthrise (original portrait view).
Source: Courtesy of NASA (Public Domain).

view" (Figure 13.3) with the earth on top, just as it is depicted at the beginning of Gore's *An Inconvenient Truth*. The Earthrise "scene" was viewed by astronauts and taken in "portrait" view, both in monochrome and color versions, as the earth emerged to the left of the moon (Poole 2008, 29). The color image was selected for dissemination, rotated to suggest the earth "rising" above the moon, and "cropped" so that the dark encompassing space was much reduced. In Poole's (2008) insightful summary, "the photograph had been altered from a Moon to an Earth perspective" (29).

Blue Marble, on the other hand, is usually adjusted to place the South Pole at the bottom of the image – although the astronaut would have seen the earth "upside down" if peering through a viewfinder to take the image (Reinart 2011) – a convention reproduced in the default setting on Google Earth as it awaits a dataset (see Gurevitch 2014).

The images, in short, reduce the strangeness of the imaging and suggest that we see what the astronauts saw. Why is this false suggestion so routinely made? Why, as well, are the photographs described as "whole" rather than "full" (think, "full" moon). The Earthrise photograph is a partial illumination. Blue Marble is a "full disk" perspective – we see as much of the earth as we possibly can, even if it appears flat, more like a map than a segment of a globe (see Poole 2008, 63).

NASA's first space mission was a meteorological imaging program, the Television Infrared Observation Satellite (TIROS) series of weather satellites, which produced almost 650,000 images between 1960 and 1966, the year of Brand's campaign. The first TIROS-1 images appeared within days of its launch. NASA, if it got wind of Brand's goading to turn its cameras to the earth, would have been puzzled by his suggestion. The earth was imaged incessantly over the entire decade. No single person could process this flood of pictures. The problem was how to select and make sense of the overwhelming flows of data that resulted. As one analyst describes, "We got the pictures from TIROS-1 in 1960 and spent the first year figuring out what we were seeing" (cited in Edwards 2010, p. 274).

Why repress the difficulty and strangeness in seeing the earth? Consider how the earth's environment appears in the Blue Marble. Brand's description of the earth suggests a precious object embedded on a black jeweler's cloth, the earth as a processed gemstone. His description draws our attention for a moment to the earth's environment – the stunning contrast of the illuminated disk situated against a homogeneous space devoid of matter and color. Never mind that the sun appears, in this picture, solely to illuminate the earth for the human eye. Instead, consider how the brilliant appearance of the earth is generated both by the spatial perspective, as discussed above, but also the manipulation of contrast between the imaged object (usually clouds in 1960s and 1970s earth imaging, but in this case the whole earth) and the background. The brightly lit earth in Blue Marble is an artifact of technical design and cropping – not what the human eye would ever see. We adjust the light of the sun through a technical program to envision the earth as it pleases us.

What, we might ask, does an unearthed eye see? The Apollo program was forced to address this question in a rather different imaging mission. Astronaut eyeballs were photographed before and after flights – and during space travel astronauts occasionally put their heads in a large photographic box (the Apollo Light Flash Moving Emulsion Detector). Why? The spacemen hallucinated while dwelling in space. If we are not embodied by the earth's atmosphere, we occasionally see white flashes of light while dwelling in the darkness of space – a light without a source of illumination (Pettit 2012). By sticking their heads inside a camera box, astronauts hoped to figure out why.

We do not see a black void when unprotected by the earth's atmosphere. The un-earthed eye registers exposure to background radiation (popularly known as "cosmic rays"). In space, the shielding effect of the earth's atmosphere is lost, and as "rays" pass through the eye, humans register the effect physically as light. A signal passes through us that we cannot process.

Box 13.2   The Apollo Program and other space programs

The Apollo Program (1961–1972) was designed and operated by the National Aeronautics and Space Administration (NASA) to facilitate human transit in space by landing an astronaut on the moon and returning the crew safely to earth. It was a program defined by the Cold War politics underpinning the space race with the Soviet Union (see Cosgrove 2001). The mission was named for Apollo, the god of sun and light (and music), and this suggests the importance of earthly detachment and cosmic perspective (see Cosgrove 2001). The Apollo Program relied on advances in the engineering of rockets, space navigation, and lunar imaging, not to mention the construction of entirely artificial habitations for making space travel livable for humans. The famous "whole earth" photographs were taken during the Apollo program, notably Earthrise (Apollo 8 in 1968) and the Blue Marble (Apollo 17 in 1972).

Visit NASA (or another country's) space program website. Choose one space mission to research. By drawing on the website information and any additional scholarly and credible sources you can locate on the mission, engage in an ecocritical exploration of its visual and verbal meanings.

Pixel

In the early 1990s, Al Gore embraced the idea of programmable earth imaging. In a manuscript titled *The New World War*, Gore (1992) argued that our perceptions of global environment were the sites of conflicts determining the future of human civilization. Industrial destabilization of the earth system had generated a concatenated series of environmental crises, yet we lacked an organizational framework for perceiving the situation properly. Gore's book offered the missing framework by extending his study of nuclear armaments to environmental matters. An editor, however, thought "ecology" was more saleable than "world war," and the text was titled *Earth in the Balance: Ecology and the Human Spirit*.

Gore's (1992) efforts led him to reprogram the iconic Blue Marble (see Figure 13.2) as a series of pixelated earths (see Figure 13.6). The blockiest version of the pixelated earth appears on the page preceding Part One of Gore's book. The second image is less fuzzy and appears before Part Two. The third image is clearer, yet still pixelated, and opens Part Three. The Blue Marble photograph as usually rendered is reproduced in the conclusion. As you move sequentially through the text, the image of the earth gains clarity with each iteration until resolving into the famous photograph. The main text ends with a tetraptych composed of these four images, a spatial display of the temporal process the reader has undergone (see Figure 13.6).

Why image the earth in this way? Why turn the planet into shimmering data sets?

The question is routed by Gore through a detour in our usual accounts of earth imaging. In place of the standard celebration of whole earth photography offered by Brand, Gore discusses an image of Abraham Lincoln. The Lincoln image was created and popularized by Leon Harmon's (1973; Harmon and Julesz 1973) experiments with the informational thresholds of perception and pattern recognition. While at Bell Labs, Harmon developed technology for digitizing photographs for graphical display on computers. He was interested in how the human eye perceived low-resolution computer images and, while creating experimental materials, he generated pictures that humans perceive as meaningful only from an appropriate spatial distance. Harmon's most famous example was the pixelated Lincoln. The image was unrecognizable from close up, but identifiable when viewed from an appropriate distance – an effect immortalized in the title of Salvador Dali's painting, "Gala looking at the Mediterranean Sea which at a distance of 20 meters is transformed into the portrait of Abraham Lincoln (Homage to Rothko)," and Dali's subsequent lithograph "Lincoln in Dalivision."

Gore's book includes a full-page pixelated photograph of Lincoln so the reader can experience this effect. If you hold page 45 of Gore's text close to your eye, you see a "meaningless jumble of light and dark squares" (45). Hold it at arm's length, however, and Lincoln's face "is clearly visible" (45). In recounting Harmon's experiment, Gore notes that the image "appeared

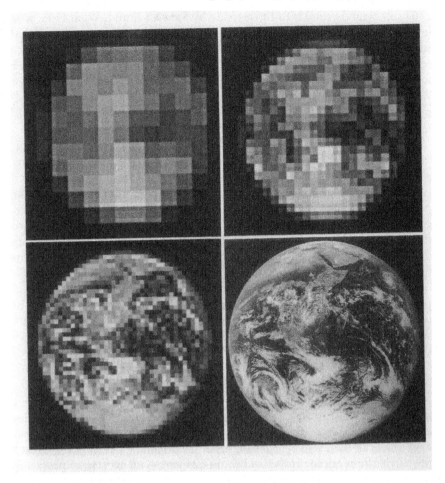

Figure 13.6 Pixel Earth.
Source: Courtesy of Todd Gipstein, Gipstein Multi-Media.

to be nothing more than an apparently random checkerboard pattern of grey squares – until viewed from a distance, when the original image of Lincoln was instantly clear" (44).

The Harmon experiment is Gore's analogue for understanding the effect of the initial circulation of "whole earth" photographs:

> Those first striking pictures taken by the Apollo astronauts of the earth floating in the blackness of space were so deeply moving because they enable us to see our planet from a new perspective – a perspective from which the preciousness and fragile beauty of the earth was suddenly clear.
>
> (44)

Gore's claim is similar to those made by Stewart Brand. What is surprising is that the basis for Gore's comparison is not relevant to the digital earths generated for his book. Harmon's image illustrates the importance of navigating space to permit the human eye to find the physical distance required to form a meaningful perception. Gore's pixelated earth does not work this way. It is part of a series and recognizable only when navigating multiple iterations in the sequence produced by "paging" through the book.

Why obscure the earth as we usually see it?

Gore sought a digital means of refreshing the cultural effect of the original whole earth photograph. The cultural shift once provoked by replacing a fuzzy human image with a recording of what astronaut eyes witnessed is replayed with digital images. The pixelated earths generated from the original photograph stand in for more primitive or unevolved stages of perception. The original photograph is the moment of insight, the standard for clarity of perception, the end point of the imaging process. Gore's earth imaging reflects the process through which we perceive and adjust our minds to our global condition.

Yet, Gore's images also demonstrate the very effect upon which contemporary earth imaging is based. Humans, in a manner of speaking, edit or reprogram how light moves through the planet by changing the composition of the atmosphere. We cannot program the sun, of course, yet we influence how it passes through, reflects from, and reshapes the planet. For Gore, night clouds (or noctilucent clouds) marked this possibility most visibly, as methane released by human activities illuminates clouds high in the atmosphere even after the sun has receded below the horizon. Yet, ozone holes and global warming, the first two global environmental crises, are also effected by industrial changes to the atmosphere that literally change how light reworks the earth (permitting more ultraviolet wavelengths to reach the earth and retaining more heat in the planet). Geoengineering proposals seek to take conscious control of this process by placing mirrors in space or sulfate aerosols in the atmosphere; in short, to edit light as a medium of life on earth.

Gore makes clear that light is programmable. In the case of the Blue Marble, Gore digitized the photograph and averaged the light intensity of discrete blocks of the original picture by using the computer program Photoshop. The sizing of the blocks varies to reflect user preferences but is uniform across the image. Each block of averaged light thus acquires a numerical value. Each number is associated with a distinct tone on a greyscale that is applied uniformly to the block when imaged. The block size, again, varies depending on the desired resolution, and the result produces a pixelated effect by eradicating the continuous variance in light intensity (this is how digital cameras generate images). In this way, photographs become fully programmable and generated as pixels.

When the light of the Blue Marble is digitized, made calculable, and rendered visually as a sequence of images, it suggests that endless images are "latent" in the imaging process, and that our perception is dependent on how light is abstracted by a computer program. The representation of the earth is a function of the desired technical resolution, and not at all what our eyes would see from space. If the book had five parts, Gore would generate more earths (say, a blockier image and a more highly resolved iteration than those contained in his text). The earth is no longer portrayed as a discrete object of appreciation for the human eye; it is now a site of malleable design and programming.

Program

The programmable earth is most obvious – and intensified as a cultural tendency – in the contemporary proliferation of digital globes like Google Earth, the popular and free software program. Users of Google Earth co-create unique observations of an environment – a capability that more widely distributes the design of earth imaging throughout a population, as people compose "the very environments they wish to travel through"

Box 13.3   Talk about it: earth imaging

Earth imaging involves the recording, storage, and processing of all radiated energy (electromagnetic radiation) that is reflected and emitted from the earth. It is usually understood in terms of remote sensing, or the study of phenomena at a distance (without making physical contact with those objects and processes under study), and it involves orbiting satellites, tracking stations, transmission infrastructure, image composition, and interpretation/analysis. Often, the satellites, stations, and infrastructure are called earth-observing systems, and there are notable efforts to integrate earth-imaging capabilities globally, especially the Global Earth Observation System of Systems (GEOSS). Image composition involves pixels, small units of programmable light, that are assigned tones (a brightness value) reflecting the average intensity of the light collected over the piece of the earth represented by the pixel (see Conway 1997). Image interpretation and analysis is a complex process, one blending the logistical constraints of maintaining technically complex and capital intensive observing capacities with the cultural history of visualization practices.

Find an example of a cosmic zoom or experiment provided by the earth-imaging program, Google Earth. How does this affect your sense of place and inform your experience of an environment? Does it confer a sense of scopic mastery (the feeling that everything can be made visible to your eyes), or does it present a confusing experience? Or something else?

(Gurevitch 2014, 97). What Gore did in the 1990s – reprogramming our perception of an iconic image – many more people can do today. As Leon Gurevitch (2014) has noted, Google Earth invests the individual with "seemingly omnipotent scopic capacities" (89) or what Caren Kaplan (2013, 24) calls "*scopic mastery,*" the feeling that everything can be made visible to a single gaze. Geophysical processes of immense scope and duration are made responsive to the human hand and eye. The earth, in brief, is reconceived from the vantage point of its potential geoengineering, and user perception is aligned with this new anthropocentric conception of geophysical change (see Gurevitch 2013, 2014, also Parks in this volume).

Consider Google Earth's "climate change tours," a visualization tool intended to influence the 2009 negotiations on climate change in Copenhagen. Introduced by Gore, the programmable climate tour is tailored to the perspective, scale, site, temporality, and preferred scenario of the software user – reproducing not the vantage point of the human eye, or the reality of a specific state of the earth, but the aspirations or needs of software user. Users witness the planet's spatial scales and temporal cycles manipulated to suit the eye within the familiar cultural form of a whole earth. Taken collectively, the climate change tours suggest numerous climates are "latent" in our atmosphere, a function of how the chemical composition of the atmosphere is programmed to process sunlight. Environmental crisis is fully ensconced in technical programming.

Conclusion

Our imaging of the earth, in Brand's account, reconfigures how humans come to inhabit the earth. The whole earth photograph impels us to reorganize our sense of environment, politics, and economics around the global scale, and to understand ourselves as parts dependent on a broader whole – the image for Brand is an argument for seeing ourselves as part of global systems. The key was photography. It disclosed how the earth appeared to the human eye given appropriate perspective and spatial remove. "What's unique, what was unique, about a photograph is that it is an analog representation of reality. It is a directly true transform of the original complex, awkward view of things. Every detail is there, like it or not" (Brand, Kelly, and Kinney 1985, 46).

Brand was idealistic but not naive about imaging. The digitization of photography both thrilled and appalled him. It was exciting to have viewers transformed into users able to craft visual experiences to meet the whims, fancies, or needs animating their engagement with imaging software. The affront was the reduction of photography to computer data and the subjection of visualization to endless fiddling and redesign, a capability ending the use of photography as "evidence for anything" (Brand et al. 1985, 42). Brand raised the issue while telling readers of his preference for analog watches – as more honest if less precise renderings of time – and speaking with anticipation of "an analog rebellion shaping up to match all this digital power" (46).

Gore digitized the Blue Marble and accepted as destiny the historical trajectory Brand hoped to oppose. Our perception of the global is malleable, programmable, and a site of political contestation, and it has long been linked to the perpetual churning and destruction of environments that military-industrial actors have occasioned. Environments, like Brand's photographs in Photoshop, are prone to endless fiddling and redesign by humans, perhaps even at the global scale, where humans fiddle with the chemistry and temperature of the global atmosphere and oceans. Brand's prized photograph, it is worth noting, fails to register such details. One can discern neither the stratospheric ozone layer nor the planetary temperature of the atmosphere or oceans in Brand's photographic imaging – knowledge that is afforded us by understanding the electromagnetic conditioning of the earth.

We should retain the original impetus of Gore's insights – that our perception of the earth is rooted in the dynamics of environmental destabilization – and ground it in Virilio's historical account of big optics. If the evolution of earth imaging and environmental volatility are coextensive, as Virilio insists, then the important point regarding big optics is not a technical distinction between analogue and digital imaging, nor of reengaging nature with our embodied senses. It is to release imaging from the strategic exigencies of military and industrial control and work through the realization that the planet is largely inaccessible to our senses (if not, unfortunately, unaffected by our collective influence). Earth imaging ultimately offers us only "a shimmering mass of proliferating data images" (Edwards 2010, 431), nothing more.

Sagan's salvaged pixel (Figure 13.1) is a portal into earth imaging as organized by big optics. It is an early marker of what Dipesh Chakrabarty (2014) has called "a growing divergence in our consciousness between the global – a singularly human story – and the planetary, a perspective to which humans are incidental" (23). The global, we might say, reflects a conception of the planet as we wish to see and dispense with it; the planetary exceeds all such hubris. It is the planetary that must disrupt the global if we hope to engage climate change: "the climate crisis is about waking up to the rude shock of the planet's otherness" (Chakrabarty 2014, 23). Sagan would have agreed. He felt cultural priority must be accorded to seeing the planet as a fragile sphere of life suffused by and dependent on the light of a single star – which, of course, was something we could not literally see at all, except as a pixel illuminated in an incomprehensibly strange environment.

Acknowledgments: I would like to acknowledge and thank the NASA Johnson Space Center Oral History Project for access to interview material with Robert Underwood and their professionalism in meeting inquires and requests in a timely fashion. Thanks also to Todd Gipstein for permission to reproduce the Blue Marble "mosaics" he created for Al Gore and for sharing information on their production. The archive of ATS-III imagery assembled and stored by The Schwerdtfeger Library, University of Wisconsin, was also a valuable source of accessible material.

I would also like to thank Jeremy Packer, in particular, as well as Leon Gurevitch, Sheryl Hamilton, Chris Dornan, and the Carleton University "Rough Cuts" gang for listening, querying, and inspiring development of this work.

Keywords

Big optics

Cosmic zoom

Electromagnetic spectrum

Geoengineering

Landscape view

Latency

Pixel

Portrait view

Programmable sequencers

Scopic mastery

Discussion questions

1   Does "pale blue dot" have the same significance to you as it does for Carl Sagan?
2   Does the ability to easily manipulate digital images signal the end of photography as evidence for anything, as Stewart Brand fears, or can programmable imaging (animations or computer simulations) help disclose truth and document reality?
3   Can you think of an embodied way of sensing or understanding climate change? How is the human experience of climate change important or unimportant?
4   What is the significance of the rotation of the Earthrise and Blue Marble photographs for popular consumption? Why do you think they rotated the images? What does this tell us about our expectations for earth imaging? What would you name the images?

Further reading/viewing

Arendt, Hannah. 1958. *The Human Condition*. Chicago: University of Chicago Press.

Elichirigoity, Fernando. 1999. *Planet Management: Limits to Growth, Computer Simulations, and the Emergence of Global Spaces*. Evanston, IL: Northwestern University Press.

Kaplan, Caren, Erik Loyer, and Ezra Clayton Daniels. 2013. "Precision Targets: GPS and the Militarization of Everyday Life." *Canadian Journal of Communication* 38.3: 397–420.

Parks, Lisa. 2013. "Earth Observation and Signal Territories: Studying US Broadcast Infrastructure through Historical Network Maps, Google Earth, and Fieldwork." *Canadian Journal of Communication* 38.3: 285–307.

Parks, Lisa, and James Schwoch, eds. 2012. *Down to Earth: Satellite Technologies, Industries, and Cultures*. New Brunswick, NJ: Rutgers University Press.

Peters, John Durham. 2015. *The Marvellous Clouds: Toward a Philosophy of Elemental Media*. Chicago: University of Chicago Press.

Ruiz, Rafico. 2014. "Arctic Infrastructures: Tele Field Notes." *Communication +1* 3.3: 1–25.

Starosielski, Nicole. 2014. *Surfacing*. http://.surfacing.in

Turner, Fred. 2006. *From Counterculture to Cyberculture: Stewart Brand, the Whole Earth Network, and the Rise of Digital Utopianism*. Chicago: Chicago University Press.

References

Anderson, Ross. 2014. "Exodus." *Aeon*. http://aeon.co/magazine/technology/the-elon-musk-interview-on-mars/

Belden-Adams, Kris. 2008. "Time Implosion in N.A.S.A's Whole Earth Photographs." *Spectator* 28.2: 23–30.

Brand, Stewart. 1977. "Why Haven't We Seen the Whole Earth?" In *The Sixties: The Decade Remembered Now, by the People Who Lived It Then*, edited by Linda Rosen Obst, 168–170. New York: Rolling Stone Press.

Brand, Stewart, Kevin Kelly, and J. Kinney. 1985. "Digital Retouching: The End of Photography as Evidence of Anything." *Whole Earth Review* July: 42–48.

Chakrabarty, Dipesh. 2014. "Climate and Capital: On Conjoined Histories." *Critical Inquiry* 41: 1–23.

Conway, Eric D. 1997. *An Introduction to Satellite Image Interpretation*. Baltimore: The Johns Hopkins University Press.

Cosgrove, Denis. 2001. *Apollo's Eye: A Cartographic Genealogy of the Earth in the Western Imagination*. Baltimore: John Hopkins University Press.

Cubitt, Sean. 1999. "Virilio and New Media." *Theory, Culture, and Society* 16: 127–142.

———. 2000. *Simulation and Social Theory*. London: Sage.

Edwards, Paul. 1996. *The Closed World: Computers and the Politics of Discourse in Cold War America*. Cambridge, MA: The MIT Press.

———. 2010. *A Vast Machine*. Cambridge, MA: The MIT Press.

Feynman, Richard. 1985. *QED: The Strange Theory of Light and Matter*. Princeton, NJ: Princeton University Press.

Gore, Al. 1992. *Earth in the Balance: Ecology and the Human Spirit*. New York: Rodale.

Guggenheim, Davis, Director. 2006. *An Inconvenient Truth: A Global Warning*. DVD. Beverly Hills: Participant Productions.

Gurevitch, Leon. 2013. "The Digital Globe as Climatic Coming Attraction: From Theatrical Release to Theatre of War." *Canadian Journal of Communication* 38.3: 333–356.

———. 2014. "Google Warming: From Media Ecology to Ecology as Media." *Convergence* 20.1: 80–107.

Harmon, Leon D. 1973. "Recognition of Faces." *Scientific American* 229: 70–82.

Harmon, Leon D., and Bela Julesz. 1973. "Masking in Visual Recognition: Effects of Two-Dimensional Filtered Noise." *Science* 180.4091: 1194–1197.

Kaplan, Caren. 2013. "The Balloon Prospect: Aerostatic Observation and the Emergence of Militarised Aeromobility." In *From Above: War, Violence, and Verticality*, edited by Peter Adey, Marie Whitehead, and Alison J. Williams, 19–40. London: Hurst.

Kelsey, Robin. 2011. "Reverse Shot: Earthrise and Blue Marble." In *New Geographies 4: Scales of the Earth*, edited by El Hadi Jazairy, 10–16. Cambridge, MA: Harvard University Press.

Kittler, Friedrich. 2010. *Optical Media*. London: Polity.

Kolbert, Elizabeth. 2014. *The Sixth Extinction: An Unnatural History*. New York: Henry Holt and Company.

O'Brien, Frank. 2010. *The Apollo Guidance Computer: Architecture and Operation*. Chichester, UK: Springer.

Packer, Jeremy, and Josh Reeves. 2013. "Romancing the Drone: Military Desire and Anthropophobia from SAGE to Swarm." *Canadian Journal of Communication* 38.3: 309–331.

Parks, Lisa. 2005. *Cultures in Orbit: Satellites and the Televisual*. Durham, NC: Duke University Press.

Pettit, Don. 2012. "Flashes of Reality: In Space I See Things That Are Not There." *Airspacemag.com*. Accessed October 20, 2014. http://www.airspacemag.com/daily-planet/flashes-of-reality-70379179/

Poole, R. 2008. *Earthrise: How Man First Saw the Earth*. New Haven, CT: Yale University Press.

Reinart, Al. 2011. "The Blue Marble Shot: Our First Complete Photograph of Earth." *The Atlantic*, April 12. http://www.theatlantic.com/technology/archive/2011/04/the-blue-marble-shot-our-first-complete-photograph-of-earth/237167/?single_page=true

Russill, Chris. 2013. "Earth-Observing Media." *Canadian Journal of Communication* 38.3: 277–284.

Sagan, Carl. 1994. *Pale Blue Dot*. New York: Random House.

Sturken, Marita, and Lisa Cartright. 2009. *Practices of Looking: An Introduction to Visual Culture*. London: Oxford University Press.

Underwood, Robert. 2000. "Edited Oral History Transcript." NASA Johnson Space Center Oral History Project. http://www.jsc.nasa.gov/history/oral_histories/UnderwoodRW/underwoodrw.htm

Virilio, Paul. 1994. "Speed and Information: Cyberspace Alarm!" *CTHEORY*. August. http://www.hnet.uci.edu/mposter/syllabi/readings/alarm.html

———. 1997. *Open Sky*. New York: Semiotext(e).

Weart, Spencer. 2001. *The Discovery of Global Warming*. Cambridge, MA: Harvard University Press.

Index